Lejeune

Lejeune

The Napoleonic Wars Through
the Experiences of an Officer
on Berthier's Staff

Volume 1

Louis-François Lejeune

LEONAUR

*Lejeune: The Napoleonic Wars Through the Experiences
of an Officer on Berthier's Staff—Volume 1*
by Louis-François Lejeune

Originally published under the title
The Memoirs of Baron Lejeune

Published by Leonaur Ltd

Copyright in this form © 2007 Leonaur Ltd

ISBN: 978-1-84677-167-5 (hardcover)
ISBN: 978-1-84677-165-1 (softcover)

http://www.leonaur.com

Publisher's Notes

In the interests of authenticity, the spellings, grammar and place names
used have been retained from the original editions.

The opinions of the authors represent a view of events in which he
was a participant related from his own perspective,
as such the text is relevant as an historical document.

The views expressed in this book are not necessarily
those of the publisher.

Contents

Introduction

The spacious times of Napoleon left ample room for many varied orbits of personal experience. The man himself is still an unexhausted subject, and anything that throws light on his character and actions must have an intense interest, no matter who writes it. Volumes upon volumes which from one point of view or another thus contribute to the history of the times still pour from the press. The 'Memoirs' of Lejeune, however, belong to a class quite distinct from these, and have a charm peculiar to themselves.

Though he was employed during the greater part of his career on the staff of Prince Berthier, Napoleon's right-hand man, and though he was therefore continually close to Napoleon, had many conversations with him, and was despatched by him personally on many missions of importance, it is not for the sake of any specially numerous or interesting anecdotes of the great man himself, or even for any very valuable additions to our general knowledge of the history of the times, that these volumes are to be commended to the attention of modern readers. The charm of them consists in this, that, cultivated, brilliant, and gallant soldier as Lejeune was, he was essentially, and always remained, an artist who had become a soldier rather than a soldier who had taken to art.

Ruskin tells us that the business of the artist is to see, 'to think perhaps sometimes when he has nothing better to do.' The saying has continually recurred to me as I have read these graphic descriptions of scenes in France, Italy, Spain, Switzerland, Germany, the Tyrol, Hungary, and Russia. From that point of view, I know nothing that approaches Lejeune's 'Memoirs.' The faculty of seeing and of vividly portraying in words or by brush the thing seen is one of the most precious granted to man. The instinctive artistic necessity which makes the eye take in all that is passing around at a time when every faculty is strained under the dire conditions of imminent personal peril, of absorption in the tremendous responsibilities involved in the command and care of men, in the stress of action, when every decision that is taken may involve the fate of an army, perhaps of a nation, is indeed a rare quality for a soldier to carry with him throughout such events as those through which an aide-de-camp on the staff of Napoleon passed during the years between Valmy and the retreat of the French army after the disaster of Leipzig.

As a collection of historical anecdotes the 'Memoirs' of Marbot[*] are immeasurably more full and complete. Whether they are, properly speaking, memoirs at all and do not deserve rather to be classed among historical compilations for which the experiences and collections of other writers have, during the years of peaceful leisure which followed the great events they describe, been laid under heavy contribution, is a doubt which has assailed almost all who have read them. As memoirs 'to serve for the history' of Napoleon, many others are more valuable than Lejeune's.

The recently published memoirs of De Menéval, for instance, throw a light upon the workings of the mind around which events in Europe for at least thirteen years pivoted, such as cannot be compared with any fresh Napoleonic glimmerings that Lejeune here and there gives us. Lejeune's are throughout palpably what they pretend to be, pen-and-ink sketches made at the time of those scenes which most impressed him as an artist, sketches developed afterwards by the help of memory but with very little extraneous assistance and little comparing of notes with others. They have therefore at the same time the charm, the value, and the weakness of composition of this kind. There is no sort of proportion in the space given to different parts of the subject. The historical importance of events gives them no claim to full treatment by Lejeune. Austerlitz and Jena, though Lejeune was present at each, are vaguely touched. No one could obtain an accurate understanding of the method of either battle or of the mode in which the skill of Napoleon was exercised in it from Lejeune's pages. Clearly Lejeune had 'something better to do' than to think about the methods employed by his master in either case. For our purposes I think he had. We have ample knowledge of what happened in both cases, and we know why it happened; but there is at least one famous

---

[*] Available in a three volume edition from Leonaur: *Volume—1 The Young Hussar*, *Volume 2—Imperial Aide-de-Camp* and *Volume 3—Colonel of Chasseurs*

dramatic scene at Austerlitz to which Lejeune has added some artistic touches, quite new to me, and so presented that it would be difficult ever to forget them again. The spontaneous illumination with which Napoleon was received by his soldiers when he visited their bivouac on the night before Austerlitz is a well-known historical incident. If, however, any one except Lejeune has recorded that the torches used consisted of the straw on which the men were lying--that, in fact, in order to light Napoleon's way, they deprived themselves both of their beds and of the rough overhead shelters they had constructed--it has altogether escaped my memory. Lejeune further tells us that this was not by any means intended as a mere demonstration, but was due to the anxiety of his soldiers lest the Emperor, who had come to visit them, should lose his way in the darkness. I shall not take the trouble to verify my memory as to the entire absence of any previous mention of these facts which give all the value to the soldiers' action as a demonstration of devotion to Napoleon, because, whether I am right or wrong, the quality of Lejeune's style in vividly presenting a scene to one and fixing it in one's memory is none the worse illustrated by the fact, if it be the fact, that others have casually mentioned, this feature of the famous illumination.

Lejeune, by a happy comparison much to the advantage of the soldier with the recklessness of George IV. when Prince of Wales in lighting a 100l. note to enable the Duke of Orleans to find a *louis d'or*, his long search for which had provoked the Prince, brings out delightfully the real nature of the men's sacrifice and its value as demonstrating their reckless devotion to their chief. This is an illustration of the kind of touches with which Lejeune not unfrequently lights up even those parts of his narrative with which he most casually deals. When, however, with a large canvas and full brush, he takes to giving us scenes in which he has been personally vividly interested, I doubt if Zola or Verestchagin has imagined anything more awful in their dramatic horror than some of those which Lejeune has given us from the siege of Saragossa, from the campaign of 1809, especially in the awful story of the capture of Ebersberg, and from the retreat from Moscow. The latter, no doubt, has been often enough described by others, but, as a rule, the peculiarity of Lejeune's work is that from his describing just what he has himself seen during a life more adventurous than any novelist could have imagined, we are usually carried through events which no one else could have described, because there was no one else on the spot with eyes to see or pen to sketch them. For in fact the whole career of Lejeune was traced for him by the master hand of a man who thoroughly understood how best to employ him. Able, as very few indeed of Napoleon's officers were, to speak languages with such fluency as often to impose on Spaniards, Italians, Germans, and to converse with Englishmen, able to make an accurate engineer's tracing from a distance of a fortress or to paint a finished picture that all Paris would crowd to see, an accomplished engineer understanding all the detailed work of a siege or a campaign, a well-trained staff-officer, above all possessing the happy tact which enabled him to go among jealous marshals and even kings and princes without exciting their wrath though charged with the delicate mission of urging them on in Napoleon's name, such a man under the great Emperor was marked out for a life of personal adventure.

I think it is safe to say that the words *Faites-moi* savoir, which meant strictly what they literally express, 'Make me know,' 'Take care that I really do thoroughly know,' are of more frequent occurrence than any others throughout the whole of Napoleon's correspondence. No one ever more keenly than Napoleon realised the impotence of the most despotic authority which does not know. To have eyes with which he could see as with his own in every part of his vast empire was the continual object of all his efforts. Who, for such a purpose, could be more suitable than the accomplished young artist who could not help seeing wherever he went, who, if he instinctively and by nature saw as an artist, had yet, when leisure permitted, devoted fifteen hours a day to mastering his profession as a soldier, who would, if he saw with an artist eye, yet describe with the military knowledge of a soldier, with the accuracy of a well-trained engineer, and with the savoir-vivre and savoir-faire of a courtier and a man of the world? Accordingly the variety of the missions with which Lejeune was entrusted was endless. Sent at one time with a detachment of cavalry for the sole purpose of making a personal report on the defences of Comorn and on the presence of any enemy in the neighbourhood of Pesth, he was able to boast that he was the only French officer who had, arms in hand, penetrated close to the capital of Hungary.

On another occasion he was employed to take over the guns surrendered by the Austrians in the Tyrol. Before the battle of Wagram he seems to have been again alone reconnoitring in front of the Austrian army when it began its night attack of which he brought back the news. He was also despatched by the Emperor to Spain to visit the King and each of the marshals, being expressly told to make the Emperor as completely aware of all that was taking place there as if he had been present in person. Each of these and other personal missions led him into situations of extraordinary danger, and in the last especially he was actually hung up for execution, having been captured by brigands, missed, only by the merest accident and his own courage, being consigned by mistake, perhaps for life, to the hulks of the Portuguese galley-slaves, and finally, having been carried as a prisoner to England, and having made his escape to Folkestone, after a series of adventures worthy of 'Brigadier Gérard,' he only barely avoided a gruesome fate, his narration of which discloses an extraordinary system of rascality. He declares that an English smuggler was reaping a murderous profit out of the desire of the French prisoners to escape. The man nominally put himself at the service of the prisoners in England, and promised to deliver them safe at Boulogne, but, afraid of being detected by the English coast-guard, he, after obtaining from the unhappy Frenchmen all the money that he could induce their friends to raise, took them out in a boat and drowned them. Lejeune states that this man had thus murdered many before he, fortunately for himself, was saved from the scoundrel's hands under circumstances which I must not describe lest I should spoil the interest of the story instead of showing what elements of exciting drama it contains.

Apart, however, from these matters of personal adventure, which, gaining as they do from his vivid powers of description, have of themselves all the attractions of a novel, it is, I think, a point which makes much for the value of the book that it is, as a rule, most full in its description of just those parts of the history which are least hackneyed, and that it is brief where we already have ample materials. Thus, having been employed personally to report to the Emperor on the second siege of Saragossa, and as an engineer in giving all the assistance he could, he devotes eighty-three pages to the details of that memorable struggle between passionate and heroic patriotic devotion and the calmer, more powerful, more scientific, and not less valiant resolution of the French army in carrying out the behests of their Emperor. That such a contest would give him scope for his descriptive powers need hardly be told. As a powerful presentment of a scene fascinating by its very horror, I can hardly imagine anything more telling than the pages

11

in which he describes the fights in the several nunneries and convents of Madrid, of which perhaps the most terrible was that amidst the ruins of the convent of St. Francis where the struggle went on from roof to cellar and whilst the Gothic gargoyles, representing dragons, vultures, and winged monsters, vomited forth upon the assailants below torrents of human gore, in the nave of the church the fight was being continued amidst coffins, bones, and broken marbles. From one of the coffins protruded the livid shrivelled features and part of the body of a bishop still wrapped in his sacerdotal robes, 'the mitred spectre swaying to and fro beneath our feet.'

But the whole story of the siege, in which the French seem to have displayed all the personal humanity that its vigorous prosecution permitted, while the Spaniards were even more actuated by passionate religious fervour, due to the fear of the priests lest the convents should be suppressed by the French, than by patriotism, recalls more closely than anything else that I have ever read the incidents of that awful catastrophe, the struggle between the fanatics of. the Temple and the Romans at the siege of Jerusalem.

Tender touches of human nature recur continually throughout, as when a young girl fifteen or sixteen years old who had lost both father and mother, after fruitless efforts to carry away her mother's body, wrapped it in her father's cloak and tried to drag it along with the cartridge-box and musket, remembering vengeance as well as filial piety, while the very Poles, who could not blame the poor child for hating them as the murderers of her parents, called out to her, first in their own language and afterwards in Spanish, 'Don't be afraid, little one.'

Few days, he tells us, passed without something of this kind occurring. To me, at all events, this personal presentation of the features of the siege from the French side comes as quite new. Certainly, however, of all the battles the one to which Lejeune contributes most new light is that of Essling. From his quality as an engineer and, at the same time, as aide-de-camp on the Emperor's staff, Lejeune had a close personal view of the battle, of the scenes at the broken bridges, and of the personal danger of the Emperor, such as no other historian of that terrible contest has possessed.

I do not think that any writer has ever given me an idea so complete of the utter exhaustion of the French army at the time when the bridges were broken down as Lejeune by his description does. Of course it has always been notorious that if the army under the Archduke John had arrived as it ought to have done to the support of Charles, the French forces on the left bank of the Danube with the Emperor must have been destroyed or captured. But viewing the situation of Lannes' corps at the time when Lejeune was personally sent to him, as graphically described by him, it looks as if a further effort on the part of even the much-shattered forces of Charles must have sufficed for the purpose. I do not think there is anywhere so graphic a picture of the scene at the small bridge, which alone remained to connect the island of Lobau with the left bank when the Emperor passed it, after it had twice already broken down, as is to be found in this book. As a specimen of Lejeune's powers of description it is perhaps worth while to give a portion of the scene.

'The river was still rising, and we had little hope of maintaining the bridge intact for any time. All our wounded were now dragging themselves to this small bridge, crowding the approach to it, each eager to be the first to cross. Driven back by carpenters, whose work they impeded, their condition was one to draw tears from all who saw it. The less mutilated amongst them endeavoured to clamber up the ropes on to the boats, but climbing one over the other they were in each other's way, and none succeeded in passing. Many wounded horses, abandoned by their owners, but accustomed to follow, pushed themselves in among these men, increasing their difficulties. All of them, huddled together on the banks and approaches to the bridge, were soon overwhelmed by the water which continued to rise. The crowd became so great that the wounded were unable to move back, and we had to look on whilst men and horses were drowned without being able to do anything to help them, for a way of retreat for the army must be secured at any price. "Let us save the Emperor!" were the words which passed from mouth to mouth. In this disaster that was our one hope; it was essential for us all that he should be neither taken prisoner nor killed; and I now went to implore Prince Berthier to do all he could to induce the Emperor to retreat to the island of Lobau whilst it was still possible. . . . At last, slowly traversing on foot the little wood which served as a place of first aid to the wounded, I had the satisfaction of leading the Emperor to the group of wounded accumulated near the bridge. All, when they saw him, seemed to recover fresh life to cry, "Vive l'Empereur!" and tried to draw yet more closely together so as to leave room for him to pass. Hitherto the Emperor's features had maintained their absolute calm, but now they suddenly relaxed, and his eyes lost their flash and their coldness as they were cast down on the ground.'

An equally graphic description follows of the cortège, of wounded soldiers, most of whom had one arm in a sling and used the other to carry Marshal Lannes, who had lost both his legs, and was borne on a litter formed of muskets, a few branches of oak, and one or two cloaks. The meeting of Lannes and the Emperor, historical as it is, receives many fresh touches from Lejeune's artistic pen. Finally, as regards this battle, we have from Lejeune, who was himself employed in preparing a boat for the Emperor, a most vivid picture of the Emperor's dangerous night voyage to the right bank after he had given the general order for the retreat of the army.

More than a hundred pages are devoted to the Russian campaign, and, numerous as have been the histories of that terrible disaster, there is a freshness about the personal narrative of his own experiences, to which Lejeune devotes himself, which makes it in many respects valuable, even if a subject which, for its full presentation, so eminently deserves the eye of an artist, did not specially lend itself to his pen. It would be impossible to do justice in brief space to all that he has to tell on this prolific subject, and I pass on to the period of Napoleon's departure for Paris, as to which, in the course of his account of his own proceedings, Lejeune brings out, with a force that I have never felt before, one very important historical feature of the case. That Napoleon the Emperor ought to have been in Paris rather than on the Niemen, for the sake even of the ruined army itself, there can be no question.

It was only because of his rapid return to France that he was able to organise the force with which he met the Allies in the 1813 campaign, received the debris of the retreating army, and for a time even restored victory to his standards. But Napoleon the General could not be separated from Napoleon the Emperor, and the desertion of the commander-in-chief was an example that was only too quickly followed by each subordinate commander in turn. When Murat showed the way the contagion spread rapidly. Lejeune himself, disguising the matter as well as he can, gives us an example, in his own person, of the method by which these desertions were carried out by numbers of general and other officers of the army. Napoleon's position was one too difficult to admit of his dealing with all the officers who had gathered in Paris in absolute violation of all military loyalty either to their Emperor or their men. At the same time nothing was more inconvenient for him than that there should be present a number of eyewitnesses who were able to describe in detail the frightful nature of the disaster, and to discount the bulletins in which he had endeavoured to minimise it. Therefore, when Lejeune, with an impudent attempt to gloss over the crime he had committed, after long delay reported his desertion of his post and his presence in Paris, Napoleon in a very mild way made an example of him. His laments and cries against Napoleon are palpably unjust, but they admirably illustrate the complete break-up of all ideas of discipline which followed the disastrous campaign of Russia, and the weakness of Napoleon's position when he could neither separate the emperor from the general in his own person, nor make the two duties consistent with each other.

It must not, however, be supposed that Lejeune's descriptive powers are employed only on the terrible and the awful. He had his full part in the gorgeous pageantries and stately ceremonial which attended the Court of Napoleon and of his vassal kings during the years of his supremacy. The beauties of nature never failed to attract him even when himself in the direst straits; and as he lands dripping from a river in which he has been nearly drowned he cannot help noting all the glories of a lovely landscape if it then comes before him. As he passed at one time or another through most of the grandest country in Europe and had much gaiety in his own life, the darker colours are continually relieved and set off by the brighter. All the elements of a varied picture are admirably presented by the man who, having the opportunity, could best see and portray the strange and wonderful events of the time. The very limitations of the book as history add especially this to their value, that so far as they go they are first-hand evidence.

To take one illustration out of many. Count Tolstoi, for purposes of his own not difficult to guess, has endeavoured to deprive his countrymen of the glory of that heroic national sacrifice, the burning of Moscow. Obviously he bases his story upon mere tradition. He strives to make it be believed that the entire conflagration was due to the carelessness of French plunderers among wooden houses. Lejeune, who was personally employed in putting out the fires, whilst he expressly admits, as every one has done, that many of them were due to French carelessness, gives evidence apparently unanswerably confuting Tolstoi

15

by anticipation, and showing that the conflagration had been organised by the Russians on an enormous scale and by most elaborate devices, and that it was these and not the carelessness of the marauders which baffled the efforts of the French authorities. In many similar instances the direct personal evidence of Lejeune is of no inconsiderable historical importance. This, perhaps, more especially applies to much of what he writes as to the gradual change in the feelings of the Spaniards towards the French, and as to other important points in the Spanish problem.

Altogether the recently republished French Memoirs, which, when they first came out, never had more than a local circulation, were well worthy of an English translation, and I feel certain that those who read them will he delighted with them from their charm, their vivacity, and their interest.

F. Maurice
Woolwich
November 30, 1896

CHAPTER 1

Earliest Recollections

My father and mother belonged to Versailles, but certain business affairs led to their settling for a time in Alsace, where I was born.

Shortly before the Revolution they returned to Versailles, and as I write I can vividly recall the belfry of the Cathedral of Strasburg, as well as the beautiful Royal Palace of Versailles, just as it appeared the day I arrived there.

I already had a taste for drawing, and one day, as I was about to begin a sketch in the park, a lady wearing a simple and elegant but somewhat *négligé* white costume approached me, followed by a *hayduc* or Hungarian hussar, who held a big sabre in one hand and in the other the lady's dainty parasol. I took off my hat respectfully without pausing in my work, replied to a few gracious questions addressed to me, and as the lady continued her walk I took no further notice of her.

At the same time the next day the lady, who I had noticed had a beautiful face and a fine figure, though she was as simply dressed as before, came up to me and asked my name. When she had heard it she said, "I know your father, and I am much attached to your uncle, who often comes to practise music with me."

From her accent I guessed that she must be an Austrian, and I replied, with a laugh, in German that I was ashamed to confess I did not know to whom I was talking.

My cheerful manner seemed to please her, and she said, "Come with me, little friend, and we will become better acquainted. You shall see some prettier bits than the one you are sketching." I accompanied her, and saw the big folding doors of the Trianon open to admit us. Attendants in the royal liveries saluted respectfully, and I caught the words, "Your majesty."

As much astonished as the peasant who took Henri IV. up behind him, I said to myself, "This, then, must be the Queen, since neither the hussar nor I can claim to be the King." It was in fact Marie Antoinette, the Archduchess of Austria, but her manner to me had been so gracious that I did not feel at all embarrassed, and went on chatting familiarly with her. The Queen offered me some fruit, and seemed to take great pleasure in pointing out to me the beauties of the Trianon, which was her own creation. Before dismissing me she presented me with a little purse embroidered in green and gold, and gave me permission to come to the Trianon again whenever I liked.

Alas! How little did we then foresee the tragic fate which was later to overwhelm her, and of which I was to be a witness!

I was still a student on the 10th of August, but I remember the massacre of the luckless Swiss soldiers, which went on for a whole week. At Passy I was struck by bullets intended for a Swiss, who knocked me over as he made his own escape, and at the Barrière Blanche another Swiss, driven perhaps by hunger from the quarries of Montmartre, where he had taken refuge, fell close to me beneath the blows of some twenty masons, who beat him to death with their plastering trowels. When the rage of the people of Paris began to subside, the triumphant singing of the "Marseillaise" was heard on every side, and at the sound of this inspiring war song battalions were formed in each quarter of the town, and many columns of troops started to join the army.

The popular excitement suddenly took a magnanimous turn, and the most timorous citizens enthusiastically enrolled themselves, eager to aid in driving back the foreign enemies who were everywhere menacing the frontier and threatening the independence of France.

The young students of literature, science, law, medicine, and art met in the Louvre in great numbers, and included Alexander Duval, Jean Baptiste Say, with many another young poet or philosopher, who now became mere common soldiers, with numerous beardless heroes who were later to rise to be generals, prefects, or senators. The band took the name of the Compagnie des Arts or the Art Corps, and the figure of Minerva was emblazoned on their banner.

Only seventeen years old then, I was, I believe, the youngest in the newly formed corps, but I managed somehow to carry the enormous amount of war material with which I was encumbered. A cardboard helmet with a horsehair crest, a cartridge box full of cartridges, a musket weighing fifteen pounds, a sabre big enough to cut off the head of Goliath, a saucepan for making and a platter to hold soup, a knapsack which my dear mother in her excess of affection had loaded to bursting and moistened with her tears, a sack to sleep in in camp or to go foraging with, bread and meat enough to last four days, a uniform of short breeches, long gaiters, and a pair of good shoes, such was what I had to carry, the weight of which I was able to ignore in the pride of the first start, but which made me realise before the very first halt that the trade of a hero is a very arduous one.

Nothing could have been gayer than our first night in the Louvre, if it had not been that in the midst of our fun a charming young fellow named Jourdain mistook a window for a door, and flinging himself against it fell into the grand court below and was killed.

One of us who had once served for a few months in a regiment of dragoons was chosen as our captain, another named Bertier became our lieutenant; and two days after our organisation and equipment were completed we defiled before the National Convention, which held its sittings in what is now the Chapel of the Tuileries.

Hérault de Séchelles was then president. About twenty-five or thirty years old, belonging to a very distinguished family of senators, he gave us an address. He was a friend of my father's, and he singled me out in the front rank, where I was placed on account of my height, and said to me: "As for you, my young friend, your arms and those of your comrades will be the ramparts of your country, and your brushes will soon commemorate our victories."

The parting with my mother was heartrending, and that with my father left a most melancholy impression. He pressed my hand as he drew me back once more, but his heart was so full he could neither weep nor speak. He embraced me without uttering a word, and never was silence more eloquent and touching. The sound of the drum and the joyful shouts of the people, who hurried to see us pass singing the "Marseillaise," somewhat dissipated our grief, and we all shouted gleefully, "We are soldiers now."

It was raining, and our first night was of a nature to disillusion the sons of well-to-do parents accustomed to comfortable beds. My billet was on a poor baker, who to make me a suitable resting-place brought out a few old flour sacks, rolling up one to serve as a bolster and giving me two others to put over me.

Tramping through the rain we arrived at Châlons-sur-Marne, where Lukner was organising a reserve force, and that general, as he said, to do us honour, placed us in the front of the camp.

The ploughed-up ground was very wet and the ruts were full of water. Before we could get any rest we had to cut down branches from the willow trees near to make conches on which to stretch ourselves. Fortunately the next day volunteers were asked for to escort a convoy, and the whole Art Corps at once offered to go. Nearly one hundred wagons were loaded with provisions for Kellermann's army at the Camp de la Lune. That very day the Prussians attacked his position, and were beaten at Valmy (September 20, 1792), but their light cavalry got behind our lines, and several squadrons reached us and attacked the convoy just as it had gained a bank lofty enough to give us the advantage of the ground. We were obliged hastily to shelter ourselves under or on our wagons and fire. The enemy lost a few men and retreated. We repaired the mischief done in this skirmish, and after marching all night we arrived at the Camp de la Lune the day after the victory. Several hundred Prussians had just been buried where they had fallen; we had to pitch our tents above their graves, and it was with our heads lying on the bodies of the unlucky victims that we took our rest after this our first expedition.

During the remainder of the campaign we did nothing but march backwards and forwards in the rain, and through the deep mud of Champagne. We were often short of bread, we were always drenched to the skin, and yet we kept up our spirits, and, as Dumouriez once discovered, the least gleam of sunshine made us quite gay. This general was one day just beginning to review some twenty thousand men drawn up in several lines before him, when one of the hares which had hitherto been allowed to multiply and grow fat under the protection of the seignorial laws, terrified by the trampling of the horses of the staff, rushed in amongst the ranks of grenadiers. The soldiers, thinking more of the hare than of the general, at once gave chase, shouting, "To the hare! To the hare!" The confusion roused up ever so many more hares, and in a few minutes the entire army was rushing helter-skelter after them. The chase lasted the whole morning, and Dumouriez, at first a good deal annoyed, ended by laughing, and in the evening he did not disdain to take his share of the vanquished, which were roasted in camp, a good many at the fires of our own bivouac hanging from twisted string, which as it unwound served very well as a spit.

The heavy autumn rains and the half-ripe grapes eaten by the Prussians caused much illness amongst them. Our men also suffered greatly from excessive fatigue. It was necessary to maintain discipline, and we were ordered into cantonments for the winter, to be reorganised.

The Art Corps was stationed near Sedan. One day several of us went together to the Château de Bouillon, a few miles off. The picturesque appearance of the towers rising from the rocks led some of us to make sketches of them from the top of a neighbouring height. We were busy with our drawing, when we saw a dozen bayonets approaching us by way of a zigzag path. Our action was so perfectly innocent that we did not feel in the least alarmed when the guard surrounded and arrested us.

The orders were to take us to the château, and in crossing the town the enraged populace tried to drag us from the hands of the soldiers, shouting, "To the lamp post! to the gallows!

death to the agents of Pitt and Coburg, who have come to make plans of our town and château!"

It was only with great difficulty that our guards saved our lives, but they did succeed in getting us safe and sound to the presence of the commander of the fort, who had ordered our arrest. He turned out to be M. de Pontbriant, captain of the Royal-Vaisseau Regiment, who had been on leave in Paris during the preceding winter, where he and I had gone through the same course. As soon as he recognised me and looked at our sketches, he overwhelmed us with excuses, and whilst we were sharing his meal he sent a messenger into the town to explain the position, so that we might go back without danger.

The time passed all too quickly, and we could hardly bring ourselves to consider the sad news which had arrived from Paris.

Captain Friant (who became Commander of the Old Guard) was ordered to join us on to other companies and form us into battalions. He had already expressed himself very well satisfied with our progress in the art of handling our weapons, when one morning, I could not imagine why, every one of us was saying to his neighbour, "We are disbanded, and we must all return to Paris!"

We at once began to run about in the streets, each with pen and paper, ready to sign certificates of citizenship and good conduct for each other. For want of a desk to write on, we used our comrades' shoulders as a table. Our knapsacks were quickly packed, and the very same day we all started independently for Paris. Those who had no money, however, joined themselves on to those who had still a little left, and five comrades went with me, each of whom possessed sixty francs in the notes then called corsets, and this small sum enabled us to reach the gates of Paris in good health. These companions of mine were my friends but also my debtors, and after we separated I never saw any of there again.

Paris was more gloomy than ever, for every one was in mourning and the greatest consternation prevailed. Every day tumbrils laden with the bodies of those who had been guillotined, passed beneath our windows on the way to the cemetery of La Madeleine. One day twenty-two victims were taken by, the eldest of whom was not more than thirty years old. These were the young and interesting Girondists and the brothers Fonfrède. Power was now in the hands of the dregs of the people, who, shouting *"Fraternité, Egalité!"* and "Down with tyrants!" called their ferocious exultation good citizenship. Every decently dressed man was to them a suspect, and was thrown into prison. One day, after making myself tidy, I was peacefully going to have my breakfast in the town, when a patrol stopped me, calling me a *muscadin* (dandy); this was the most fashionable term of opprobrium just then. I was marched off, dragged about all day long from one guard-room to another, and at last shut up with a number of others in the basement of the Church of St. Martin. It was not until ten o'clock at night that we were taken before Henriot, then in supreme authority in Paris. Our crime was the wearing of white linen and clean clothes. Our judges having heard who we were, still hesitated to release us, and it was midnight before we were set free and could get our breakfast.

Provisions, especially bread, were very dear, and life became beset with difficulties. Work served as a distraction from our many woes, and I had resumed my studies, when, one day on my way to one of the courses I was going through, I found myself involved in a huge crowd obstructing the Rue St. Honoré as it pressed on towards the Oratoire. Every window, every roof, was densely packed with spectators, and on every side the obscene song, "Madame veto promised," &c., was being shouted out with fiendish and delirious glee.

Troops were already approaching, escorting a cart in which a woman was seated with a priest beside her and several executioners standing behind them. The procession was moving with slowness, so as to prolong the agony of the victim and pander to the eager curiosity of the hundred thousand spectators who had gathered to gloat on the terrible sight. I began to tremble violently, and my heart almost ceased to beat when I realised whom I was about to see again; but nearly crushed to death in the crowd retreat was impossible, and it was with grief indeed that I recognised the lady who had admitted me to the Trianon with

23

such graceful kindness. It was the Queen, Marie Antoinette, in just such a white costume as she had worn on the day when I had the honour of accompanying her to the Trianon. She bore herself like a saint, and the priest who was exhorting her looked far more miserable than she did.

At this melancholy spectacle many eyes filled with tears, but, hemmed in by the menacing crowds, not one generous soul had the courage or the strength to give a single cry for mercy. With me, too, that cry died away upon my lips for fear of the populace, and I have never ceased to reproach myself for my cowardice ever since.

Under such melancholy circumstances as these, I heard without regret that all young men from eighteen to twenty-five years old were called out to join the army; it would be more cheerful in camp than in the streets of Paris. I was now eighteen years old, and I started once more.

CHAPTER 2

The Campaigns in Holland

It had been the custom to appoint as officers in the army only those of noble birth, but nearly all the nobles had emigrated, and the first thing to strike us was the ignorance of many of the generals who had taken their places. I was a sergeant of infantry, and one day, when I was serving at Pérenne under General Calendini, a brave Italian soldier, he was studying a general map of Europe to find out how best to manoeuvre his troops in the Sambre, and he seemed dreadfully worried because the short cuts were not marked on it!

A little later I was transferred to the artillery, a service in which the work suited me much better. Meanwhile the Austrian army, which had taken possession of our strongholds in the north and was marching on Paris, gave us battle near the gates of Guise, where it was at last arrested, beaten, and compelled to retreat. The very evening of the struggle, General Lacour, chief of the staff, sent a horse, which had been captured, to me with the orders, "Gallop off, work your horse to death if you like, but take this order to Jacob, who is twelve leagues from here; follow the movements of his division, and come back and report to me."

The courageous example set by this general a short time before had contributed greatly to the glorious defence of the lines at Wissembourg by General Hoche (December 26, 1793), which had won him the grade of general of division. This general took a fancy to me and kept me with him as an aide-de-camp. He could only just read and sign his name, but he was a fine fellow, and his courage was indomitable. He had previously been for a long time chief shoemaker to an infantry regiment.

A few days later Jacob's division succeeded in crossing the Ourthe, a narrow but deep river with very steep banks, which covered the Austrian position. As the troops went down towards the river in columns, I was ordered to seek a fordable place. I found one. The attack was sharp, and the division got over (August 18, 1794). This lucky hit of mine led the three representatives of the people, Alquier, Ducos, and Lacoste, to send for me to give me the brevet of assistant lieutenant of engineers, and to send me in that capacity to take part in the winter campaign of the army of the North then on the way to conquer Holland.

The winter of 1795-1796 was extremely severe, but it favoured our advance into Holland, as the rivers, the well-filled dykes, and even the Texel channel, were frozen over, and our cavalry seized the Dutch fleet, riding across the ice right up to the vessels.

When we were at La Haye, two of my fellow engineers named Bontemps and Ferrus and I were attached to the staff of General Vandamme. He led us one day to the edge of the great canal to await a boat full of emigrants who were being taken to Ostend, to be sent out of the country occupied by the army. We were anxious to assuage the terrible sufferings of our unfortunate fellow countrymen and women, amongst whom I recognised the Comtesse de Neuilly, whom I had several times seen at Versailles. It was difficult to recognise her as she left the boat, carrying in her hand all that was left of her possessions tied up in a little handkerchief. Her feet were frozen, and she could hardly walk. Her daughter, a girl of about sixteen, benumbed with the cold, slipped on the plank and fell into the black and muddy waters of the canal. The ice broke and she disappeared, but some of us jumped in after her. She was rescued; we gave her a cloak, and took her, all dripping as she was, with her mother to our quarters in the Stadtholder's Palace, where they were both well cared for, provided with clothes, passports, and money. The collection we made, to which every one was eager to contribute, gave them twenty-five *louis d'or*. Twenty-five years afterwards I met these ladies together at a ball in the house of M. de Bourienne at Paris, whither they returned after the Restoration.

We were, however, very poor in Holland. Our pay was given to us in *assignats*, which we could not pass in the country we were in; this was supplemented from the treasure chest of the army by eight francs a month in specie--no one, whatever his rank in the regiment, got more. I was obliged to sell my rations to buy forage for my horse and pay my washerwoman.

My poverty was, however, nothing to that endured by my father in Paris at the same time, and a little later I had the gratification of being able to help him. The Dutch Government being very rich in specie was disposed to treat us liberally, and the General-in-Chief got the municipalities to give each officer a sum equal to the full value of his assignats for a month. Thanks to this, I got four thousand francs together in a few months, and sent them to my father. This little packet of gold coin must have seemed to him a vast treasure, when one loaf of bread cost fifty francs in *assignats*!

The order to attack the enemy reached us in the summer of 1795, and I was one of a body of officers who received instructions to make ready for the passage of the Rhine by our army.

We hired at a great cost in Holland a number of strong boats, which were got ready to receive beams, planks, the roadways of bridges, and everything necessary for constructing several bridges in a few hours. This fleet, which numbered more than one hundred sailing vessels, was towed up the Rhine by about six hundred horses aided by the wind.

We reached the frontier of the Duchy of Berg on September 6, 1795, and during the night three beautiful bridges of boats, with masts and rigging complete and flags flying, were flung across the river below Düsseldorf. The army of Jourdan from its position on the left bank of the Rhine covered the construction of the bridges by a brisk cannonade, whilst the advanced guard of our army was carried over to the right bank in flat-bottomed boats manned with rowers.

Neither the depth of the water, the firing, nor the vigorous defence of their entrenchments by the enemy, arrested our progress, and we entered Düsseldorf the same day. The Lefebvre division, which led the way, well sustained the reputation which had won for it the name of the Infernal Column, and had a large share in the victory which established us on the right bank of the river.

In the retreat which soon followed, I was sent beyond Bamberg to prepare for the crossing of the Redritz by the numerous rearguard commanded by Brigadier-General Ney. I was lucky enough to find several ferry boats near the most suitable place, which I arranged end to end, and several great beams of floating wood, which I placed side by side, covering them over with the planks of all the fences in the village of Obersk and making three bridges, one for the artillery and cavalry, the other two for the infantry. The rearguard passed over easily, and we burnt the boats as soon as the enemy appeared. During the short time we were occupied with these works, the unfortunate peasants were constantly appealing to me for protection against the marauders who were pillaging their houses, and I ran great danger in opposing the undisciplined soldiers, many of whom resisted my authority. In the last house whose owners appealed to me for help, more than thirty soldiers were quarrelling over the very garments of the women and children. I was alone against them all, and not being able to attack them in front, I resorted to a manoeuvre, and climbing up to the granary, I advanced upon the crowd, sword in hand, and quickly drove the whole party down before me. I met with no resistance, but just as I was, as I thought, closing the door on the last of them, a peasant called out that one fellow was still there, whilst a ball pierced the door and broke the step on which I was placing my foot. I was unable to catch the culprit, who ran faster than I could, and I went back to my bridges.

The Directory had now succeeded the Convention. Paris, saturated with blood, at length began to be ashamed of her horrible orgies, and her inhabitants, eagerly resuming their old mode of life, were passing rapidly from one extreme to another, and seemed more greedy of pleasure than ever. Fêtes, entertainments, and balls became ever more numerous, and friends in meeting each other again embraced, as they would the day after escape from some terrible catastrophe. On my return, however, instead of giving myself up to these gaieties, I devoted fifteen hours a day to earnest study, in the hope of properly qualifying myself for my new profession. I was much encouraged in my work by General Dejean, of the Engineers, side by side with whom I had followed the campaign in Holland. One day he took me aside and said, "I want you to dine with me to meet Moreau; there will only be we three." During the meal, Dejean, whilst talking of the late campaign in Germany, said to the illustrious commander-in-chief, "Why did you not drive off the representatives of the people, who worried you so with their cruel treatment of your soldiers?"

"There's no doubt," answered Moreau, "that I ought to have had them hanged, marched on Paris, treated their accomplices in a similar manner, and rescued France by seizing the supreme power. I really did think of it, but somehow the execution of such a scheme suited neither my tastes nor my character."

The Minister of War had now summoned to Paris some forty officers, who had been serving as I had in the Engineer Corps without having left the School of Mézières; and to ascertain whether we were up to our work, he ordered us to be examined by a commission.

An examination day always excites more or less painful emotions, and I was by no means free from nervousness about this one. It arrived in due course, and to appear before the committee I donned the uniform faced with black velvet which was then adopted nearly everywhere by engineers, and which I should be very grieved to have to give up. It was pouring with rain, the various signboards in the street were swinging about in the wind, and a garland of ivy, the usual decoration of Bacchus, which was displayed outside a wine seller's shop, was flung at my feet. I picked up the crown, accepting it as a happy augury for me, and awaited my turn with a quiet spirit. I felt very uneasy, however, when I was questioned closely and in an almost disagreeable manner. Indeed, when I went the next day to call on the examiners, I asked the Abbé Bossut, who was one of them, why he had been so anxious to put me out. To which he replied, "I wanted to sift the matter to the bottom; but you need not grumble."

A few days later, General Alexandre Berthier, whom I had not then the honour of knowing, invited me to breakfast, and at our *tête-à-tête* meal he told me that I was retained in the Engineer Corps with the rank of captain, and offered to take me with him as aide-de-camp to the reserve force, of which he was just about to resume the command. I expressed my delight and my gratitude to the minister for my appointment, and in my heart I thanked the crown of ivy for keeping faith with me.

A little later we started for Geneva via Dijon, and at Lausanne the First Consul joined us, and placed himself at the head of the army.

The first mission entrusted to me was to take some bags of gold to the curés of Valois with which to pay the peasants who were to help drag our artillery over the Alps, and to obtain some provisions and wine from the hospice of St. Bernard. With infinite trouble the dismounted guns were carried one by one over the mountain, whilst the cavalry and troops passed over without any serious mischances. The whole army met again in the valley of Aosta, and marched without delay upon Fort Bard, routing as it went the Austrian troops which attempted to defend the approaches.

The position of Fort Bard was such that it would not have done to pass it without taking possession of it. We managed to hoist some cannon up a mountain which the very goats would have found it difficult to scale, a battery was quickly established, and fire was opened on the fort. An assault was at the same time attempted without success. On this occasion I had a very anxious time, for the general, on leaving to lead the assault, instructed me to wait for him at head quarters. I was brokenhearted at receiving an order which prevented me from distinguishing myself, and it was very difficult to obey when I heard the cannonading begin. My longing for action finally overcame my sense of duty, and trembling lest I should be noticed, I ran to the batteries. The assault was just over when I got there, and the General caught me near him. He looked very much annoyed at my presence, and said, "As you have quitted your post, you can take this order and recall that company, which has got into a bad position." This was a very arduous mission, and one from which I was not likely to return alive. I started, and approached the fort by creeping along behind some piles of stones; but presently this shelter came to an end, and I had more than a hundred steps to go without any cover, under the fire of some two hundred guns pointing almost straight at me.

I confess that I hesitated a moment, for I was rather in the position of a hare within range of the guns of approaching hunters by whom she has not yet been discovered. But those I was to recall were losing men; the whole army, placed in a kind of amphitheatre, seemed to be gazing down on me, and feeling that my honour was at stake, I dashed on muttering to myself, "Audacity alone can succeed!" and in a few bounds I crossed the open space. The brave Captain Bigi had his jaw broken beside me, but I escaped untouched, and I led the company to shelter, carrying the wounded with us. A few hours later the fort capitulated, and our route was clear before us.

In the many tasks allotted to me, the dangers on the battle field were not always the worst. Once I had to go and tell a division arriving from Lugano to join us, when a fearful storm was lashing into fury the lake I had to cross. It was not without a considerable bribe in gold that I was able to induce four fishermen to take me over in their boat; and when they did, they flung themselves on their knees and said their prayers, as they rowed me towards Lugano. In some parts, too, the roads were infested with brigands, who menaced the lives of officers travelling alone carrying orders.

Amongst the many missions I had entrusted to me, after the taking of Turin, was that of helping to make the bridges of boats over the Po, to push on the work and to return and inform the general when it would be finished.

It took some sixty hours in a drenching downpour of rain to collect the boats, rafts, beams, ropes, and anchors necessary for making the bridges and dragging them all to the most suitable place. At midnight on June 5 all was finished, but meanwhile my horses had disappeared. Nevertheless I had somehow to get over the two or three leagues between me and Pavia, to carry the news so eagerly looked for. Hungry, soaked through with the rain, and exhausted with fatigue increased by the struggle in the pitch dark through the deep mud of the ploughed-up ground, I was almost sinking beneath the weight of my wet cloak and my accumulated troubles, and nothing but the fear of retarding our success by my failure could have kept me up, when an artilleryman on horseback happened to pass me. I begged him, at first in vain, to help me out of my predicament by lending me his horse. He declared he was as tired as I was, and not until I offered him two *louis d'or* did he consent to take me up behind him and carry me to head quarters.

On June 6, before sunrise, the whole army had crossed the river on our bridges of boats, and advanced upon the enemy. When I and my party reached the borders of the Scrivia, it had overflowed its banks. We were obliged to wait, but time was precious, and as soon as the water had sunk a little, and we thought it would not be higher than our waists, we tried to wade over, but the current was so strong that even the horses could not stand against it. The happy thought then struck me of linking our arms together and dashing over by whole sections at a time. This answered admirably; the sun soon dried our wet garments, our bath had only given us a better appetite; but in spite of the absence of provisions we kept up our spirits, and arrived in time to take part, fasting as we were, in the battle of Marengo.

The necessity of leaving garrisons behind us at Turin, Pavia, Milan, Tortona, and elsewhere had greatly diminished our numbers, which were not one-third as large as those of the enemy. However, former successes had made us bold, and three divisions of ours under Lannes, Victor, and Chambarlhac, resolutely attacked the vast lines of the Austrians. About three o'clock in the afternoon our forces were becoming exhausted, and the First Consul consented to a retreat, which was effected in as orderly a manner as at a review, but we had lost ground and many men, and were now some two leagues behindhand.

The First Consul, full of anxiety about the issue of the day, sent me to hasten the approach of the Desaix division, for which he was waiting. Our ranks were already beginning to be a little disorganised, when I met that general about half a league from the field of battle.

His troops were marching as gaily as if they were bound for a ball; he made them deploy in the vineyards as they approached the enemy, and open fire on a column of about 8,000 Hungarian grenadiers, the leading battalions of which halted opposite to him, in order to deliver a point-blank fire. It was at this moment that General Desaix was killed. The other Hungarian battalions, instead of halting; too, so as to maintain their proper distances for manoeuvring, all pressed on in confusion, till it was quite impossible for them to deploy.

General Kellermann, commanding a body of cavalry, noted the confusion, and, without consulting any one, acted on the spur of the moment, and just when the Hungarian troops were huddled together and unable to offer any resistance, he charged into their midst at the head of the 400 horsemen under him, and completely routed them. The column of picked troops flung down their arms, and the Austrian army, numbering three times as many men as ours, was driven behind the village of Marengo. The genius of the First Consul showed him how best to turn this to account, and that very evening he dictated his own terms to General Melas, who consented to abandon Italy.

The First Consul and my own general returned to Paris, whither I followed them.

CHAPTER 3

Austerlitz and Jena

I was working away at painting when I was summoned to follow Marshal Berthier to the camp of Boulogne in the capacity of an orderly officer.

Every one knows how Napoleon, when he heard that war with him had been declared by the Austrians through the invasion by them of the territory of our allies the Bavarians, led the army from the camp at Boulogne to the shores of the Danube.

As for me, I had already taken a considerable share in all the eager sending to and fro of despatches, the embarkations, the manoeuvres of troops, &c., and I had ordered my post-horses to follow the Imperial staff to Alsace, when Marshal Berthier gave me orders from the Emperor not to leave Boulogne till I had sent off by the quickest route for Germany 300,000 pairs of shoes to be delivered to me for the military stores. At the words remain and shoes I felt stupefied, and, fell into utter despair. What had been the good of all my study, I said to myself, if I was to become a mere escort of shoes? Still, I put my whole heart into the matter, but the difficulties were very great, and I was not able to rejoin the Emperor until October 14, 1805, whilst the battle of Elchingen was going on.

In giving the Emperor an account of my mission, and saying to him, "The shoes are there," I could not help grumbling at his having reduced me to the position of a mere army contractor, and deprived me of the honour of being present at the beginning of the campaign, to which he replied with a smile: "What a child you are! You don't seem to understand the importance of the service you have just rendered; shoes help on marches, and marches win battles; you will get your turn as well as every one else." A day or two later, October 17, 1805, General Mack signed the capitulation of Ulm. It was a fine sight to see all the splendid Austrian and Hungarian regiments file by in their full-dress uniforms, all looking as fresh as possible still, for it was but eight days since the campaign began. The French army was drawn up in divisions opposite the town and facing the heights of the Michael Berg, which rises like an amphitheatre behind it and looks down upon the left bank of the Danube, where the Austrians were marching past. This was of course a glorious spectacle for us, but at the same time rather an affecting one, for we could not but remember that the fortunes of war are fluctuating.

The army resumed its march immediately afterwards, Marshal Murat, with an energy which did much to insure us the victory, driving the enemy before him. Accustomed to overcome every obstacle, he cared but little for the fate of those he came across. But everything was by no means *couleur de rose*; it was now November 4, 1805, it was cold, and ground and trees in the Amstetten forest were alike covered with masses of snow, which produced a very remarkable effect on those of us who came from the South of Europe and had never before realised how beautiful nature can be in the winter. In this particular instance everything was robed in the most gleaming attire; the silvery rime softening the rich colours of the decaying oak leaves and the sombre vegetation of the pines. The frozen drapery, combined with the mist in which everything was more or less enveloped, gave a soft mysterious charm to the surrounding objects, producing a most beautiful picture. Lit up by the sunshine, thousands of long icicles, such as those which sometimes droop from our fountains and water wheels, hung like shining lustres from the trees. Never did ballroom shine with so many diamonds; the long branches of the oaks, pines, and other forest trees were weighed down by the masses of hoar frost, whilst the snow converted their summits into rounded roofs, forming beneath them grottoes resembling those of the Pyrenean mountains with their shining stalactites and graceful columns. I called the attention of Marshal Murat to the beauty of the scene as we rode rapidly beneath the frozen vaults, pursuing a rearguard of cavalry which was fleeing before us, and we were still admiring the grandeur of the northern scene when a break in the forest suddenly revealed a very unexpected sight of a totally different character.

Eight Austrian and Hungarian regiments drawn up in order of battle awaited us unmoved at the entrance to the defile. Murat had very few men with him, yet he had the audacity to attack them. It was now the enemy's turn to charge us, which they did with splendid gallantry, and it was very difficult for us, though we turned right about at once, to get back to the protection of the pass. The enemy overtook us, their ranks were mingled with our rearguard, our men were swept down, many were taken prisoners, and we ourselves were in danger of being captured. Murat's horse was killed under him, mine fell in the confused rush down the steep path, and I was flung off. I should have been crushed by the onrush before I could get out of the way if I had not flung myself under the shelter of two pieces of cannon which a young officer of artillery, fresh from college, had the presence of mind to place in position in the middle of the path. The *mêlée* was truly terrible, and swords were already clashing above our heads, when the young officer, having with admirable *sang-froid* made sure that his guns were properly pointed, sprang between the two cannons, fuse in hand, and just as he was going to be cut down, in less time than it takes to tell, he fired. The grape shot, with which the two cannons were charged, swept down the whole of the head of the enemy's column, which, spread out as it was across the slope of the entrance to the forest, presented a wide surface. Not one single shot of the double discharge missed its victim; the shock brought down on our heads the masses of snow in the trees, and as if by enchantment the squadrons of the enemy disappeared in a cloud of smoke and a storm of snow mixed with great death-dealing icicles, which, falling from a height of more than one hundred feet, crashed upon the helmets of the fugitives with a resounding noise. A sudden panic seized the Austrians, and they took to flight. Murat saw his opportunity, returned to the charge, and gave chase to the enemy. In the end we halted eight leagues farther on on the road to Vienna. I regret that I cannot give the name of the young artillery officer to whom we owed our success. I had not time to ask him what it was, but I know that Murat intended to recommend him for promotion.

We soon reached Vienna, but we only halted there for a short time, and pressed on in our pursuit of the Austrians and Russians. They meanwhile had managed to get near to Olmütz, a fortress in a strong position on a lofty plateau. There, protected by the fort, the enemy halted, apparently with the intention of giving us battle. Napoleon, however, was far too clever to leave to the Austrians and Russians, who were altogether more than 120,000 strong, the advantages of so fine a position, especially as the French army, owing to the number of garrisons left behind en route to secure the retention of the districts conquered, was now reduced to some 60,000 men. The Emperor therefore sent me to reconnoitre the country round Brünn, to which he meant to try and entice the Russians, and give them battle on ground where the advantage would be on the side of the French. Napoleon himself was determined to choose the position, and with this end in view he drew back his advanced guard for several miles towards the heights, which seemed fitted by nature to be the theatre of an event of such tremendous importance as the coming battle.

This feigned movement of retreat did not fail to restore confidence to the enemy; they resumed the offensive, followed us, and fell into the trap.

On December 1, 1805, we were drawn up awaiting the enemy's forces, which soon appeared and halted when they saw how well prepared we were to receive them.

On the morning of the same day I was sent with an order from the Major-General to Marshal Bernadotte, whom I found on the height called Sokolnitz at the foot of a cross on which was a life-sized figure of Christ painted red. The marshal had had a fire lighted, and was standing near as naked to the waist as the Christ, performing some wonderful gymnastic exercise with his arms. I asked him what in the world he was doing stripped like that in the bitter cold? and he replied, "My dear fellow, I am bracing myself by taking an air bath." Little did he think then, when he was trying to get used to the climate, that he would one day be king of a northern country.

The day of December 1st was passed on either side in preparations as for some grand fête, and an hour after the darkness fell, the two armies, their dispositions satisfactorily made, settled down to rest in profound silence, broken only by the sound of chatting round the bivouac fires, where the soldiers merrily talked over past successes or those which they counted on achieving in the future. I shared the bivouac of the staff of Marshal Berthier, and it was a very lively one, for one of our comrades, M. Longchamps, who had been detained in France, had only been able to join us that day, and during his journey he had composed some verses which very aptly hit off the rapidity of our march. The arrival of this merry companion, who brought letters from home for each of us, was the most charming episode of the day.

The letters from our families, the portraits, and in some cases the love letters brought by the friendly singer, the Tokay wine which we drank straight from the casks through straws, the crackling of the bivouac fire, with the presentiment of a victory on the morrow, combined to raise our spirits to the highest pitch. By degrees, however, one after the other fell asleep, the songs ceased, and we were all closely wrapped in our cloaks and stretched comfortably on a little straw beneath the twinkling stars, when we were aroused by shouts of joy and the glare of brilliant illuminations.

Whilst we had been sleeping, our general had been keeping watch and completing his preparations. His army was but half as strong as that of the enemy. His soldiers had hitherto always been victorious; but with so small a force to deploy in the vast plains on which we were encamped, it was of the utmost importance to him to know whether the confidence of the troops in their own superiority would again be sufficient to make up for their inferiority in numbers. It had therefore occurred to him to go on foot, accompanied by Marshal Berthier only, throughout the camp, and listen unnoticed to the chat of the soldiers round their fires. By eleven o'clock he had already traversed a great distance, when he was recognised. The soldiers, surprised at finding him in the midst of them, and afraid that he might lose his way going back to his head quarters (which consisted merely of a fire near his carriage), hastened to break up the shelters they had made of branches and straw, to use them as torches to light their Emperor home. One bivouac after another took up the task, and in less than a quarter of an hour 60,000 torches lit up the camp, whilst passionate cries of "*Vive l'Empereur!*" resounded on every side. The shouts and the illumination alarmed the enemy, who, fearing a surprise, came from every side to reconnoitre our outposts and remained under arms all night. The Emperor meanwhile, rendered happy and secure by the proofs of affection he had just received from his whole army, was able to sleep in peace and security.

Only those who know the difficulty of securing a little straw to sleep on in camp can appreciate the sacrifice made by the men in burning all their beds to light their general home. The Prince of Wales, it is said, once lit a hundred-pound note, and held it burning for five minutes, to enable his friend the Duke of Orleans to look for a *louis d'or* he had dropped when playing cards, but this lesson in dignity for the Duke cannot as an example of unselfish devotion be compared with the action of our soldiers in thus proving their love and enthusiasm for their illustrious chief.

This memorable evening, this beautiful winter night was succeeded by the rising of the brilliant sun of Austerlitz.

The 2nd of December was the anniversary of the coronation of the Emperor, and it was eight o'clock in the morning when the sun appeared above the horizon of Moravia as pure and radiant as in the brightest days of spring.

A light mist subdued the brilliancy of the scene, but we could distinctly make out the 120,000 bayonets gleaming; in the sunshine as they slowly approached us, forming a crescent as vast as the horizon. This manoeuvre was intended to threaten our right wing, intervene between us and the town of Brünn, which was about four or five miles off, cut off our retreat towards Vienna, take us prisoners, and probably send us eventually to freeze to death in Siberia.

The right wing of the Russians advancing by the Olmütz road met the divisions under Suchet and Caffarelli, supported by a division of cuirassiers. The Russian general, thinking that the position would be a difficult one to attack, ordered his regiments to put their haversacks down on the ground where they stood, and when they were relieved of what he thought would be an embarrassing weight in the struggle, he gave the order to charge, saying to his men, "You will get the French haversacks, they are full of gold!" The attack was indeed a spirited one, but our cannon caused some little confusion. Our cuirassiers noticed this, and in spite of the terrible fire from the Russians they flung themselves upon the enemy, overthrowing more than 10,000 men and taking them prisoners. Ten thousand haversacks ranged in rows remained in our possession; but our booty, vast as it appeared, resolved itself into 10,000 little black boxes or rather triptych reliquaries, each containing an image of St. Christopher carrying the infant Saviour over the water, with an equal number of pieces of black bread containing a good deal more straw and bran than barley or wheat. Such was the sacred and simple baggage of the Russians!

On the right of this position the village of Pratzen was set on fire by the first balls from the Russian guns. The enemy was, however, defeated there also, driven back or taken prisoners. The Vandamme, Saint-Hilaire, and Legrand divisions occupied the centre opposite Austerlitz on the heights of Krecznowitz. The enemy made most strenuous efforts here, and the struggle was prolonged. Our troops suffered greatly, and were beginning to lose ground, when the Emperor sent his own Guard and came in person to their support. The arrival of the Imperial Guard enabled us to resume the offensive. A picked corps of the Russian cavalry was just charging when Colonel Morland at the head of the elite of the French army flung himself upon them, overthrew them together with their artillery in the deep ravine of the Krecznowitz stream, pursuing them to the very foot of the castle of Austerlitz, the property of Prince Kaunitz. Colonel

Morland was killed, and General Kapp wounded in the mêlée. I was in the thick of it too, and returned at the same time as the general to report to the Emperor. The return was really more dangerous than the charge, for the enemy pelted us with shells. A chasseur of the Guard, who was already wounded, disappeared from my side with his horse, a shell having exploded inside the latter and blown both victims to pieces, leaving literally nothing but their shattered bones.

This brilliant struggle had taken place in the central division of our army, whilst the right was going through the most terrible experiences.

The enemy persevered with the greatest obstinacy in the attack, with a view to turning our right wing. A hot fusillade had been going on ever since eight in the morning, and the fortunes of the day fluctuated greatly opposite the villages of Tellnitz and Menitz. The Emperor sent me to Marshal Davout, who was on our extreme right, with an order to push forward to the support of the centre. When I arrived the marshal had already taken the initiative, and had been fighting for an hour in the village of Menitz. His troops had been three times repulsed, and three times he had driven out the Russians. The wide Rue de Menitz, which was some four or five hundred yards long, was literally choked up with the dead and wounded of both armies, piled one on top of another, and it was all but impossible to ride over the heaps of mutilated bodies and weapons. Marshal Davout's infantry, however, managed to debouch from the village in spite of the resistance of the Russians, who were finally repulsed by the hot fire opened on them from the Saint-Hilaire and Legrand divisions, who pursued there for some distance. On my way back to the Emperor with M. de Sopranzy and some twenty dragoons, we found ourselves compelled to pass through a Russian column. One of the generals in a very simple uniform with a few troopers tried to bar our passage, but we pushed right through them and wounded the general in the arm, whilst M. de Sopranzy seized the bridle of his horse and we dragged him along with us to our own ranks. I asked him his name, and he replied, "I am the Baron de Wimpffen." He was in fact first cousin of Lieutenant-General Baron de Wimpffen, who held high rank in the French service, and was an intimate friend of my father's. The Emperor, to whom we presented our prisoner, received him very courteously, and ordered his own surgeon, M.Yvan, to dress his wounds. Then, noticing that I was very much heated and bathed in sweat, he ordered a page in waiting to go and fetch me a glass of Bordeaux from his private canteen, which I drank with the toast, "Success to the Emperor!"

This little scene took place on a high mound above the village of Augesd, opposite the lakes, or rather the big ponds, formed by the Tellnitz dyke. Meanwhile the Austro-Russian corps, driven back by Marshal Davout and unable to rejoin the main body at Austerlitz, were endeavouring to escape by way of the Tellnitz dyke, and thus to reach the road to Hungary; but the Height was already occupied by the artillery of the Guard, and the cavalry alone ventured to risk the passage, galloping by under a hail of grape shot, whilst the infantry, hesitating what to do, finally imagined that their only chance of safety was to try and cross the ponds dividing them from the other side on the ice floating on their surfaces. A few men, indeed, might have got over safely; but when a number had reached the middle of the water, the ice began to crack beneath their weight. They paused, and the troops behind them pushing on, there were soon some 6,000 men collected in a dense crowd on the swaying slippery ice. There was a pause, and then in the brief space of a couple of minutes the whole mass with arms and baggage disappeared beneath the broken-up ice, not one man escaping or even appearing again at the top of the water. We looked down upon the churning, rippling waves produced by the struggles of so many human creatures swallowed up so suddenly, and a thrill of horror ran through us all. Very soon the fractured ice, broken up by the useless efforts of those beneath it, sank again into repose, the clouds were once more reflected on its gleaming surface, and we knew that all was over. Much of the Russian artillery remained still harnessed at the edge of the waters or overturned in the ponds, and later it was melted down to form the Austerlitz Column set up in Paris in the Place Vendôme. Just as the waters closed over the last relics of the army which in the morning had all but surrounded us, the sun went down behind a mass of clouds on the horizon, snow began to fall very much as a curtain does after the last scene at a theatre, and the Emperor, Marshal Berthier, Marshal Soult, their various staffs, and I set off to find a shelter from the bitter cold of the night, making our way with the greatest difficulty through the dense darkness amongst the dead, the wounded, and the prisoners, of whom there were an immense number.

On the vast battle-field, which was many miles in extent, there was but one little shelter, the post-house where travellers changed horses on the Olmütz road. The small amount of space in it was crowded with wounded, and I passed the night on the snow under an apple tree in the garden without fire or so much as a wisp of straw. It was intensely cold though the day had been so fine, but I counted myself lucky, and I was indeed a thousand times more fortunate than the 20,000 poor wretches lying out on the ground not far from me, all wounded, many dying, without fires and quite unattended.

Our prisoners told us that when our cavalry charge reached the gates of Austerlitz, the Russian and Austrian Emperors Alexander I. and Francis II. were looking down upon the battle from the castle. We should have been doubly venturesome had we known that a few more sabre cuts might have won us so costly a prize as these two crowned heads. It was this circumstance which led to the battle of Austerlitz being also called that of the three emperors.

I was ordered to make a topographical survey of the battle field, and I also made sketches of the chief points of interest, writing on them the most remarkable incidents which had occurred at each spot. On the fifth day, as I was crossing the blood-stained battle field covered with the dead, I came upon a group of fourteen Russians, who when wounded had crawled close to each other for the sake of warmth. Twelve were already dead, but two still lived, their hollow cheeks, furrowed with the tears they had shed, bearing witness to the agony they had endured. They made touching signs to me, entreating me to help them. I at once fetched some peasants from Soloknitz, and made them carry the poor fellows to a place of security. No words could describe the radiancy of their looks when they found that they were being lifted on to the rough stretchers of branches the peasants had made. One of them, who knew but one word of French, kept on repeating, "Monsieur, monsieur!" I put them under the care of our surgeons, and rejoined the Emperor at Vienna. Before he left the army he gave many of us rewards for our behaviour in the field, and I was made captain of a battalion of engineers.

I returned to France by way of Bavaria, and passing again through Munich I had the honour of being received by the King of Bavaria, who loaded me with favours. I had known him since I was a mere child at Strasburg, where he had been colonel of a French regiment.

He would not let me leave Munich till he had taken me to see the brothers Senefelder, who had just invented the art of lithography. The results obtained by them appeared to me incredible, and they wished me to try my hand at the work. I stopped with them for some hours, and made a sketch with their crayons on one of their stones. I then left them, and an hour later, to my great surprise, they sent the stone to me with twenty impressions of my design. I took these proofs with me to Paris, and showed them to the Emperor, who at once recognised the immense value of the invention, and he told me to follow it up, but I found very few people disposed to aid me, and other affairs soon called me away. It was not until 1812 that lithography was really introduced into France, and began to yield far better results than those achieved by the original inventors. I had the honour of bringing the first specimen into France, but it was the talented Madame la Comtesse de Molien, wife of the Minister of the Treasury, who was the first to make generally known the great value of the invention.

We were hardly back in Paris before the fêtes began celebrating the successes of the campaign of 1805; but fresh preparations were being made for war, and my painting was again and again interrupted by the various missions entrusted to me. I had to take orders from the Major-General to the various corps the Emperor was collecting in Bavaria and Saxony to oppose the King of Prussia, whose army was already formidable and prepared to attack.

On October 9 the Prussians commenced hostilities at Schleitz by attacking the cavalry of Prince Murat. On the 10th Marshal Lannes took thirty pieces of cannon. In one of the charges of this eventful day Prince Louis of Prussia, nephew of the King, was killed by a sabre cut. On the 12th Marshal Davout took possession of eighteen pontoon bridges ready for use.

On the 13th the armies continued to approach each other in order of battle at right angles, and in the evening the plain of Jena appeared to be perfectly encircled with the watch fires of the two or three hundred thousand Prussians who rested in security, confident in their vast numbers.

The fires of the French army, on the other hand, hidden by the irregularities of the ground, were scarcely visible, and the apparent distance of the enemy still further encouraged the confidence of the Prussians. The night was fine and calm, and from the heights we occupied on the plateau above the plain of Jena the view of the illuminated camp below was magnificent. We felt as if we were preparing for a brilliant fête on the morrow, and the sentinels on either side chatted together at their outposts without any inclination to fight, as if in time of peace.

On October 14th, 1806, just before sunrise a thick fog came on and wrapped the whole district in gloom for several hours. The Emperor wished to turn the darkness to account by delaying the action long enough to allow our reserves and cavalry to come up, but the impatience of our troops led to the outposts opening fire on the enemy about nine o'clock. The whole line followed the movement, emerging through wide openings cleared and tested beforehand under Marshal Lannes.

The Prussians were also anxious to wait till the fog cleared away, but our attack roused them from their inaction, and their whole line also began to manoeuvre, changing front and marching upon Jena on their left. About eleven o'clock we could see their infantry advancing and deploying with precision, whilst their artillery arrived at a gallop at the head of an immense body of cavalry. When the two armies, marching towards each other, were nearly within musket shot, the 800 Prussian and French cannon simultaneously opened fire and exchanged salvoes. The thunder of the terrible discharge dispersed the fog, and soon nothing intercepted the rays of the sun but the smoke, which reproduced above the heads of the combatants the ranks in which they stood.

The whole army then engaged, and for some time the struggle was indecisive; but the Emperor, hearing that Marshal Ney and a portion of Murat's cavalry had come up, ordered a general attack. The shock was terrible. The Prussian cavalry in their furious charge shattered themselves upon our bayonets, and our grape shot and cavalry completed their destruction. The Prussian divisions were mingled in a confused mass, in which every ball from our guns struck down some hundred victims, whilst the forces of the enemy were divided.

General Rüchel fled towards our left wing, and the King of Prussia turned towards Magdeburg.

The fall of night put an end to the fighting, but not to the pursuit of fugitives, and the victories of Jena and of Auerstädt, which Marshal Davout won the same day, left in our hands 200 flags with the black eagle, more than 40,000 prisoners, 500 pieces of artillery, with the baggage, pontoon trains, and stores of the Prussians, who left 30,000 dead upon the field, with an immense number of wounded. The King of Prussia himself was wounded, as were also the two Dukes of Brunswick, the elder (who had made war on us in Champagne) so seriously that he died a few days later. Prince Henry, brother of the King, Prince Hohenlohe, the Marshal von Mollendorff, General von Tauenzin, General Rüchel, and thirty other superior officers, were either killed or wounded, and in consequence of this terrible defeat the whole of Prussia as far as the Vistula fell into our hands in a few days.

The Grand Duchess of Brunswick, sister of Frederick the Great, was then living in a château near Potsdam, and I was sent to carry to her the respectful greetings of Napoleon, and to offer on his behalf to do her any service in his power. This princess, her heart wrung with the terrible disasters which had overtaken the kingdom so much aggrandised by her brother, was also grieving bitterly over the loss of her husband and her nephew Prince Henry, both killed at Jena. Still her Royal Highness controlled her emotions in a wonderful way, received me kindly, expressed her gratitude to the Emperor for his magnanimity, but asked only to have some of her property secured to her, and would not allow me to leave with her the guard of honour I had orders to place at her disposal.

Following up our successes we stopped for a few days at Posen, and the grandees of Poland came to do homage to the Emperor in their Oriental costumes. The contrast of the costly robes, the valuable furs, and the richly decorated weapons of the nobles with the wretched garments of the peasants, and the difference between the noble dignified bearing of the masters and the abject demeanour of the serfs, impressed me painfully, and the state of things in Poland was quite a revelation to me. The castles of the nobles with their gorgeous internal decorations were surrounded with rough huts, the thatched roofs tumbling to pieces, beneath which serfs and domestic animals such as pigs and poultry were huddled together in misery, protected but little from the weather. Vast stretches of sand, here and there sparsely cultivated, alternating with gloomy pine forests, with the tumbledown huts void of all comforts for the inmates, gave to the country such a desolate poverty-stricken appearance, that our soldiers, used to their fair land of France, said to each other with a smile, "They call this a country, do they? A fine country it is, too, where if you ask for bread (kleba) the only answer you get is *gué gué gué* (I haven't got any), or if you ask for water you are told *zara zara* (presently). It's not our idea of a country, anyhow."

A Pole brought up in the midst of such privations at once becomes a hero in war. The moujik, bent with toil and huddled beneath his sheepskin fastened at the waist with a rope of straw, becomes a spirited horseman as soon as he dons the plumed *schapska* and brandishes his Lance with its floating pennon. His horse from the desolate Ukraine, which in his winter gear, with his long flowing mane reaching almost to the ground, seems crushed by the weight he carries, now holds himself up proudly, not a whit less ready for the battle field than his master. The Poles received us with enthusiasm as brothers and liberators. They were aided to form regiments, very soon 10,000 joined our army, and the Emperor picked out a corps of the best of them to join his own guard.

What struck us most in the big town of Warsaw was that everywhere in the streets, the promenades, and the salons, we heard French spoken as perfectly as in Paris.

The memory of the terrible Suvoroff was still recent. That general had burnt half the city of Warsaw, and destroyed with his artillery its finest buildings, without being able to make the inhabitants open their gates. He was also cruel enough to have the whole population of Praga, a suburb on the left bank of the Vistula, massacred in the night without distinction of age or sex. The people of Warsaw looked upon us as the avengers of Suvoroff's atrocities. Kosciuszko, the valiant defender of the independence of Poland, had found consolation for his woes in our ranks. There was but one sentiment with regard to the Russians, and no matter with whom we conversed the same opinions were expressed in excellent French. The ladies of Warsaw were as eager for our success as were their husbands and brothers, and so great was their sympathy for France that when, in 1813, six years later, Austrian troops occupied Warsaw, and the general in command, the Archduke Ferdinand, invited the ladies to a fête given by him, they all declined to go. The Prince, irritated by their contempt, sent them an invitation to a second fête, giving them to understand that he would punish those who did not attend it. This time they went, but they were all dressed in mourning, and none of them would dance, each one pleading as an excuse that she had lost a brother or some other relative in the war. Many of these ladies were very beautiful, with fair complexions and good figures; they were, moreover, as graceful as the Creole women so often are. Their lively yet dignified manners, and cordial reception of us, led us to hope for a pleasant winter in their society, but more serious matters than balls quickly summoned us elsewhere.

Prince Poniatowski, nephew of the last King of Prussia, had awaited our coming in his palace at Warsaw, and he now eagerly placed himself at the head of the Poles who had taken service under our Emperor. General Dombrowski, another Pole, was already in command of a French division. The French army crossed the Vistula on December 18th and 19th, 1806, whilst the Russians were advancing in force to the support of their allies the Prussians.

Amongst the dense forests of pines, where we sank knee deep in the miry soil, we again cane across the Cossacks, Kalmucks, Khirgesses and Tartars from the Ural districts, with whom we had first made acquaintance at Austerlitz a year ago. We found the Russians at Pultusk and Golymin, and the Augereau and Davout divisions were there engaged in a fierce struggle. The miry nature of the ground added to the horrors of the combat. The Russian loss was very great. The luckless wounded had not the strength to drag themselves out of the mud to join their comrades in retreat, and were ridden down and crushed beneath their own artillery and that of the French in pursuit. No efforts, however strenuous, on the part of the teams of horses could enable them to drag their loads through the quagmire, soaked with blood and made up of the flesh of thousands of victims kneaded with the mire into a revolting mass which clogged the wheels, and the Russians were compelled to abandon all their artillery, including ninety cannon. A great number of prisoners also fell into our hands. Marshals Lannes and Davout carried off the chief honours of the day (December 26th, 1806). The next morning, when we were awaiting the signal for departure, my comrades asked me to make a sketch on the wall of the room we were in of some episode of the recent struggle in the town. They pointed a few bits of charcoal for me, and I sketched a dozen men and horses, the size of life, choosing some of the mounted Cossacks, whose quaint appearance had struck me and who had deafened us with their yells whilst they riddled us with their arrows. My companions, delighted with the faithfulness of the representation, scribbled the name of the artist at the bottom of the drawing, but the trumpet call to mount sounded before I could finish it. The Pole who owned the house set store on this souvenir of the French, preserved it carefully, and changed the sign of his inn to that of the "French Cossacks." Thirty-three years afterwards some young Polish refugees whom I met at Toulouse recognised my name through having seen it beneath the picture on the wall of the inn at Pultusk. My more serious works will probably not last as long as the sketch, which has brought so much custom to this Polish inn.

During the night of the following day I had orders to summon the Legrand division in all haste to cut off the retreat of a fugitive corps. The snow was falling, and it was pitch dark. I had no guide and nothing to direct me through the pine forests and over the quagmires, but fortunately the latter were now frozen over and pretty firm. I had been wandering vaguely about with no idea of my bearings for some two hours, when I came upon the bivouac of a few chasseurs of the guard who had lost their way. Waiting for light, they were cooking the results of a little foraging in a big saucepan; some rice, a few fowls, and a goose or two, all boiled down together, had produced a most inviting hotchpotch, seasoned with such an appetite as it is not given to the great ones of the earth to know. The brave fellows invited me to share their supper, and my portion of their stew renovated my forces, exhausted by fatigue.

After a halt of a few minutes only, I resumed my search, and I had gone about a mile when I heard some luckless Frenchman shouting, swearing, and calling for help. He and his horse were sinking in a bog, the ice on the top having broken beneath their weight. I was only able to approach with difficulty, for my horse refused to advance on such treacherous ground. But I thought I recognised the voice, and shouted, "Who is it?" The answer came back, "It's you, Lejeune, is it? I am in the greatest danger. My horse has sunk to the neck, and I am up to the waist in mud. I am exhausted with my struggles and benumbed with cold; for pity's sake get me out of this terrible pit. I shall be swallowed up directly." It was General Legrand, the very man I was looking for, but, like myself, he was also ignorant what had become of his men and in peril of his life.

Not being able to fasten up my horse, and fearing to lose him, I wrapped his head up in my cloak, and thus blinded he remained perfectly still. I then approached the General on foot, and our combined efforts at last resulted in his getting to terra firmer, whilst his horse, relieved of the weight of the rider, managed to get out of the mud. We then went off to try and find the lost division. First we made out a few scattered fires, and then came upon the infantry, which were able to reach at daybreak the point to which I had orders to take them. The enemy in retreat had had no better road than we, and after defending them for some time they abandoned to us a good many pieces of cannon which had stuck in the mud.

General Legrand, whom I had just rescued from danger, was a fine fellow some six feet high, with a manly presence and a somewhat imperious manner, but a noble character. A little later he married General Scherer's daughter, who was perhaps the prettiest girl in Paris. She was the very ideal of a heroine of romance, such as the old chroniclers loved to paint. Her light golden hair floated from a dainty head set upon a charming figure, and resembled the fleeting mists which gather about the rising sun, and exhale in the morning air the scent of the flowers they have caressed during the night.

The stern and dignified warrior with his strong athletic limbs, yielding so gently and submissively to the lightest whim of his young bride, was like a new Hercules bound and conquered by love. The Emperor liked his generals to marry, and often aided with liberal gifts to bring about unions which would otherwise have been difficult if not impossible.

CHAPTER 4

Eylau, Friedland, Tilsit

We pursued the Russians through the forests for several days, but there was no fighting except a little skirmishing on the part of the advanced guard. The Emperor then halted a few days to reorganise the army, which was much exhausted with the long struggle, and our head quarters were in a stable at Golymin, where we were all crowded together on the straw. Our privations did not at all damp our spirits, and one evening the Emperor and Prince Berthier stopped a few minutes to hear us sing airs from the latest operas of Paris.

We exchanged new-year visits in the mud of Pultusk, and the Emperor returned for a short time to Warsaw, whither we followed as his suite on January 2nd, 1809. The ninety cannon we had taken had arrived before us, carriages and all.

A few days later the Emperor was ready to resume the campaign, and sent me to demand from the King of Saxony the troops he had promised. That venerable monarch, and his consort, the sister of the Queen of Bavaria, received me with many demonstrations of respect and expressions of devotion to the Emperor. The King placed all the luxuries of his palace at my disposal. Never since my childhood had I ridden in a sedan chair, and I thoroughly enjoyed being carried about by men in grand liveries in the fine structures assigned to me by the Grand Marshal for my various excursions in Dresden. The Picture Gallery and the Treasury were both thrown open to me, and in the latter I was specially struck, amongst the quantities of remarkable objects, with the many huge pearls, and the number of diamonds, including a green one. I greatly admired the pictures in the world-famous collection, notably the *Notte* of Correggio, considered his masterpiece; the *Madonna di San Sisto*, most admired of Raphael's virgins; Gerard Douw's *Woman with Dropsy;* and *The Cemetery* by Ruysdael, &c.

In a very short time the troops were collected, and I started at the head of the first column. The rain had swollen many of the streams, and inundations compelled us to halt at Görlitz at the same time as a French battalion following our route. The wine shops of the town were soon full of the soldiers of the two nations fraternising glass in hand.

I left the Saxons *en route*, and rejoined the Emperor, who had just left Warsaw to open the campaign of 1807. The thaw on the Vistula had broken down the bridges, and only a golden bribe would induce a boatman to trust himself and his frail craft amongst the floating ice to take me to the other side of the river. In spite of my every effort to press on, I did not reach the Emperor till February 8, the Sunday before Lent.

On the day before, the Augereau, Davout, and Ney divisions, with Murat's cavalry and the Imperial Guard, had bivouacked opposite and round about Eylau on ground covered with snow.

On the 8th, before six o'clock in the morning, the Russians took the initiative by attacking us all along our line. Several of our battalions were surprised and fled in disorder through Eylau, under the impression that they were pursued. This panic was, however, soon allayed, order was restored, and the battle which had begun on the frozen ponds outside Eylau became general. Several times during the day snow fell for an hour at a time in such quantities that we could not see two paces before us, and bodies of troops in movement lost their bearings. Now and then the cavalry crossed the enemy's lines, and did considerable mischief amongst their ranks; but, on the other hand, the Russian horsemen performed prodigies of valour, and the battle field was soon covered with the dead, 300 cannon on either side pouring out a hail of grape shot at close quarters and working terrible havoc. Marshal Augereau was wounded, and his corps, left without a leader, suffered horribly; his infantry, drawn up in squares, was positively annihilated where it stood.

The squadrons of the Emperor's Guard twice dashed through the Russian army, disabling more than 20,000 men, and sabreing the artillerymen at their posts. They would have assured victory to the French if the falling of the snow had not prevented us from seeing clearly and co-operating properly. The struggle had lasted for twelve hours, and the issue was still uncertain when, as night fell, Marshal Davout succeeded in outflanking the enemy on the right at Schmoditten, whilst Marshal Ney did the same on the left at Altdorf.

The enemy defended these two positions with desperation until eight o'clock in the evening, and at last managed to retreat during the night under cover of the darkness, leaving 7,000 dead upon the field, whilst every road was encumbered with thousands of wounded. This eight days' struggle cost the Russians 15,000 men in killed and wounded, 15,000 prisoners, thirty flags, and forty-five pieces of artillery.

We passed the night on the snow, wishing impatiently for the return of daylight, which, when it came, revealed to us a terrible sight, the gloom of which was intensified by the low-lying threatening clouds, heavy with snow ready to fall. Every detail of the struggle, the position of the lines, the squares with the places where the cavalry had charged, were clearly marked upon the ground by heaps of corpses. Many wounded, too numerous for help to be given them at once, had crept close to each other for the sake of warmth, whilst here and there horses wounded to death were dragging their entrails over the snow, piteously neighing to us or to their late riders for help in their suffering. I saw one of these poor creatures with but three legs licking the face of his owner, who was standing gazing at his injured steed with an expression of the greatest consternation. He had but a morsel of bread for himself, but he gave it to his horse. The Emperor was as grieved as we were at the frightful sufferings he could do so little to relieve. He gave up several days to doing what was possible, and one day he paused near a group of wounded Russians, whilst his surgeon Yvan dressed their wounds. The Russians, guessing from the respect with which he was treated that he was the Czar of the French, invoked blessings on his head, kissing his foot and stirrups. His whole time was given up now to seeing that the wounded received proper care, and he insisted on the Russians being as well treated as the French. After the battle of Eylau, the Russian army retreated towards Königsberg, and took up a position beyond some narrow but deep and muddy streams, which we could not have crossed but for our portable artillery bridges. Our outposts were stationed on the banks of the streams.

It was now necessary for the French army to rally its scattered forces and to replace men lost in the murderous struggle. Moreover, the Emperor had left behind him three fortresses which it was necessary for him to take lest they should harass his rear when he should attempt to drive the Russians beyond the Niemen. These fortresses were Stralsund in Swedish Pomerania, defended by a Swedish army held in check by Marshal Mortier; Colberg on the Baltic, defended by the Prussians and besieged by General Loisin; and lastly, Danzig, one of the largest fortified towns of Germany, at the mouth of the Vistula, containing a numerous garrison, which might greatly interfere with our operations. There was no doubt that these three towns had to be taken, and, as an officer of engineers, I was commissioned to go to and fro, urging on the besiegers, and bringing them the Emperor's orders.

In due course I found myself with Marshal Mortier outside Stralsund, within the walls of which he had driven the Swedes, where, in spite of all the efforts of King Gustavus Adolphus, they were completely blockaded, and compelled to take refuge in the island of Rügen, divided from the mainland by the narrow sound on which the town is built. Gustavus Adolphus, thinking that he could emulate the exploits of King Charles XII. as easily as he could don the uniform of a soldier, was in reality quite unable to cope with the situation. His weakness of character had alienated his subjects, and was as much the cause of his defeat as was the success of the French arms. He remembered that Charles XII. had passed a night on watch at the gates of Stralsund, so he too spent one as a sentinel on the same spot. A little later he hoped to cut Marshal Mortier off from the main body of his army, and he embarked his Swedes for that purpose near Passvalk, but he was defeated and lost all his men.

When I returned from Stralsund, I found the Emperor at Osterode, where he was receiving the Turkish ambassadors from the Sultan and General von Kleist, aide-de-camp of the King of Prussia, who had brought proposals of peace which were perfectly inadmissible. The Emperor instructed me to escort the Prussian envoy as far as our outposts. This led to one of the most comic episodes of my military career. The General was doubtless a brave man enough as a rule, but he was the most arrant coward in a carriage I ever had the good fortune to meet. I gave him a guard of honour to accompany his carriage and sat beside him myself. We started at night and had to traverse some twenty or thirty miles of very bad road in the woods. As we bumped over the roots of trees and in and out of ruts we were a good deal shaken about, and every time the brave General lost his equilibrium he clutched hold of me, screaming, "We are lost! we are lost!' His anxiety manifested itself in the most extraordinary manner. He insisted on the carriage being carried by peasants, and I told off a dozen, who bore lighted torches in one hand whilst they held up the carriage with the other, with the aid of ropes fastened on either side, so that there was no further danger of our being tumbled into the mud. We were kept in position like the masts of a vessel, or like banners carried in procession and kept steady in the wind by long ribbons. The gay young officers forming our escort laughed so much at the absurd arrangement and at the terror of our guest, that I was obliged to dismiss them at daylight lest I should not be able to enforce proper respect for the envoy. He fully appreciated my care and courtesy, and rewarded me later by protecting me in a far more serious danger than that of being upset in the mud.

There was a neutral space of about seven or eight leagues in extent between the outposts of the two armies, and I did not choose to leave the General till he was safe with his own people, so I went with him to the gates of Ortelsburg, where a body of Cossacks advanced towards us, lances in rest, shouting,

"*Honi?*" (Who goes there? Who are you?) To which General von Kleist answered, "*Zoni*" (friends). But the Cossacks as they approached our open carriage recognised my French uniform before anything else, and in a moment, with faces full of rage and hatred, they aimed some twenty lances at my breast, whilst Von Kleist, whose life was in danger as well as mine, only with the greatest difficulty managed to make the Cossacks understand that he was an envoy returning without drum or trumpet to announce him, and that I was his escort. The men, full of suspicion of us, took us both prisoners pending the decision of the King of Prussia in our case, and I was shut up at Ortelsburg for three days. The General, however, who was quickly recognised by the Cossack officers in the town, refused to leave me lest some harm should befall me, and during the time of my detention all the Cossacks belonging to the division occupying the place came to stare at us as if we were lions in a menagerie, crowding into our room and spending whole nights in the snow in the streets outside, though there were twenty-eight degrees of frost, sleeping with the bridles of their little steeds called *konias* on their arms, as peacefully as we could have done in the most comfortable of beds. These Cossacks were many of them handsome fellows, and much to their amusement I took portraits of several with a pencil on a bit of paper. On the third day the Emperor of Russia sent his aide-de-camp, Colonel Prince Sokoreff, to release me from my tedious imprisonment, and to escort me on my way to the outposts. I took leave of General von Kleist, but met him again at Berlin a few years later when he was commander-in-chief of one of the big Prussian armies.

On my return to Osterode, the Emperor listened with interest to my account of my adventures, especially to what I told him about the Cossacks who could hit an enemy with their lances at a distance of more than four yards. He asked me what I thought of introducing their weapon into the French army, and when I replied that I thought it would be a good thing to do so, he told me to design a suitable costume for a corps of French lancers.

Marshal Murat coming in during this conversation, the Emperor said to him: "You are to equip a hundred men in the costume Lejeune will design, and at once instruct them how to use the lance." Murat approved of the rough sketch I made; he chose the colours, and formed the hundred men into the guard of the Grand Duchy of Berg. The Emperor was much pleased with the result, and later he introduced whole regiments of lancers into his own guard and the army, retaining the uniform I had designed.

Soon after this I was sent to Marshal Brune, whose corps, with that of Marshal Mortier besieging Stralsund, was engaged in the manoeuvres against the Swedes. Marshal Brune, after several successes, had granted an armistice of ten days. The King of Sweden availed himself of this to ask for an interview; and the Marshal having done me the honour to consult me, I said it would be a capital thing if we could break off the alliance which the Swedes had formed with the Prussians and Russians. The Marshal then agreed to the proposed rendezvous, and he took me with him in his carriage to the Bridge of Auklam, spanning the river which formed the boundary.

We were very much surprised to find no outposts on the bridge; still, we ventured to cross it with our escort and push on to meet the Swedes. After traversing some four leagues without meeting a creature we reached the large village of Schlatkow, all the doors in which were closed, whilst the streets were absolutely deserted. Very much put out at this state of things, we had just told our coachman to turn back, when the gates of a big hostelry were suddenly flung back by some Swedish officers, who ordered our carriages to enter a yard in which a bodyguard of cavalry was drawn up in order of battle. The gates were at once shut, and we found ourselves separated from our escort. We were very much astonished, for it seemed as if we had fallen into an ambush. We alighted from our carriage, however, and were escorted to a room where the aides-de-camp of the King received the Marshal with every demonstration of respect.

The King, though notice of our arrival was at once given

to him, kept us waiting a long time, and our annoyance was no doubt reflected in our faces, for a dead silence succeeded the interchange of compliments.

At last the King sent to ask the Marshal to go to him alone in a private room, and one of the royal bodyguard took up his station at the door. Presently we heard a very animated, almost an angry, conversation going on within. The party waiting outside consisted of Colonel Mathis, Colonel Saint-Raymond, and myself, all three strong determined French officers; three Swedish aides-de-camp, and a French gentleman wearing the Cross of St. Louis and the gold-laced uniform of a lieutenant-general of the old French army. It was the Duke of Vienne, an emigrant serving in the ranks of our enemies, and he looked at us with anything but a pleasant expression. The situation became more and more strained, and, convinced that we should have to sell our lives as dearly as we could, I had just whispered to my comrades, Colonels Mathis and Saint-Raymond, "I'll deal with the King and the sentinel, you see to the others," and we were standing on the *qui-vive* at our posts, sword in hand, when the Marshal came out pale, grave, and disguising the anger he felt. I was near the door, and I got a glimpse of the King standing up wearing a caricature of the costume of Charles XII. and gazing at us. The Marshal, fearing that I meant to go into the room, took my hand and said, "Let us be off!" The carriages were waiting; we got in; the guards, still under arms, opened the big gates, and we started, followed by our escort.

Alone in the carriage with the Marshal, he told me what had passed that I might tell the Emperor. Gustavus, though he had been beaten ten times in succession by the Marshal, had actually proposed to him that he should desert to the enemy with his army, and, joining the allies, aid in placing Louis XVIII. upon the French throne. "The legitimate king of your country," he had said, "will make you Generalissimo of his army and that of the allies, and will place under your orders the troops which the Duke of Vienne, who is now with me, can dispose of." These troops were three or four old emigrants, who had not so much as a sword amongst them. This speech was moreover interlarded with curses of the Emperor Napoleon. Marshal Brune, who felt how imprudent he had been to venture into the Swedish quarters so far from his army, was obliged to disguise his indignation and to listen to the whole of the infamous propositions, to come scatheless out of a situation which his physical strength and our resolute courage could only have made yet more desperate.

Acting on the Marshal's instructions, I now rejoined the Emperor at Finkenstein, where he occupied rather a pretty château near several lakes or big ponds, now half frozen over, amusing himself by hunting the wild swans by which they were frequented.

At Finkenstein the Emperor received the ambassadors from Persia, with Mirza-Riza-Khan at their head, who came to congratulate him on his victories over their enemies the Russians. In the neighbouring forests were great troops of elands, which are bigger than stags and have huge antlers. We spent the few days we had to spare in the chase of these fine creatures, which are very difficult to hunt. We succeeded in bringing down a few. When we got back from our excursions over snow and ice amongst the gloomy pine and fir forests, we warmed ourselves at the stoves of the well-heated conservatories of the château, where strawberries, plums, and cherries were successfully cultivated. The snow was now beginning to melt, and spring was approaching. Marshal Lefebvre was besieging Danzig, defended by Marshal Kalkreuth with 20,000 Prussians, by whom many sorties were made. The Emperor sent me to Marshal Lefebvre to press on the siege, and I took part in many remarkable episodes. The first was at a sortie of the Prussians by way of Hagelsburg, where they were vigorously repulsed; and the second was the affair of Veichselmunde, where a considerable body of the Russian army attacked us in the hope of compelling us to raise the siege and capturing our artillery. The troops under Marshal Lefebvre drove back the sorties, whilst those under Marshal Lannes and General Oudinot repulsed the Russians. During the battle I rode a horse lent to me by Marshal Lefebvre, and on my way back to head quarters in the evening a ball from Bischofsberg shattered a rock beneath me, and the fragments killed my horse on the spot. I remained flat on my face on the ground for some time before I could get up. The effects of the shock and the pain of my bruises soon went off; I was not really wounded, and I was able to drag myself to head quarters, where the rejoicings over the victory soon quite restored me. I started the same night to take the good news to the Emperor.

A few days later he sent me back again to urge on the siege of Danzig, which was rendered extremely arduous by the skill with which the defence was conducted by Marshal Kalkreuth.

We had already crowned the covered way, and effected the descent of the ditch, when on May 19th an English sloop of war with twenty-four guns tried to run the blockade and get into the town by way of an arm of the Vistula which winds through the meadows round Danzig. The bold commander of the vessel hoped to break down every obstacle with discharges of grape shot from his cannon. He had actually got within range of the town, having met with no more formidable obstacles than a few simple booms, which were easily broken through. He was not, however, prepared for the sudden attack opened upon him by several companies of our sharpshooters, who rushed across the meadows and fired a volley into the ship from both sides of the stream, mowing down the sailors and bringing the sloop to a standstill. Without helmsmen, and with sails flapping helplessly, the vessel drifted to the side of the stream and grounded; the soldiers sprang on board and took 150 prisoners as well as the valuable cargo of weapons, ammunition, and provisions which the commander had intended for the use of the garrison of the beleaguered city.

All the best engineer officers of the French army were collected together under General Chasseloup at the siege of Danzig, and the operations were conducted with great rapidity, though not fast enough to please the Emperor, who, at a distance from the scene of action, did not realise that fresh obstacles were thrown in our way every day by the skill of the directors of the defence. My fellow officers were therefore by no means pleased to see a messenger arrive from head quarters with orders to stimulate their zeal, and they revenged themselves on me by making me cross in the open from one parallel to another at all the most dangerous points of the saps. Two of the boldest of my tormentors, named Bodzon and Delange, however, were punished for their useless temerity by being wounded, I meanwhile pretending that I saw nothing unusual in their behaviour. The descent of the ditch had been effected at the principal point; our sap had reached the enceinte, and Marshal Lefebvre was as impatient as we were to get into the town and to put an end to the tedious operations, which had now been going on for a month, and cost us many lives every day. One day the Marshal, angry at all the delays, took me by the arm and began banging with his fist at the base of a wall, pierced by the sap, shouting in his Alsatian brogue, "Make a hole here, and I'll be the first to go through it."

Meanwhile the walls were falling under our bombardment, and a practicable breach had at last just been made. Troops were ready for the assault, and the decisive blow was to be struck the next morning, May 24th, 1807, when Marshal Kalkreuth capitulated. I took the good news to the Emperor.

On June 1st the Emperor went to Danzig to examine its condition, gave orders that the damage done in the siege should be repaired, and that the town should be restored to a state of defence. He then hurried back to Finkenstein, where negotiations for peace had been begun by the Russians. On June 5, when Napoleon hoped to end the campaign by a favourable treaty, the Russians, who had only pretended to want peace with a view to throwing the French off their guard, made a general and unexpected attack all along our lines.

Hostilities being thus renewed by the Russians, our whole army was again led against them, and during eight days they sustained one reverse after another, and were several times compelled to retreat, and pursued on the route to Königsberg and Friedland.

On the 7th I received orders from the Emperor to go and press on the operations at the siege of Colberg.

General Loison, who was conducting the siege, and General Chainbarlier, commandant of the engineers, took me round the

trenches, which had been opened ten or twelve days before opposite the fort of Volfsberg, at about half a cannon-shot from
the town itself. This fort, which had inflicted a great deal of mischief on us, was so much damaged by our artillery that I could
not dissemble my surprise that it had not fallen into our hands
several days before.

"Well, my dear fellow," was the reply I got, "if you find it so
easy, take it yourself."

I accepted the challenge, and set to work at once. I began by
demanding 300 picked men who would be willing to join me,
and I had assigned to me 100 French, 100 Italian, and 100 Polish
grenadiers, commanded by three brave captains, namely, Beau-
fort d'Hautpoul and Rohault de Fleury of the engineers, with
Bécli of the Italian legion.

Whilst these troops were approaching the trench, I took a
drummer, and advancing with him to the fort, I ordered him to
beat the rappel. I wanted to reconnoitre and to parley with the
enemy. I made my way thus right up to the barrier of the fort,
and was able to convince myself that the glacis and the bottom
of the ditch were bristling with spikes and military pits in good
condition. The commandant did not keep me waiting, but appeared at once, and I advised him to withdraw before the assault
of a fort which seemed to me no longer tenable, but the grand
defence of which did him honour. He agreed with me that his
position was most critical, but added that he could not surrender
without orders from the Governor of Colberg. I gave him half
an hour to get those orders, and withdrew, employing the interval in giving my instructions to my three columns, telling them
exactly what they were to do, but not allowing a single man to
show himself beforehand.

At the time named I took my drummer again and went towards the fort. I had not taken twenty steps from our trenches
before the cannon opened fire on me, the discharge covering me
with dust. The answer was clear enough. I gave the signal for the
assault by raising my sword instead of the white handkerchief I
had been holding, with the cry of "Columns to advance!"

With the rapidity of a flash of lightning my 300 men were over the parapet of the trench and dashing forward in the direction ordered. I did not wait a single instant for them to come up, but made straight for the barrier, getting there just in time to see the garrison running away. I called out to them in German, "Right about face!" and, astonished at the command in their own language, they obeyed. I drew them up in line between myself and the fort, and they never suspected that they had been made to serve as a screen between me and the hail of shot from the bastions. The next moment the walls and every point of vantage of the fort swarmed with my grenadiers, and I ordered them to shoot down the first Prussian who moved from the spot where I had posted him. I then made my way into the casemates, which the gunners had not been able to leave. The brave fellows received me with a threat to set fire to their powder and blow us all up together. They would no doubt have done so if I had taken the matter seriously; but calling up all my tact and retaining my presence of mind, I answered them gaily, disarmed their anger, and avoided an explosion. They left the casemates, and I made them set fire to the four blinded batteries flanking the fort from right to left, which were completely burnt down. Our engineer officers then set to work to install us in the fort and establish our communications.

As long as I kept the Prussians drawn up in line between us and the town, the town could not fire on us, and the day passed without the exchange of a shot, as if there were an armistice. Several Prussian officers, amongst others the young partisan Schill, who had won some celebrity, came to chat with us, and they assured us that Colberg would never be taken.

Towards evening, when our defensive works were complete and we were well under cover, we felt we no longer needed the presence of our Prussians; and not wishing to encumber myself with prisoners, I set free one by one the men who had saved us much bloodshed by coming between us and several hundred balls. The last Prussian had scarcely left when the firing from Colberg recommenced, and the very first shot mortally wounded General Teulié, who survived but two days, and killed on the spot two engineer officers who were chatting with him and did not choose to take the precaution of drawing back. This foolhardy ostentation of courage cost France the lives of many gallant warriors, with no result to the country but accustoming their subordinates to despise death and to be ready to face all manner of dangers.

During the night we pushed forward our parallel with its communications in advance of the fort, so as to get within reach of the town, which kept faith with us by making a most vigorous defence. I myself aimed some dozen bombs at a Swedish frigate, the huge balls from which struck us in the rear, destroying our men and our defences. Two of my bombs struck the water so near the vessel that she raised anchor and fled out into the offing. Never was siege trench more vigorously assailed than was ours on that terrible day. General Loison, who had but one arm left, seeing his men falling all around him, flung up his empty sleeve, hoping that it would be carried off instead of the head of some poor artilleryman. We were at such close quarters with the enemy that every shot told on either side. General Chambarlier advanced to the attack on the opposite side to the fort we had taken, and from that moment our success became more and more assured; whilst at the same time we realised how useful outlying forts are for prolonging the defence and retarding the fall of a stronghold protected by them.

Leaving everything in such good train, I hastened back to the Emperor to tell him of our success, and to take part in the grand struggle for which preparation was being made when I left him. During the interval our army had been gaining ground, and, in spite of all my haste, I did not arrive at Friedland till the evening after the battle, which was just ending after lasting no less than sixteen hours.

On June 13th the Russians, in retreat on the right bank of the Alle, noticed that our light cavalry, in endeavouring to bar their way to Königsberg, where their magazines were situated, had taken possession of Friedland, and Prince Bagration ordered a large body of cavalry to charge our advance guard, routing them and compelling them to retire behind the advancing infantry of General Oudiriot.

This temporary success encouraged the Commander-in-Chief of the Russians, General Bennigsen, to hope for victory, and during the night and the next morning he made his army cross, by way of Friedland, from the right to the left of the Alle, with a view to attacking us. He thus left in his rear the very narrow bridge of Friedland, and a deep river with very steep banks. This position, it was evident at a glance, was a very bad one in which to give battle, and his only excuse was that he greatly underestimated the numbers of the French.

Meanwhile the Emperor had ordered our cavalry under Prince Murat and Marshal Davout to advance upon Königsberg, so as to get there before the Russians, whilst Marshal Soult was marching on Kreuznach, Marshal Lannes on Domnau, Marshals Ney and Mortier on Lampasch, and General Victor and the Imperial Guard on Friedland.

The Emperor was waiting for these various corps to get into position, when he received the news on the morning of June 14th of the offensive movement of the Russians.

He mounted immediately, and galloped rapidly over the eight or ten leagues which separated him from the field of battle, reaching it about noon. Imagining that the Russians had only made an attack to cover the retreat of their rear guard, he was very much surprised to hear a prolonged and vigorous cannonade. In his anxiety he urged on his Arab steed, with which few other horses could keep up, and quickly found himself among a number of wounded, who were retreating towards the ambulances. Amongst them he recognised Colonel Reynaud of the 15th regiment of the line, and stopped to ask him what had happened, if his regiment had retreated, and under what circumstances he had been wounded. Reynaud, who had been struck by a ball, replied that, tired of seeing his regiment inactive under a decimating fire, he had ordered it to advance and charge the enemy's guns in the hope of carrying some of them, but that a trench he had not been able to see had arrested the men, of whom he had lost 1,500 on its brink. He added: "On the plateau of Friedland, behind the position I had hoped to take, the enemy has just massed an immense number of men, certainly not less than 80,000."

The Emperor, still in error as to the state of things, thought this account exaggerated, and exclaimed, "That is not true!" to which Reynaud, irritated at being disbelieved, answered, "Well, I swear by my head that the numbers I have stated are there, and that there will be hot work.' The Emperor's only reply was to dash his spurs into his Arab, which bounded furiously forward, carrying its master into the very midst of the sharpshooters.

The united corps of grenadiers under General Oudinot, supported by General Grouchy's dragoons and General Nansouty's cuirassiers, had been engaged since daybreak opposite the village of Posthenen, by way of which the Russians were endeavouring to debauch with a view to a vigorous attack on us. Many charges of cavalry had taken place on the flanks of this village, whilst our infantry had been driven from it five or six times after taking possession of it. From every one of these charges our cuirassiers had brought back many prisoners, but the enemy, still supposing they had but the small body of men they could see to deal with, directed a furious cannonade upon the place, whilst the main body of the French army was rapidly gaining ground in the direction of Königsberg and had advanced nearly a league and a half beyond Friedland.

Such was the state of things when the Emperor arrived on the scene of battle. He now saw plainly enough the formidable forces reported to him, and realised what mighty issues were at stake. It was now past noon, and having calculated the time required for the various corps to get to the front, he fixed five o'clock as the time for a general attack, and sent messengers in every direction with these orders.

At that time the whole army was drawn up in line; Marshal Ney on the right, Marshal Lannes in the centre, Marshal Mortier on the left, and General Victor with the reserve force. The entire force of Bennigsen was in position opposite to them, in front of and on the right and left of Friedland.

A salvoe of artillery gave the signal, and Marshal Ney issued with his corps from the wood which had hidden them from the enemy, and advanced upon the Russians in columns of divisions with shouldered arms at a rapid pace.

Immediately a swarm of some five to six thousand Cossacks, Kalmucks and Khirgesses and Bashkirs, covering a mass of regular cavalry, surrounded our infantry, hoping to dismay them with their wild charges and yells. But our dragoons advanced at a gallop, swept aside and drove back this irregular cavalry, whilst General Victor came up to protect the artillery of General Senarmont, who was thundering at the enemy's lines from a battery of thirty pieces, and Marshal Ney marching straight ahead attacked and drove back with bayonet charges a considerable body of Russians, driving men and horses into the ravine and the river, where many of them were drowned.

Whilst this was going on on our right, Marshal Mortier on the left charged the enemy in front of him and drove it also back on Friedland, where the Russians were now massed in great numbers.

At the same time, with a concerted action no one but the Emperor could have brought about, Marshal Lannes with the Oudinot and Verdier divisions attacked the centre of the Russians concentrated at Friedland, and drove them back, in spite of charge after charge of their cavalry, which with reckless bravery endeavoured in vain to check the advance of our columns.

Marshal Ney, having quickly destroyed the forces which had opposed him, now approached Friedland by his left and attempted to enter it. The Russian guard, infantry and cavalry together, rushed to oppose his movement, and for a moment threw the Marshal's troops into confusion, making them lose ground. But Marshal Dupont saw what was going on, attacked the Russian guard in the rear, and drove it back. With scarcely room to move in the narrow ravines by which they endeavoured to retreat, nearly all the men of the guard fell in a general massacre, and their generals Pahlen and Markof were killed.

All the Russian forces on the right of Friedland were driven back by Marshals Lannes and Mortier, and forced to retreat by way of the difficult fords of the Alle. Great numbers were drowned, and quantities of artillery and baggage were left embedded in the mud. Every house in the little town of Friedland was crowded with wounded Russians, and the reserve forces of the enemy made superhuman efforts to prevent our entering it. But we advanced all the same, and the fighting went on in the streets, which became literally choked with the bodies of men and horses killed by shot or bayonet. At last as the sun went down the French found themselves masters of the town, and with no more enemies to repulse. They were able to take breath once more, and their repose was broken only by an occasional discharge from the cannon on the heights of the right bank of the Alle, and by the hunger and thirst they could not satisfy.

It was just at the end of this glorious day that I arrived panting for breath with the good news of the approaching fall of Colberg. The Emperor and Prince Berthier were just dismounting near the town when I came up to them. I had no sooner begun to tell of my having taken the outlying fort of Colberg by assault, than the Emperor interrupted me, saying with a bright and friendly smile, "I too have taken my village of Colberg today, and everything else which checked my advance. Friedland is worth Austerlitz, Jena, and Marengo, the anniversary of which I celebrate to-day! That will do now; go and rest. I have got to work!"

I went off to find my comrades, who were bivouacking in a field of wheat, our men taking the straw to feed the horses. I flung myself down beside them, and they told me all that had happened that day and how my young brother, a second-lieutenant in a picked corps, had been wounded in the morning. I went off to find him, but could not do so for several days. At last, however, I came upon him in a château to which he had retired, and where he was being carefully nursed by five or six pretty women. A ball had wounded him in the leg, but without fracturing the bone, and he recovered well and rapidly. It was with great regret that he left his kind hosts at the end of the campaign, after the signing of the Peace of Tilsit, when I went to fetch him and to take him to Paris as a convalescent. It was not quite six months before the battle of Friedland that I had fetched him in my carriage from the military college at Fontainebleau, and taken him to join his regiment at Jena. When we parted I said as I embraced him, "I wish you three things, a wound, advancement, and the cross of honour." A few days after Friedland all these wishes were accomplished, for the young soldier was raised to the rank of lieutenant, and General Oudinot, who had noted his brave bearing in the battle, gave him the cross of honour, then a very rarely granted recompense. I had the pleasure to gain for him in addition to all this six months" leave of absence, which he passed at home with me.

But I must return to the Imperial head quarters at Friedland. Some 18,000 Russian corpses encumbered the ground round the Emperor's bivouac, with more dead horses than I had ever seen elsewhere, for the enemy's cavalry had suffered terribly.

On June 15th the pursuit of the enemy was continued, and we entered Vehlau, where the Germans, men and women alike, freed from the yoke of the Russians, who had treated them badly, received us with open arms. In their retreat the Russians everywhere set fire to their magazines, and cut or burnt the bridges. Reaching the Pregel on the 16th, we found the bridges all burnt, and the Emperor had several new ones thrown across the river. The same day the Russians abandoned Königsberg, leaving that fine city crowded with wounded and with stores of weapons and provisions of all kinds. Marshal Soult established himself there with his corps, whilst Prince Murat continued the pursuit of the retreating army. Every day a skirmish took place with the Russians, and the Prince secured 5,000 prisoners with seventeen cannon, making his entry into Tilsit on the 19th, in spite of the opposition of a swarm of Kalmucks and Tartars, who discharged their arrows with considerable skill to the accompaniment of piercing yells. The nomad cavalry then galloped over the wooden bridge of Tilsit, and hastily set fire to it.

The Emperor and his staff entered Tilsit on the afternoon of the 19th. The enemy had not had time to do much mischief, and in the farms and homesteads on the fertile borders of the Niemen we found plenty of the forage for the horses and provisions for the men of which our army was in such urgent need.

After sustaining in a few days such heavy losses, the Emperor Alexander realised the necessity of putting an end to the disastrous war by making peace, and he sent one of his generals,

Prince Labanoff, to Marshal Berthier to propose an armistice. The Emperor at once granted an audience to the Russian Plenipotentiary, receiving him in a most friendly manner, and the preliminaries of peace were ready for signature on the 21st.

The day after we learnt that the Emperors Alexander and Napoleon proposed meeting in a boat on the Niemen between the two armies, to talk over the final terms of peace. General Lariboisière, commander of the French artillery, at once ordered a huge raft to be made, on which a beautiful pavilion was to be erected for the reception of the two Emperors. Whilst awaiting the interview, Napoleon occupied himself in reviewing the troops, reorganising them, and disposing them so as to make them present as good an appearance as if they had not suffered at all in their arduous campaign. He was very much aided in this by the fine condition of his Guard, which had not been into action since the battle of Eylau, and looked as well in the camp at Tilsit as ever they did in a parade at Paris.

At noon on June 25th, 1809, the banks on either side of the river were covered with immense crowds, presenting a most picturesque appearance. On the Russian side were the soldiers from the Caucasus and the Don, with their bows and arrows, their lances and their barbaric armour, whilst on the other the French warriors in their gleaming uniforms were picturesquely grouped in the careless disorder of times of peace, on roofs, trees, and every point of vantage on the banks of the Niemen.

At half-past twelve two boats draped with flags, one bearing the white ensign of the Emperor of Russia with its double-headed black eagle, the other the national flag of France, left the banks at the same moment and approached the raft. As they alighted on it the Emperors cordially shook hands and passed into the tent prepared for them, round which were stationed a number of Russian and French sentinels.

The interview between the monarchs lasted two hours, during which I remained standing in a little boat which I had so placed as to command the best possible general view of the memorable scene and of the banks crowded with spectators on either side of the beautiful river. I made a sketch of it all, which was afterwards engraved; and when the Emperor left the raft at the end of the two hours I was allowed to go on board. My friend Bontemps reverently took possession of the pens and writing-case used in signing the treaty which was to secure peace to Europe for many happy years. If what M. de Talleyrand, Prince of Benevento, wrote to me in 1817 is still true, these three precious relics connected with the memory of an event of such importance must have very greatly deteriorated in value. I knew that the Prince's large fortune had been acquired under the Empire, so I begged him to give his support to the authors of an historical work on our campaigns and victories. He replied, "Victories are only interesting as long as the advantages they procured are retained; the results of the work of the Empire no longer exist, and they cease to be remembered as politics change. I cannot help those on whose behalf you appeal to me."

On June 26th the two Emperors met again on the Niemen, and directly afterwards the Emperor Alexander took up his residence in Tilsit, where he was treated with all possible honour and consideration. On the 27th we witnessed the arrival of the venerable Marshal Kalkreuth, who bad so heroically defended Dantzig. The King of Prussia and the Grand Duke Constantine arrived the next day. We helped to do honour to all these royal visitors, and the time was fully occupied with fêtes, brilliant parades, and dinners, washed down with plenty of punch. The Grand Duke Constantine had the square features of a Kalmuck, and resembled his father Paul I., whom I had seen at Strasburg when I was a child, but he had a fine figure, held himself well, and his courage in mounting the wildest horses was only equalled by his extraordinary skill in controlling them. He delighted in showing off his skill to us in the slippery streets of Tilsit, where the dangers of these hazardous feats were, of course, greatly increased. Another equally remarkable sight, and one we often went to see, was that of the encampments on the right bank of the Niemen of the wild hordes from the North. We liked to study their customs, their quaint flat features, and their Oriental costumes, to listen to their songs, and watch their skill with their bows and arrows, giving prizes to the best marksmen. Their arrows would pierce an apple at a distance of a hundred yards more often than our pistol shots could hit a button at twenty-five. I made sketches of a good many of these Tartars, Kalmucks, and Khirgesses.

In the midst of these warlike recreations the young, beautiful, and graceful Queen of Prussia arrived, and the feminine attractions at Tilsit now made us all more polite than ever, so that for some days the town wore the aspect of a Court.

Meanwhile the Emperor had quitted Tilsit and was on his way to Paris, whither I followed him in the suite of Marshal Berthier.

CHAPTER 5

From Poland to Spain

The enthusiasm with which we were received in Paris on our arrival there fifteen days after the Emperor can be imagined. Our time was passed in fêtes and rejoicings, and many thanksgiving services were held, including the chanting of a solemn *Te Deum* with appropriate ceremony in the Cathedral of Notre-Dame on the Emperor's birthday (August 15th, 1809).

Marshal Berthier was raised to the dignity of Vice-Constable of the Empire, and my share in the rewards given was a ribbon and a sum of money. Probably now (1845) I should have been made a Marshal of France for the same services.

I resumed my painting with a happy heart, and had a good many of my pictures engraved.

I had scarcely got to Paris, however, before I received orders from the Emperor to go to Dantzig and Warsaw to examine the army on the Vistula, and return to report on its condition. Then when I got back once more to Paris I had to start off again with my horses and carriages for Burgos in Spain.

I passed rapidly from the cold dreary and sandy flats of Poland to the beautiful country of Spain, where beneath the warm sunshine of the South fresh verdure and sweet-smelling flowers flourish even on the slopes of the lofty mountains.

The troops of the Emperor had been received as friends throughout the Peninsula, and now occupied Pampeluna, Burgos, Madrid, Cordova, and Barcelona. In Portugal Junot held Lisbon in place of the Princes of the Royal Family of Braganza, who had embarked for Brazil. Everywhere our soldiers were welcomed as liberators, and all along my route I found towns, villages, and even isolated houses prepared to celebrate the expected arrival of the Emperor. On every road laurel branches had been cut down to form triumphal arches beneath which the Emperor of Europe, the redresser of the grievances of the people, was to pass. My comrades and I, who had come to announce his approach, came in for some of the enthusiasm which his presence was later to arouse.

The Spaniards had long been discontented at the position occupied by Manuel de Godoy, surnamed the Prince of the Peace, who had risen from the ranks to the position of Prime Minister, and was now absolute master of Spain. Our troops had been welcomed in Spain itself; Spanish sailors had shed their blood in our service at Trafalgar; a Spanish army, under the Marquis de la Romaña, had fought side by side with the French in the remote districts of Germany, and the loyal populace, who now received us as if we were their brothers, impatiently awaited the day when the emperor should arrive at Madrid. They hoped that he would remove the hated minister and restore the royal authority to Charles IV. or place it in the hands of his son Ferdinand, Prince of Asturias, who was unfortunately on very bad terms with his father.

The friends of the Prince of Asturias took advantage of the family dissensions to prepare an *émeute* against the Minister, Don Godoy, who, defended though he was by the royal carabineers, was to be assassinated and burnt in his palace. In the struggle the King was compelled to abdicate in favour of his son, but the very same day he wrote to the Emperor protesting against this forced resignation of his throne and asking him to become the arbiter of his fate.

The Emperor received the news at Bayonne, and summoned the Prince of Asturias before him to give an account of his conduct. About the same time a rumour began to spread amongst us that the Emperor meant to place the crown of Spain on the head of one of his own brothers or generals, and the event proved that the rumour was not without foundation.

The Emperor, however, was still hesitating, when Talleyrand said to him on April 24th, 1808, "What policy suggests, justice authorises". Needless to say the Spanish did not agree with him.

Murat was now at Madrid at the head of an army, and in compliance with the wish of the Emperor he lost no time in urging the Prince of Asturias to go to Bayonne.

That prince having taken the title of King of Spain after the revolution of Aranjuez, set off accompanied by a hundred men belonging to his father's bodyguard, to which an escort so strong had been added that I could not help suspecting that he was to be taken prisoner. An officer who was a friend of mine went on in advance, taking with him back to France the sword of Francis I. He had received certain confidential instructions, and the grief he manifested at their tenor confirmed me in the opinion I had formed as to the false and cruel position in which we were soon to find ourselves.

I had the honour of saluting the Prince of Asturias as he rode through Burgos surrounded by his guards and preceded and followed by strong detachments of French cavalry. I was sorely tempted to give him a private hint to escape and not to go to Bayonne, but to save a prince who inspired me with very little personal interest I should have had to betray the Emperor. The situation was very grave, and with deep regret I confined myself to my narrow round of duties, leaving wider issues in the hands of Providence.

On his arrival at Vittoria the Prince began to suspect the trap prepared for him, and under various pretexts put off his departure. But the task of taking him to Bayonne had been confided to a man who knew what he was about, and when the unlucky Prince realised the impossibility of escaping from his escort, he allowed himself to be led whither they would without resistance. Those Frenchmen who had any foresight and who were without unworthy ambition shuddered at the way in which a loyal nation was about to be treated, whilst others who hoped for profit to themselves applauded the measures about to be taken, which, moreover, they were told were necessary for the regeneration of an effete race of monarchs no longer equal to the task of government.

About the same time a scene took place at Pampeluna, serious enough in its bearing yet also amusing, which did much to open the eyes of the Spanish to the nature of the protection they were to receive from the French armies they had welcomed so cordially.

General Darmagnac, with several French regiments, had been received in the town of Pampeluna, but the citadel was still occupied by Spaniards, when the French general, inspired by secret orders, sought about for some means of surprising the garrison.

For several days the country had been covered with snow, and our soldiers amused themselves with pelting each other with snowballs upon the glacis of the fort. The Spanish soldiers looking down from their lofty ramparts took a lively interest in the sport, and Darmagnac, hearing of this, turned it very cleverly to account. He increased the number of combatants and passed the word to them. Amidst shouts of laughter the first assailants were covered with a hail of pellets of snow and forced to retreat. They could only escape by taking refuge in the citadel, and the friendly Spaniards hurled all the snow from the parapets on to the victors and received the defeated within their gates and in their casemates, gaily helping to prolong the struggle. But the aim of the French had been achieved: the gates had been stormed, and the French battalion, bringing out their hidden weapons, took possession of the citadel, and set to work to insure its retention.

King Charles IV. and his Queen soon followed their son and betook themselves to Bayonne, receiving every possible honour all along their route. On their arrival the Prince of Asturias, with those of the Spanish nobles assembled at Bayonne, hastened to do them homage, but the King waved them back, saying in a severe tone, "Have you not outraged my white hairs enough?' on which they all retired covered with confusion.

The Emperor and Empress lost no time in calling upon their August visitors, and after the first compliments had been exchanged, the old King and Queen with true Spanish prolixity treated the Emperor to a long account of the ingratitude of their son and all the insults he had heaped on them during the last month. After listening to the long explanations the Emperor refused to recognise the abdication of Charles IV. and restored to him his royal prerogatives. This decision irritated the people of Madrid, who were very proud of the victory they had won at Aranjuez on March 19th, when they had dethroned their king. They refused to recognise his authority, and the French were often insulted. Hostile gatherings became daily more numerous and menacing, and at last on May 2 our officers and men were attacked in the streets, and the Grand Duke of Berg caused the assembly to be beaten. The French garrison rushed out and attacked the rebels. The enemy had already taken possession of the arsenal, where they seized 10,000 muskets, but our musketry fire, with the discharge of grape shot from our guns, and the charges of our cavalry, dispersed their numerous gatherings. They then went into the houses to aim at us from the windows, but our soldiers forced open the doors and 2,000 mutineers perished at the point of the bayonet. The armed peasants who flocked in from the country to take part in the revolt were pursued by our cavalry, who cut down and killed a great number. The Spanish troops took absolutely no part in the rising of the people, and order was soon restored.

Very much the same thing happened at Burgos, where I was on the same day, and the results were exactly similar. I was just going to make a sketch, on the Arlanson Quay, of the beautiful bas-relief on the gate of the bridge, when I heard the cry, "Death to the French!" and several musket shots.

I ran as fast as I could to the guard in the Plaza Mayor, where our troops were under arms and ready for battle. It was the same with the rest of the French soldiers in the town, and, sudden as was the attack of the conspirators, they did not succeed in surprising or taking a single one of our posts.

We lost a few men from cross shots, but the shots fired by the compact crowd, which charged us at a run, exhausted their ammunition and left them disarmed, whilst our repeated orderly discharges at close quarters soon swept the place clear of our assailants. Marshal Berthier, with troops hastily called out, hurried to our assistance. The whole affair lasted but one hour, and order and discipline were everywhere completely restored. I must do the people of Burgos the justice to add that not a single assassination took place on this occasion.

After the events of May 2nd, the Grand Duke of Berg established a *junta* at Madrid for the management of affairs, and he was recognised as its head with the title of Lieutenant-General of the kingdom. On this eventful day he had saved the life of Don Godoy, Prince of the Peace, when the people had tried to burn him in the palace in which he had been compelled to take refuge. A few days later the Grand Duke sent Don Godoy to Bayonne in safety. If the Emperor had had the wisdom to prevent the rising of May 2nd, and had constituted himself judge of the misdeeds with which the Prince of the Peace was charged, and after condemning him had allowed him to escape, he would have met the wishes of the people of Spain; and, whilst leaving to them their own princes, he would have gained all he really wanted in their country. The conduct of the Emperor under the circumstances seemed to be altogether opposed to his usual able policy. The events which had occurred caused universal uneasiness, and I remember that my friends Alfred de Noailles and Ferreri, who lived with me, talked a great deal about how these things would affect France.

There was very great excitement in Spain, and we at Burgos were eager for news from Bayonne. One day we heard that Ferdinand VII., the Prince of Asturias, had been sent as a prisoner to Valencia, the next that the King and Queen of Spain with the Prince of the Peace were on their way to Fontainebleau. A little later I received orders to join the Emperor immediately.

I started at once at full speed, and in twenty-three hours I had done the 110 leagues between Burgos and Bayonne. Directly I arrived Berthier took me to the Emperor, who said to me, "I know you are fond of Bernadotte, and I have chosen you to take him some news which will please him. In consequence of the disputes between the King and Queen of Spain and their son, I have accepted their abdication of the throne in favour of my brother Joseph, King of Naples; go and tell Bernadotte, who is his father-in-law, he will be gratified. You will tell the Marquis de la Romaña and the troops under his orders the same thing, and add that in my brother they will have a king who, by his attention to their wishes and care for their success and glory, will merit their affection. In fact, tell them all the good things I think about my brother. Go and rest for an hour, and then start again. Berthier will give you the despatches"

One hour of rest ! Not much surely for a man who had just arrived from such a journey as mine. But never mind, I could have a swim in the Adour, and snatch a hasty meal. That would be enough to freshen me up, and there would just be time whilst the light carriage was being got ready in which I was to be shut up for eight days and nights on my way from Bayonne to the remote districts of Jutland, then occupied by the troops under Bernadotte.

I passed through Paris, Brussels, and Hanover, stopped at Hamburg to see the French Minister, M. de Bourrienne, who had heard nothing as yet of the events which had taken place at Bayonne, and who made me promise to call on him again on my way back. I pressed on by way of Holstein, and beyond Schleswig, where I found Marshal Bernadotte.

That officer did me the honour to receive me as an old friend, and after celebrating my arrival and the news I brought him by a fête, he allowed me to pursue my way to the Marquis de la Romaña, whom I found at Viborg in the midst of the encampment of the 10,000 Spaniards under his command. The very cold reception he gave to the tidings I brought from Bayonne left me in no doubt as to his feelings with regard to them; but for all that, after asking me a great many questions on the subject of what I had recently seen in Spain, and about which he really seemed as well informed as I was, he called his officers together to tell me before them and in their name that, however great might be their regret at losing the princes whom they had been taught to love from their childhood, they would be no less faithful to the new king, and then begged me to convey to him the assurance of their respectful homage.

In the conversations which succeeded this interview, many officers expressed their satisfaction at the prospect of serving a king who would probably be as much beloved at Madrid as at Naples, where he was adored; others, on the contrary, were evidently depressed and hid their real feelings under an assumed demeanour. I felt it would be prudent to avoid discussion as much as possible, and I left them with an assurance that the Emperor would appreciate their noble services, and that he would be happy to treat them with as much affection as if they had originally been his subjects.

Bernadotte gave two charming fêtes in my honour on the Schleswig lakes, reassured me as to the loyalty of the Spaniards, in which he firmly believed, told me to congratulate his brother from him and to ask the Emperor to recall him from the North, where he felt the cold very much, and to summon him to the South, where he would be delighted to serve him. He loaded my carriage with valuable presents, and at last allowed me to take my leave.

At Hamburg, M. de Bourrienne also fêted me. I had sent my carriage on to Altona so as to rejoin the Minister without loss of time. After the fête I was escorted by the guests to the shore, near to which the boat belonging to the French Consulate, with sails set, flags flying, and rowers in their places, was waiting to take me out of the Elbe.

M. de Bourrienne, taking me aside just before I started, confided to me his discontent with the position in which he found himself, letting me see how very keenly he felt the Emperor's constant refusal to meet his wishes. I saw how very much he had the matter at heart, and promised to plead his cause with the Emperor. I made my adieux to the company present, and as my boat moved away I waved my handkerchief in response to the friendly gestures of those I was leaving.

Back again in my carriage, which I found at Altona, I had plenty of food for reflection in all I had seen and heard. I thought of the dreary country I was leaving, of which commerce alone relieves the monotony, though the chief roads naturally open to it are closed by the vigilance of the customs officers. I thought of the Elbe, once crowded with a forest of masts, which is now deserted and where not a single vessel is ever seen to arrive; I pondered on the ingenuity with which contraband goods were introduced, and the rigour of the blockade evaded, and remembered with amusement a scene I had witnessed the day before at Hamburg, where I had scarcely been able to get to the gate through the dense crowd assembled there, attracted by a spectacle which was curious enough. For some little time the *octroi* officers had been quite distressed by the mortality which apparently prevailed in the town, for every day numbers of victims were carried out to be buried in the cemetery beyond the walls. Funerals succeeded each other with the most alarming rapidity, till one day an officer of the *octroi* happened to put to his lips a probe he had plunged into one of the many cartloads of sand daily brought into the town to be used in building. The probe tasted sweet, and it was discovered that the contents of the cart were really brown sugar with a sprinkling of sand at the top. This roused the man's suspicions; he was put thoroughly on his guard, and searched the contents of the next hearses which passed back from the cemetery. They were all full of sugar and calico! The crowd laughed and applauded when the discovery was made, but all the same they were very sorry that their trade had received such a check, for the ingenious device had brought them not a little prosperity without really costing the life of a single citizen of Hamburg.

I again passed through Paris and pushed on for Bayonne. I went straight to the Emperor on my arrival to give him an account of my mission, and he questioned me about the mood the Spaniards were in when I left. He then said, "And what is Bourrienne doing?" I described the farewell ceremony before I left Hamburg, and fulfilled my promise to the French Minister by putting his case before the Emperor. He listened with interest and replied, "I like Bourrienne very much, but you must tell him how much I regret having to refuse his request" and in this refusal the Emperor persisted.

During my absence things had taken a very unlucky turn in Spain. The triumphal arches put up in honour of the Liberator had been torn down by the enraged people, and the Emperor, defeated in his object, had to prepare for the reconquest of the Peninsula by force of arms. He found Spain in fact neither so docile nor so rich as it had appeared when her people had turned to him with confidence, admiration, and affection.

On every side the Spanish were turning against the French army. The clergy of the chief churches of Seville, Valencia, Valladolid, and Saragossa were trying to arouse the patriotic zeal of the people, and the blood of our countrymen was being shed in every provincial town.

The catastrophe of Baylen had taken place, and the news of it reached Madrid the very day King Joseph made his entry. The same tidings came to the camp outside Valencia just as Marshal Moncey was expecting the arrival of his heavy guns to commence the siege, and it revived the courage of the defenders of Saragossa.

Under this melancholy conjunction of circumstances the King found it prudent to leave Madrid on August 1 and withdraw to Burgos, whilst Marshal Moncey, abandoning the idea of taking Valencia, withdrew to Catalonia with his army, taking with him fifty pieces of cannon he had captured. Meanwhile Lefebvre-Desnouettes, not having troops enough to occupy Saragossa, raised the siege.

These various successes inflamed the ardour of the Spanish nation, and on every side regular armies were formed and bands of guerrillas were raised, rendering our communications very difficult. England took the most extraordinary interest in promoting the war, making the greatest sacrifices in the Spanish cause, sending over generals, men, arms, and money. The English advances made to the Marquis de la Romaña in Denmark had been not without success, and that general, whilst pretending to Bernadotte that he was still faithful to us, embarked as many of his officers and men as he could win over on a number of English vessels and shortly afterwards landed them at Coruña.

It was at this juncture that the meeting at Erfurt took place. The Emperor of Russia was really passionately attached to Napoleon. He sincerely admired the French Emperor's genius and all the grand successes he had recently achieved. One evening Alexander was chatting enthusiastically about his friend to Count Daru, whom he, however, asked to explain why Napoleon had created an order of nobility in France when he had been so fortunate as not to find one about the throne when he had ascended it. The Russian Emperor was no doubt thinking how the Russian nobility, held as they are in slavish servility, often revenge themselves, as is the way of slaves, by murdering their master. He knew how many of the Czars had been assassinated, and the fate of his own father Paul I. was no doubt present in his mind. With no presentiment of the doom he was to meet himself ten years later, the Emperor in this conversation talked of the institution of an order of nobility rather as a menace to than a support of the throne, and of all the deeds of Napoleon this creation of a nobility was the only one of which he did not recognise the utility.

The troops in Germany, set free by the restoration of peace in the North, crossed France and the Pyrenees on their way to Spain, receiving everywhere a regular ovation, fêtes and banquets being held, and songs composed in their honour, till they became perfectly intoxicated with enthusiasm. Our seasoned disciplined warriors, led by skilful chiefs, were now to begin a fresh struggle, this time with a brave nation imbued with love of independence.

The French troops poured in in great numbers, crossed the Bidassoa in good order, and pushed on for Galicia, Castille, and Aragon in advance of the Emperor, who arrived at the same time at Bayonne and lost not a moment in following the army to Spain.

My entry into Irun in the suite of the Emperor was a very different thing from my arrival there the first time, when I believed I was heralding his approach. Then the Alcalde and corregidors had come to meet me, and conducted me to the best quarters in the town, where they had given me an excellent meal and placed a very comfortable bed at my disposal, after pointing out the hotel and triumphal arch prepared for the Emperor. This time I found myself at eleven o'clock on a pitch-dark night, entering a town encumbered with troops, where I could get neither food nor shelter for myself, forage nor stabling for my horses, and where daybreak revealed to me the fact that the couch, which after all had not been a hard one, on which I had snatched a little repose during the night, was nothing more or less than a heap of dried dung, such as is painfully collected by the Spanish peasants with which to manure a few square feet of soil.

In his advance upon Madrid, the Emperor's first care was to attack the troops which harassed his march on either flank, so as to leave no enemy in the rear.

When we re-entered Burgos on November 20th, our friends were all gone, called to the war or dispersed by terror, and the town, which had been pillaged after the battle, was still in the most terrible disorder. The Emperor only stopped two days, and the Imperial head quarters were transferred to Lerma on the 22nd, and on the 23rd to Aranda. Whatever may have been the consideration shown by our advanced guard for the inoffensive inhabitants of the towns we passed through, they all fled before us, fearing reprisals for the assassinations of which some of them had been guilty, and abandoning to us their houses, convents, and churches, which had, however, already been broken into and pillaged. These buildings, deserted as they were, offered irresistible temptation to the cupidity of our soldiers, and, in spite of the severe punishments inflicted by their officers, every inch of them was ransacked from the chapels to the crypts, the very tombs being rifled, and all that could be removed carried off.

When we halted at Aranda, the Emperor wished to leave the enemy in doubt as to which route he would take for Madrid, and with this end in view he divided his forces, one half going by way of the Guadarrama and the other by the pass of the Somo-Sierra. The latter was the shorter way, but much easier to defend on account of the narrowness of the mountain defile. It would therefore most likely be guarded by a smaller number of troops than the other route, and on this account the Emperor decided on it.

On the 29th the Emperor and his suite had established their head quarters at the base of the Somo-Sierra, where they were joined by Marshal Victor, who at once led his troops into the pass through a fog so dense that they could not see two paces before them. In spite of this the Marshal made his men climb into the forests on either side of the main road, the enemy having occupied the summits, where they considered themselves impregnable behind the deep excavations they had made. General Bertrand, one of the aides-de-camp of the Emperor, had instructions to repair the road and render it practicable for our cavalry and artillery. Napoleon, however, impatient at the delay caused by the necessary work, told me to push a reconnaissance into the mountain till I came upon the enemy, when I was to return and report as to their numbers and position. I soon came up with General Bertrand, who had not yet completed his task, and then pressed on by a rapid ascent. I had traversed about a couple of miles without seeing any one, when a Pole who was one of my party made me a sign that he could hear the Spaniards talking.

I dismounted at once, gave him my horse to hold, and crept noiselessly forward till I was arrested by the sound of falling earth, behind which a number of people were talking Spanish. I then turned aside and walked along the edge of the road to try and find out the extent of the entrenchment, which seemed to me to contain some twelve or fifteen guns. After having reconnoitred the position so far as was possible in the dense fog, I was returning down the mountain to my horse, when, after taking some five or six steps, I suddenly found myself face to face with a battalion silently advancing upon me. Although quite close to the men, the fog was so thick that I at first took them for a French corps, and I said to the officer marching at their head, "You had better not advance in this direction. There is a ravine you cannot cross" At the words the whole column took aim at me, and I shouted as I came nearer, "Do not fire! Do not fire! I am French!' At that very instant I discovered my error, for it was a Spanish corps climbing up from the base of the mountain. My position was indeed critical, and I hastened to call out in Spanish, "Do not fire! do not fire! I have three regiments here which will cut you to pieces; the best thing you can do is to surrender to me who can do you no harm"

The Spaniards seemed uncertain what to do, and hesitated, whether because they were afraid of firing on their own people, or believed in the three regiments I had referred to I don't know, but they quickly dispersed on the left and disappeared in the fog, their leader with them, who was in such haste to be gone that he left his horse and cloak behind him, so as to escape more easily across the rocks. Their panic saved my life, and as soon as they were out of sight I ran back to my men. I hastened to return to the Emperor, and told him all I had done. I found him very much put out at the delays he had met with, and he said to me, "You are making fun of me" He saw that I was greatly annoyed at the reception he gave me, and recognising the danger I had run in his service, he made me repeat what I had said about the artillery of the enemy and the state of the road. He then ordered General Montbrun to advance with his cavalry, in spite of all obstacles, protected by the infantry, which had now had time to crown the heights.

Montbrun at the head of a body of Polish cavalry galloped up the mountain, fell upon the Spanish entrenchments, and sabred some of the artillerymen at their posts; but the roughness of the ground, combined with the volley of grape shot which met him, overthrew the head of his column, and compelled him to retreat and rally his men beyond the range of the guns. In the thick of the hail of shot the Poles recognised the Emperor himself, and almost without waiting for the word of command from their chief the gallant Kosciusko, they returned to the charge, overcame all the obstacles which had deterred them at first, carrying everything before them, and penetrating into the very heart of the formidable position of the Spaniards, who were unable in the fog to see how very small the attacking column was. The Cavalry of the Guard followed the movement; every one of the Spanish gunners in charge of the sixteen cannon defending the pass was cut down.

During this struggle the infantry under Marshal Victor had succeeded in scaling the heights and dominating the position of the enemy, and our Poles, protected as they were by their fire, completely routed the thirteen or fourteen thousand men defending the approaches to the defile of Somo-Sierra. The fog, the rocks, and the woods combined to protect the Spaniards in their flight, and we made few prisoners, but we took all their cannon, and they left nearly 2,000 men upon the ground. As we climbed the mountain I pointed out to the Emperor the horse and cloak abandoned by the Spanish officer I had met; the bridle was still entangled in the folds of the cloak, and the horse, thinking, perhaps, that his master was sleeping, had remained patiently standing where he was, like many a faithful dog which we had seen awaiting death on the battle field beside the corpse of his owner.

The Emperor was able to verify some of the other details I had mentioned to him, and they were of a nature to excite his just indignation. During the preceding days the Spanish had made a few prisoners, and they had been barbarously executed by strangling. Not daring to leave behind them such damning proofs of their barbarity, they had made a hurried attempt to conceal the bodies, which had been hastily hidden, tied two and two together, beneath an arch of the bridge spanning the road where I had seen them when I was climbing up on foot. Some few of the poor wretches, of whom there were about fifteen, were still breathing, and help was given to them. Just at this moment some prisoners, including several monks and superior officers, were brought to the Emperor, and he reproached them with their cruelty, threatening to serve them in the same fashion, but he was really too generous for that, and no harm was done to them.

The fog gradually cleared away, and we were able to contemplate with delight a battle field bristling with entrenchments and redoubts, strewn with abandoned cannon, dead and wounded. The site was an admirable one, and later this scene furnished me with a fine subject for a picture, in which I introduced all the details which had particularly struck me in the morning, when, thanks to Providence, I had such a marvellous escape.

On December 2nd we were before Madrid, which was in a state of the wildest excitement. The pavement had been torn up in all the streets to serve as barricades. The houses were loopholed, thousands of bales of wool served as epaulments at the gates and in all the public squares, and 100 cannon defended the various entrenchments. But divided counsels prevailed in the town, some wanting to open the gates to us to save bloodshed, whilst others were for defence. The latter strangled the Marquis of Parles because he was supposed to be favourable to us, and they were minded to murder M. de Soulages, the aide-de-camp of Marshal Bessières, who was entrusted by their leader with proposals of peace. The tocsin was rung from every church, the drums everywhere beat to arms, and 50,000 armed peasants who had flocked in from the country joined the garrison, shouting as they perambulated the streets, "Down with the French!"

When on December 2nd the Emperor went the round of the lines of our outposts, the soldiers remembered that it was the anniversary of his coronation and of Austerlitz, and greeted him with such shouts of "*Vive l'Empereur!*" that they were heard at the gates of Madrid. They longed to enter the city, and very soon Marshal Bessières enabled them to do so.

His preliminary dispositions made, the Marshal summoned the Marquis of Castelar, President of the Junta, to surrender in the cause of humanity, and thus to avert the horrors which would result from an assault of the town. The Marquis replied by sending a general to parley with us, and we saw him arrive under the surveillance of some twenty ferocious-looking guards, who behaved in a very arrogant fashion. The Envoy was told that the Emperor wished to spare a city so beautiful as Madrid, containing so many sensible men and peaceful families, who were worthy of all consideration, and that it would grieve him to the heart if he had to reduce the town by force of arms.

Marshal Victor had already placed his divisions in the positions they were to occupy in the attack, the firing had everywhere begun, the danger was indeed imminent. The General was sent back to the town, and the Emperor, profiting by the brilliant light of the moon, made a vigorous attack on the suburbs, eager to get the siege over as quickly as possible.

The suburbs, which were badly defended, were quickly taken, and the rest of the night, which was almost as light as day, was occupied in placing our artillery. After this first success Marshal Berthier sent into the town a Spanish officer of artillery, who had been taken prisoner in the Somo-Sierra pass, with instructions to tell his fellow-countrymen and the Governor how well able we were to reduce the city. Whilst that officer was engaged in his mission a battery of thirty pieces of cannon kept up a hot fire on the town, demolishing a barrack with part of the *enceinte* and making a breach in the palace of Buen Retiro. Another battery of twenty howitzers meanwhile made a feigned attack on the other side of the town, doing some damage. The Spanish officer now returned from his mission, bringing with him a letter from the Governor, who said that as he was dependent upon the Junta he begged for time to make known the gravity of the situation to the people, and entreated the Emperor to grant an armistice of a few hours.

Berthier sent back word that the Emperor granted this request, and had ordered the firing to cease everywhere.

One party of outposts after another now brought in the prisoners they had taken, and from these unfortunate fellows we heard of the scenes of disorder which were taking place in the town, and of the cruel way in which the armed peasants, who wished to defend the town to the last, treated those inhabitants who wanted to surrender it for the sake of saving their property.

The day was passed in reconnoitring various points of the town and in active preparations for its assault; but as night was beginning to fall, a number of envoys from the town arrived at our bivouac, and we took them to the tent of Marshal Berthier. They dwelt upon all the difficulties of their position in a town where during the last four months many generals had been hanged or otherwise put to death, and they pleaded to have the next day (the 4th) to bring the people to reason. The Marshal took them to the Emperor, who made their feel the whole weight of his indignation, telling them that he knew well enough how those at the head of affairs, instead of making the people listen to counsels of conciliation, misled them and excited them to resistance: "They allowed French prisoners and merchants to be massacred when honour demanded their protection; it was they who gave up the women of Roussillon to the Spanish soldiers; it was they who ordered the treacherous bombardment of my ships at Cadiz when we were on friendly terms; only a few days ago they ordered the strangling of Frenchmen in Madrid. They have violated the treaty of the capitulation of Baylen in an atrocious manner, and now they ask me to grant an amnesty to Madrid. Is it likely ? . . . However, you can go back to the town and say that I promise all peaceable citizens oblivion of the past and protection of their religion. I give you till sunrise tomorrow; but don't come talking to me about the people again unless it is to announce their submission, or it will be all up with you. Now be off!"

The presence of the Emperor himself before their walls, and the threats he was known to have uttered, greatly intimidated the people of the town, who were moreover disheartened by the great losses they had sustained the night before. The more mutinous amongst them, too, when they saw some of the troops of the line disband, withdrew during the night, not daring to face the worse perils which were approaching.

The notables of the town, thus relieved of the presence of this dangerous element in their midst, threw themselves on the generosity of the Emperor, and the Governor of Madrid, Don Fernando Vera, with General Morla arrived in our camp at six o'clock on the morning of the 4th to announce the submission of the town.

A general amnesty was at once proclaimed, communications were reopened, and General Belliard was made Governor of Madrid, where he quickly established such perfect order that the shops were reopened the very day of his nomination, whilst the people hastened to remove all trace of the miseries of the siege by taking down the barricades and repairing the streets.

The Emperor, accompanied by Major-General Prince Berthier, who had been with him in the Castle of San Martino, did not enter the town till the 8th, but his arrival had been heralded by the issuing of various proclamations and decrees.

With a view to appealing; to the eyes of the populace as he had previously appealed to their reason, and hoping to dispose them to accept with pride an alliance with so rich and powerful a nation as the French, the Emperor ordered that his Guard and all the troops should appear in their most gorgeous uniforms at the review he intended to hold on the Prado. We all got ourselves up in gala array, so as to be worthy of the grand occasion. Fashion, which controls the costumes of soldiers as rigorously as those of ladies, has changed so much since then that the day will doubtless come when many will be interested in knowing what uniforms were worn by orderly officers on occasions such as this, so I will describe the garments of the little group to which I belonged.

The aides-de-camp of Major-General Prince Berthier had been chosen from amongst the sons of the highest families of France; and, either by accident or by choice, we were all tall young fellows with good figures. The Prince had ordered me some years before to design a special uniform, and I had suggested something in the Hungarian style – a black cloth *pelisse*, a white *dolman* with gold braid and fur, wide breeches, and a shako of scarlet cloth surmounted by an *aigrette* of white heron's plumes. The different details of the costume were enriched with plenty of gold braid, cord, and buttons; and a rich sash of black and gold silk, a small cartridge pouch, a sabretache, and a Damascene sabre completed the get-up. Our parade horses were of Arab breed, greyish white in colour, with long floating silky manes; their bridles, like those of the hussars, gleaming with gold braid and tassels; whilst the saddle was covered with a panther's skin festooned with gold and scarlet. My young friend Alfred de Noailles looked grand in this costume, which set off his fine figure and handsome features. His manner, too, was very distinguished and chivalrous, and his heart was as good as his form was beautiful. I can scarcely refrain from tears when I think how he and many other fine young heroes were soon afterwards to be mown down at my side by an enemy's fire. Even at the head of the Imperial Guard we presented a remarkable appearance; and, though I should be charged with conceit for thus recalling the incidents of a time so remote, I cannot help declaring that I really never saw anything finer or more brilliant of its kind than our cavalcade of six aides-de-camp as we entered Madrid. The Emperor and Marshal Berthier looked at us in quite a paternal manner, and congratulated us on our smart appearance.

The sun had been shining continuously for the last eight days, and everywhere under its genial influence flowers were bursting into bloom. The review was favoured with bright weather and a clear sky, and went off admirably; but there were few spectators, and very little enthusiasm amongst those few. Yet most of the Spanish hoped much from the restoration, under the Emperor and his brother, of constitutional government; but their fears of a reaction led them to maintain a prudent reserve. The ladies, however, with a little more political prescience, were not quite so reserved in their demonstrations, and we noticed a good many pretty little feet carefully shod but not perhaps very carefully hidden. Many small hands, too, fluttered fans with thoroughly Castilian grace and vivacity, and waved a friendly greeting to those of us who were known to their owners; and the coquettish black lace mantillas were parted to give us a glimpse of beautiful dark oval eyes with long lashes, gazing out at us with a sweet and gentle expression. This review and fête illustrated forcibly alike the pomp, the grandeur, and the stern vicissitudes of war, as well as the power of the fair dames of Castille to lead their conquerors captive by their grace, their charm, and by their lively and witty conversation. True, the dark scowling looks of the stern hidalgos in the crowd, with their cloaks drawn up and their wide *sombreros* pulled down so that only the black eyes gleaming with rage and jealousy could be seen, cast a decided gloom on an otherwise bright picture, but this only made the general effect all the more piquant for us.

After the review we went to visit the King's Palace, and saw the grand pictures by Raphael, Murillo, and Velasquez; the remarkable emerald; the huge nugget brought over by Vasco da Gama; and the gigantic skeleton of a mammoth in the Natural History collection. We then returned to San Martino, leaving Madrid with regret, for we could have enjoyed resting there after all the fatigues of war.

CHAPTER 6

Benavente, Astorga, Valladolid

The English, hoping to make us uneasy at Madrid, and wishing to encourage the people of the neighbouring districts to resist us, had sent a few agents to Zamora and Salamanca, who were to deceive us into thinking their army was approaching, whereas they really were making in force for Valladolid and Valencia on their left, towards Marshal Soult, more than fifty leagues from our right flank, so as to threaten our communications with France in that direction.

The Emperor, warned of this movement, ordered me to push forward a strong reconnaissance in the rear of the enemy towards Toro, by way of Avila, and to return to give him all the information possible as to the movements of the English forces.

I started on December 19th. Hitherto it had been very hot, quite like summer; but now the weather suddenly became cold. The ground was covered with snow, and it was with difficulty that I crossed the Guadarrama mountains, along which two of our cavalry divisions, that under Coulaincourt and Laboussaye's dragoons, were posted in echelon. The latter general gave me eighteen hundred dragoons, and at their head I marched upon Fontiveres, where I arrived without noise at midnight. I let the horses rest for an hour, surrounding my camp with vedettes, to guard against being surprised and denounced by the Spaniards, who were so clever in reporting our numbers, after which I started at a brisk trot to go and surround Palacios, where the road between Salamanca and Madrid branches off, and where I hoped to surprise a few detachments of the enemy, make them prisoners, and get some news. We arrived at

Palacios a little before daybreak, in a heavy fall of snow, which helped us to hide our approach.

After posting my guards round Palacios, and in the plaza mayor of that town, and ordering them to keep perfect silence, I went to the house of the Alcalde, who had been woke by the noise made by our horses, though it was deadened by the snow. He was just hurrying out in alarm when I arrived, and I prevented him from leaving the house. He at once asked me to whom he had the honour of speaking, and, profiting by his uncertainty, I replied in Spanish, "What, don't you know your own friends?" At these words he beamed with joy, and exclaimed, "Ah, you are English?" I gave him a sign to speak low, whispering, "Hush! hush! the French are not far off; they are pursuing us. Ever since we left Madrid we have been trying to rejoin the English army, which we expected to find here. Just show me in which direction it is."

He answered immediately: "The rearguard, under General Ward, were here yesterday with the Hamilton division, but have now left for Medina; they were following the Commander-in-Chief, General Moore, who is marching to-day on Valladolid, with the Fraser, Spencer, and Beresford divisions, to support the Marquis de la Romana. But you must make haste to be off, for a body of French cavalry some 1,800 strong arrived at Fontiveres at midnight, and may be here any minute."

"My dear Alcalde," I said, "I congratulate you on being so well informed, and am very much obliged to you for giving me all these details, which I shall certainly turn to account at once. But every instant is precious. Tell me how many men Ward and Hamilton had with them." At this question he hesitated, and interrupting me, he said, "Wait a minute; I had an express messenger from head quarters here this very night, who saw everything; he will be able to tell you all about it better than I can." The rascal of an Alcalde wanted to get away from me into the street, to make sure whether we really were English; but I insisted on his sending his servant for the messenger, instead of going himself. The servant went off, and the Alcalde and I had hardly exchanged half a dozen words before the messenger hurried in, trembling with excitement, and nearly dead with terror at having found the town occupied by troops, whom he took to be French. The Alcalde, however, directly he saw him, called out, "These gentlemen are English." The messenger, seeing my scarlet trousers and shako, also took me for an Englishman, and in his joy and relief he kissed my hands and answered all my questions, describing to me very clearly the positions of Generals Baird and Hill, the number of horses, of guns, and of battalions, the direction he had seen them take, &c., winding up by saying that their skilful manoeuvring would lead to the French getting a tremendous thrashing.

During this conversation the Colonel of dragoons who had accompanied me was warming himself at the *brasero* without speaking at all, but now he undid his overcoat to shake the snow from it, and the Alcalde caught sight of the Cross of the Legion of Honour on his breast. He went up to the Colonel, touched the cross, and said to me, "*Pero, Señor Oficial, esta cruz no es Inglesa!*" (But, Sir Officer, that cross is not English!) I replied, "Yes, yes, it is; damn it! it is a cross of the order established in honour of the battle of Aboukir, won by Nelson; don't you see that the ribbon is the colour of the British flag?"

This answer did not seem to satisfy him, and approaching the messenger, he whispered in his ear, "*Creo que son Franceses!*" (I believe they are French!) I heard, and as naturally as I could I placed myself between them and tried to divert their attention. But the messenger began to stammer in his speech, and the Alcalde, getting more and more uneasy, presently exclaimed in a low voice, 'son Franceses!" (They are French!) Then, dropping all disguise, I shouted, "Yes, we are French! and now I will force you to finish telling me the rest of what I have learnt by stratagem." The messenger was really only a wretched spy in the pay of the English, a poor half-starved creature, more like a tipstaff than anything, with a pinched and shrivelled skin, looking as if he had had nothing but garlic to eat for months. His feet, shod only with sandals of grey thread, his thin legs cased in laced gaiters, his scanty leather breeches open at the knee, his wide drooping sash disguising the leanness of his body, his brown vest all too short, the red handkerchief twisted into a rope and worn on his head, which it left bare at the top, his shaven scalp and long matted hair, his heavy eyebrows almost meeting in his terror, his glittering eyes and gleaming teeth, combined to make up a grotesque and grovelling appearance, such as provokes the rope or the bastinado. His gestures of terror betrayed clearly enough what he expected. He flung himself at my feet and begged for mercy. I made him get up; it was my business to turn him to account, not to ill-treat him, but his brains were in such a muddle with his fright that I could get no more out of him, and the Alcalde, who was also in a great fright, now evaded my questions.

Meanwhile my guards had arrested General Don José Valdes and a few stragglers who were trying to escape from Palacios, where they had slept, and they were now brought to me as prisoners. I interrogated them each separately, and though their answers were evasive enough I managed to make sure that I was behind the English army, which was gathering up all its strength to attack our right wing. I recognised the necessity of alarming the enemy as promptly as possible, and in the presence of my prisoners I ordered the Alcalde to have provisions prepared for 20,000 men and forage for 4,000 horses, who would arrive in the course of the day, and of whom we were the advance guard. I had no desire to encumber myself with prisoners, so I now released my captives, allowing them to continue their route, and just before they left I repeated my orders to the Alcalde to see about the provisions for our army as quickly as possible. I then told my Colonel not to remain behind for more than a few hours after me to rest his horses, but to rejoin his division as soon as possible. I exchanged my weary post-horse for the fresh mount I had taken from General Valdes, ordered a young guide, who thought I was English, to get on to the messenger's horse, and started at a gallop by the shortest route to rejoin the Emperor.

I was not without anxiety in thus crossing without escort a hostile country where in the last few days Colonel Mirabeau, Captain Menard, and two or three other officers engaged in various missions had been assassinated. But full of confidence in the fact that my costume was deceptive, and that I could speak six foreign languages fluently, I thought of nothing but how best to serve the French cause, and this gave me the presence of mind, energy, and nerve which carried me safely through my enterprise. My chief difficulty was in getting the postillions at the post-houses to give me relays of horses quickly enough for me to get off before the crowds which everywhere collected on my arrival were strong enough to stop me. Never before, perhaps, had the horrible English oath done better service than it did on this journey of mine. The liberal use of gold and of the magic words "Damn it!" won me success beyond my hopes. For all that, I was delayed by a rather serious contretemps some ten or twelve leagues from Palacios. It was late in the day, and the night was evidently going to be pitch dark, when my guide found he no longer knew the way. There were no relays of horses to be had in the village we were approaching, and there was nothing for it but for me to go to the Alcalde, who was also the innkeeper, and ask him to help me. I made my request in English as if I were an English officer, but before answering he looked me well over with an anxious expression, finally observing, "We have no horses here, and you are French. If I let you leave now, you will probably be murdered by the peasants of this village. You had better not come in here, where there are a lot of fellows who will combine against you; but if you like to go up to a room I will show you, I'll bring you some food and you can rest in security. I will also give your horses some oats, and find you a guide."

What was I to do? It seemed as dangerous to stop as to go on. If only it were a clear night, if only I knew the way, if only I could tell our bearings . . . The songs I could hear from the adjoining rooms were not calculated to reassure me, for the patriotic national hymn was being shouted out, "*Vivir in cadenas, mejor es morir*" (Better to die than to live in chains). On the other hand, the offer of the Alcalde seemed genuine enough, and without hesitating long I said to him, "If you look at me you will see that I am able to sell my life dearly; but your honest face inspires me with confidence, and I will trust you." A few minutes after I had reached my room, my host brought me some first-rate Spanish bread, some fish seasoned with red pepper, and some rancio from the Peñas valley. I tossed off a few bumpers, stretched myself out on my bed of straw with my sword beside me, pondered a bit on the importance of my mission, and commending myself to God, I slept the deep sleep of a man exhausted with fatigue.

At three in the morning I saw a ray of light stream through the keyhole, and heard my door opened gently. It was the Alcalde, who, seeing me sitting up on the alert, made me a sign to be silent, and coming up to me said: "All is ready." He at first refused to take payment, but in the end accepted a gold piece, led me to my horses, told the new guide he had procured to take good care of the English officer, held my stirrup as I mounted, and shook me cordially by the hand with the air of a man who knows he has done a good action, finally dismissing me with hearty Spanish words of farewell, "*Vaya Usted con Dios!*" (God be with you!)

About noon I had crossed San Vicente, and reached Valdea amongst the mountains. The priest of the village and a few peasants were in the street when I was changing horses, and overwhelmed me with questions whilst my horse was being saddled. I gave myself out as an Englishman, the bearer of a flag of truce commissioned to arrange for an exchange of prisoners. This account was accepted in good faith till the priest, who was a sharp fellow and more suspicious than the peasants, walked round me, and noticing a golden eagle on my sabretache he said, pointing at it, "*señor, las aguilas non son reales* (Sir, eagles are not royal). Why do you wear that eagle if you are English?" "It is the sabre of a French officer I took prisoner," I answered, drawing out the blade; "look what good steel it is, although it was not made at Toledo!" As I brandished it, laughing and boasting of my prowess with the aim of keeping inquisitive folk at a distance, my horses were led up ready, and I mounted, glad enough to get away from the priest, who knew too much about the difference between Imperial and Royal armorial bearings. The noise I heard behind me as I rode off showed me that I had had a narrow escape. A terrible storm hindered me still farther in my journey, and I did not reach the town of San Raphael at the foot of the Guadarrama mountains till midnight.

On December 2nd, during my absence, the Emperor had heard from the reports of his Marshals of the bold advance of the English on our right flank. He at once went to Madrid, and at the head of the troops of the centre he was advancing to cut off the retreat of the enemy. I found the whole of the Imperial Guard at San Raphael. The storm had been so terrible on the mountain that many men and horses had been swept over precipices, where they had perished. The Grenadiers, exhausted with fatigue, were sleeping on the frozen ground covered with masses of snow and ice beside their fires, which were all but extinguished by the rain and hail, which were still falling. Some 10,000 men without any shelter at all were gathered about the chapel and one or two little huts near by, belonging to the officiating priest of San Raphael, which was a great resort of pilgrims, and where the Emperor had been compelled to halt to rally his troops, dispersed and delayed by the storm. I dismounted at the door of the chapel, and was taken at once to the Emperor, who was standing up studying some maps.

"Ah! there you are!" he exclaimed. "I was uneasy about you. Have you brought me good news?" I told him all the details I had been able to collect as to the movements of Generals Moore and De la Romaña, and my report, combined with the accounts brought by others, confirmed him in his intention of pressing on his march to surprise the English. He made me tell him the subterfuge by means of which I had got all my information, and managed to return to him safe and sound. He laughed like a child when I described the fright I had given the Alcalde, the express messenger, and the prisoners of Palacios, and after asking a great many questions about the state of the road and the nature of the district I had traversed, he laid aside the gracious, fascinating manner natural to him, and resuming the Imperial gravity he said in a tone of command, "That will do; go and rest."

Rest! That was anything but easy. There was not a square foot of shelter from the rain not already invaded by sleepers piled one on top of the other, so I went to the door of the chapel, and amongst the snoring soldiers I took my stand by one of the fires which was still smouldering, and as I stood there gazing sadly into the embers, which threw out but little heat, and watched them being quenched by the rain, I mused on our dreams of happiness, which, like our camp fires, had been so bright at first, but were equally fleeting. Feeling very low-spirited, I had just tightened my sash to dull the pangs of hunger, when I felt a touch from behind me, and something was forced into my hands. I turned sharply round and found Josserand, the Emperor's steward, at my elbow, who had come to cheer me up. "Hush! hush!" he whispered. "Take this, sent to you by the Emperor; but don't let any one see it, because he can't do as much for every one." I was much too polite to refuse some supper. I begged Josserand to thank the Emperor for thinking of me when he had such weighty affairs on his mind, and the good fellow smuggled into my hands a flask of Bordeaux wine with some bread and a bit of pâté de foie gras made from some luckless goose or duck of Toulouse or Strasburg, I'm sure I don't know which, but anyhow the Emperor's gift was exceedingly good eating. I turned my back on the fire, the light from which might have betrayed me and made others jealous. I no longer saw the embers which had suggested such melancholy reflections, and as I did full justice to the present sent to me by his Majesty my confidence in Providence returned, I once more believed in an ever generous Power ready to forgive our ingratitude, and I was ashamed that I had ever doubted it.

An hour later, and long before daybreak, the signal to start was given in silence, passed from one to the other without sound of drum or trumpet. Each man as he rose shivering with cold broke and shook off the ice with which he was covered, and went to mount his horse or take his place in the ranks, and the column resumed its march. The rain still poured down, and the roads were all but impassable; we had met with no such mud anywhere else but in Poland and Champagne. The terrible state of the roads greatly retarded our march. The enemy, having just heard of the departure of the Emperor from Madrid, had hastily abandoned the plan of attack and commenced the retreat on Coruña. But for the delays the English army would have been caught between two fires, and it would have been very difficult for it to escape destruction. On the 25th we were at Tardesillas on the Douro, where we greatly harassed the English rearguard, and on the 26th our advanced guard crossed the Esla torrent and entered Benavente. It was a pretty fine night, and the water having temporarily subsided our cavalry were able to ford the river, but we were scarcely over when the rain began again.

The English vedettes retired at our approach, and just as we were charging into Benavente in pursuit of them several squadrons of the enemy came into action, presenting a bold front so as to give other squadrons time to turn us and cut off our retreat. Lefebvre-Desnouettes was at the head of the Chasseurs of the Imperial Guard, and emboldened by the tried courage of the troops he commanded, he did not pay enough attention to this manoeuvre of the enemy, and draw back soon enough, so that the English hemmed us in all round in our retreat. Lefebvre-Desnouettes was taken prisoner with a hundred of his men, whilst I was one of the few who escaped back to the stream, which had meanwhile become so greatly swollen that it could only be crossed by swimming. I was a good swimmer, and I did not hesitate to make my horse plunge in, dropping the reins and clinging on only by his mane. The whirling and rushing of the water made me quite giddy, and when I got to the other side I was chilled to the bone, and very much surprised to find myself still alive. A few Chasseurs were drowned, but about a hundred escaped as I did from being cut or shot down, taken prisoners, or swept away in the water. But, alas! what strange quarters and painful experiences awaited me in the village to which I went to rejoin head quarters, and try and find somewhere to rest with a fire to dry my clothes! The houses were deserted by their inhabitants, but crowded with the troops prevented from crossing by the swelling of the torrent. Every shelter was full of men and horses, and I had a long struggle, worse than any I had had with the English, before I could get the privileged Imperial Guard to let me have a corner where I could place my beloved horses under cover from the rain. In the rapid movements of a war such as that we were engaged in, the care of our horses was of vital importance, for on them victory often depended.

When I got to the but which formed the head quarters, I found spread out an abundant repast such as the care of the Chief of the Staff usually managed to secure for the aides-de-camp. Still very wet but warmed up a little by a good meal, I set off to try and find an unoccupied corner in which I could stretch my weary limbs and get a nap. I found one at last, a humble place enough, where the master of the house had plucked his plump gallinas or fowls. I put a plank over a pile of blood-stained feathers and down, rolled myself up in my cloak, and lying down on my rather rickety couch I was already happily wrapt in a deep sleep when the door of my retreat was suddenly knocked in. Startled by the noise I sat up, thus throwing too much weight on the middle of my perch; I broke it and tumbled into the feathers, which rose up in clouds about me. The intruder was one of the two brothers Stoffel, who had quite recently left the Spanish service and joined our head quarters as interpreters. As much bothered with the rain as I was, but not quite so inured to hardship, he too was trying to find a dry corner to rest in, and, candle in hand, thinking only of his own comfort, he took no notice of the unhappy wretch flung by his entrance into a heap of stinking feathers, and I, enraged at finding my hopes of a sleep destroyed by the breaking of my plank, shouted out angrily, "What do you want?" My appearance and position doubtless led the intruder to suppose that I was of the lowest rank, for he answered brusquely enough, "I want a bed." "Well," I replied, "you see there are none here, and you have made me destroy my only chance of a sleep." Seeing him still insensible to my sufferings, I jumped up, exclaiming, "sir, when people see a French officer they take their hats off." Whether he understood or not he kept his head covered, and in my rage at his indifference I flung his hat on to the stairs, and gave him a push in the same direction. I then picked the door up, intending to shut it on him, but he stumbled away shouting at me with a strong German accent, "*Fous êtes un prutal!*" (You're a brute!) and disappeared. Left alone in the dark I had great difficulty in rearranging my bed, but by hook or by crook I managed to fix it up, and was soon asleep again, my happy dreams undisturbed by fear of the consequences the untoward incident might have.

The next day the army resumed its march on Benavente, which had been hastily abandoned by the English, who were afraid of being surrounded there. A melancholy sight, which upset us all very much, met our eyes when we entered the town. The English horses were less accustomed to the fatigues and privations of war than ours, and a very great many of them had been wounded in the legs or on the withers, so that they were unable to follow the army. Unwilling to abandon them to the enemy, who might have nursed their back to health and used them, their masters had barbarously hamstrung them, and the appearance of five or six hundred beautiful creatures thus mutilated moved us almost to tears. Even the Spanish were indignant at this cruelty, and, disposed as they were to look on their allies as heathens, they came to the conclusion that the poor horses had been mutilated in this way as a sacrifice to idols.

The Emperor entered Astorga on January 1st, 1809, after gloriously winding up the year 1808 by the successes his armies had everywhere achieved, throwing into disorder the whole English army, which was hastily retreating towards Coruña. Marshal Soult received instructions to pursue hotly and drive the enemy into the sea, and the Emperor and his suite halted a few days at Astorga to direct the various operations.

The new year's gift I was to receive on January 2nd was not at all in harmony with the rejoicing of the first day of the year. I was on duty and alone in the ante-room at head quarters, when M. Stoffel, the elder brother of the officer of that naive who had tumbled me into the feathers a few days before, carne in and said to me very politely, "Until recently, sir, the foreign officers on the staff had every reason to congratulate themselves on the courtesy and consideration shown to them by you; you never treated them with the haughty disdain of some of your brother officers, who, proud of their titles, often gave us cause of complaint, and it is with regret that I learn that you have lately taken to sharing their want of respect for us." "I know what you mean," I answered. "You are speaking on behalf of your brother." "Yes," he said, "and as foreigners, whose courage is not yet proved, we cannot allow the incident to pass over without demanding satisfaction." "As you refer to proving your courage, I am afraid the excuses I could offer to your brother would not satisfy him. I am on duty till noon: but at one o'clock I shall be at your service. My brother, who is returning from Lisbon, will be here then with his regiment, and we will have a family council." "That will suit us, sir," was the reply. "I will return at one o'clock," and he took his leave.

"What a bother!" I said to myself. "I, who detest the stupid prejudice which makes it impossible to avoid a duel, am now dragged into one myself. The fear of appearing a coward really is a piece of culpable pusillanimity, and it is a proof rather of want of courage than of the reverse not to dare to express one's aversion to risking one's life in a single combat when there are plenty of other opportunities of proving one's valour in presence of a thousand dangers. Might not a duel deprive my country of two of its best defenders? Does a duel make a skilful rogue and bully respectable? Or is an honest fellow who falls beneath the sword of a swashbuckler contemptible?" Such were the questions I put to myself, and it struck me that it really would be a good thing to look upon the two parties to a duel as mentally afflicted, one because he was fool enough to insult the other, and the other because the insult has inflicted on him a mental injury. This state of things once admitted, the seconds, who are able to judge of the cause of quarrel calmly and dispassionately, should be bound in honour, and by certain rules to be agreed upon, to effect a reconciliation in every case. Society and civilisation would doubtless gain greatly by the abolition of the barbarous custom of rushing to a duel to atone for one offence by committing a yet greater one, resulting often in the death of the innocent party. I was still musing on this weakness of humanity when at the hour appointed M. Stoffel reappeared.

In spite of myself I was really as much under the tyranny of the point of honour as any one, and I gaily accompanied M. Stoffel to the place where I expected to find my brother with his regiment. But, alas! on his return from Portugal he had been ordered elsewhere with his corps, and I was unable to find him. "It doesn't matter, however," I said to M. Stoffel; "you must be second for both of us, and I have full confidence in myself." We found his brother awaiting us outside the ramparts. Snow had been falling heavily for the last two days, and it lay on the ground more than four inches deep, so that there was not a clear space suitable for our trial of skill. Seeking about we re-entered the town by a breach where traces of the assault could still be seen, and finally fixed on a spot rather freer from snow in the vaults of a hospital which had been broken open by the same cannonade which had thrown down the walls. Several dead bodies completely stripped lay upon the flagstones awaiting burial, and here and there the blood-stained ground was strewn with quantities of grain. Tired of hunting for a suitable place, we dragged a few of the horrible witnesses out of our way, and swept a space clear of rubbish with some bundles of faggots which were ready to our hands. In thus removing the blood and grain covering the stories we uncovered several inscriptions marking the resting places of the dead, and I confess that my heart sank a little when I came upon my own names, Ludovico Francisco. But I soon conquered the qualms which I attributed rather to disgust than fear; we stripped before crossing swords, the elder brother, sole spectator of the scene, holding our clothes, which would have been soiled if they had been laid on the ground.

I was in no mood to brook further delay, and I made a vigorous attack upon my adversary, who prudently withdrew before me, awaiting his chance of taking me off my guard; but I gave him no time for that, and he had retreated some ten paces when I drove him against the wall, and seizing his right arm with my left hand I held the point of my sabre at his breast. Our faces nearly touched. I felt none of the ferocious courage which would have enabled nee to drive my blade home in the body of one who had done nothing to offend me, but as I had to beware of a surprise I sprang back and resumed my guard. A second time my adversary was pinned against the wall in the gloomiest part of the vault and threatened in the same manner. Still unwilling to kill him, I said, "Must I?" His eyes glared at me menacingly, but terror prevented him from answering. I could not make up my mind to sacrifice him, and feeling a little doubtful of the brother, who was behind me, I sprang back to my original position, and wiping my sabre, my hands, and my face, all splashed with our blood, I said, "That is enough for the present; but if you are not satisfied yet we can meet again," and I left them. It was not till long afterwards that I learnt of what service my frank audacity had been to me, for my adversary turned out to be a very noted fencer. We neither of us received any but slight wounds, but we were both a good deal scratched. The affair lasted so short a time that we were both able to appear an hour later at the review, held by the Emperor, of the Lorson and Laborde divisions, which had just joined us at Astorga. No one even noticed our disfigurement.

That same day one of my friends, General Franceschi, a very clever sculptor, who had been with me in the Compagnie des Arts and had now risen to the rank of Major-General, had a brilliant affair with the troops under the Marquis de la Romaña, by whom the army under Marshal Soult had been surrounded, General Franceschi took 1,500 prisoners at Mansilla.

The English endeavoured to hold Prieras and Villafranca, but were dislodged by General Merle on January 3rd. During the six preceding days 10,000 Spanish and more than 1,500 English had been taken prisoners. In the last affair we lost a very interesting man, one of the flower of the army on account of his fine figure, his courteous bearing, and his chivalrous courage. He bore the distinguished name of Colbert, to which his conduct added fresh lustre. In advancing through the outposts with our skirmishers to attack the enemy, he received a ball in the forehead. The gallant young general was deeply regretted; he left behind him a widow, a son, and two brothers. Madame de Colbert was the daughter of the Comte de Canclaux, a general of engineers, to whom I had been under great obligations in previous campaigns.

When we entered Villafranca, we again met with the horrible spectacle of some 500 fine horses which had been brutally murdered.

On January 15th, after having seen their powder magazines blown up, accidentally or of a purpose, at Coruña, the English gave us battle outside that town. The embarkation of the wounded had already commenced, and they were probably anxious to cover that difficult operation.

Taking advantage of the heights of Elvina, their position was favourable, but Marshal Soult's attack was so vigorous that they lost all their guns, some 3,000 men, their commander-in-chief, Sir John Moore, an admirable leader, whose loss was deeply regretted in England, and many generals, including Lord Crawford, Sir David Baird, Lord Stanhope, and others who fell in the terrible struggle. On the 16th the town of Coruña was bombarded, and whilst the beach outside was covered with all that was left of the British army, struggling to reach the ships, the flames and smoke of the burning houses rose up from different quarters of the town, an explosion of some magazine of powder occurring every now and then. From the heights on which we were placed we looked down upon a scene of indescribable confusion on the seashore, greater even than that in some invaded anthill. At last when the day broke on January 17th the British ships, all sails set, gradually receded from view on the horizon, bound for England, and carrying with them the melancholy remnant of the English army.

The magistrates of Coruña now succeeded in bringing about a capitulation, and two days later Marshal Soult entered the town. In addition to many abandoned guns, the French found 500 English horses still living and unhurt, which it had not been possible to embark. Perhaps the fact that their owners were weary of cruelty had saved their lives.

The Emperor, taking it for granted that the enemy, who were flying in disorder before the troops he had sent in pursuit with orders to completely destroy them, would not be able to rally or attempt any offensive movement, left Astorga on January 5th, to return by way of Benavente to Valladolid, where he intended to await the end of the campaign. In passing through Tordesillas he lodged in what was once the old palace of the Moorish kings, but had been transformed into a convent of Benedictine nuns. He asked to be presented to the Abbess, a woman of great energy and ability, then in her eightieth year, and overwhelmed her with courtesy, granting her everything she asked, showering generous gifts on the community and raising the greatest enthusiasm for himself amongst the sixty nuns of the convent, who had been told but a month before that he was a regular cannibal.

On January 7th at Valladolid the Emperor was anxious to express his gratitude to certain Benedictine nuns who had saved the lives of several soldiers when they were being hunted through the streets by a rabble covered with the blood of the French they had murdered. The nuns, in the true spirit of Christianity and hospitality, had reserved for the French the right of sanctuary at the altars of the churches, and in thus snatching away their victims had roused the fury of the populace against themselves. The Emperor with Marshal Berthier and their respective staffs went to the Benedictine convent to thank the nuns in person, and to offer to grant them anything they wished.

This sort of thing, taken with our victories, did much to cheer us all, and if only the Emperor had not been discredited by the greed of some of his generals, his own generous heart would have helped him more than all his armies to win over the Spanish to his cause.

The news of the embarkation of the English at Coruña and of their complete disappearance from Spain reached the Emperor at Valladolid, and leaving his orders with the army, he set out for Paris. Before he left, however, Marshal Berthier took me to him, as he wished to give me a duplicate of the order he had sent to Marshal Lannes. The Marshal was appointed commander-in-chief of the army besieging Saragossa, and I now received instructions to tell him to press on that operation by every means in his power. I was also to take part in the siege as an engineer officer, and I was placed under the orders of one of the Emperor's aides-de-camp, General Lacoste, commander of the siege train. The shortest route being impracticable, I went by way of Burgos, where my old friends had returned to their quarters. I crossed the Ebro at Miranda, and skirted along the left bank of that river as far as Tudela, where I found the Marshal, who had been detained there for some time by a slight indisposition. I gave him the news from the army, and went on, arriving outside Saragossa a few days before he did. There, beneath the olive trees and in view of the belfries of the town, I began an altogether new kind of life, as adventurous as that of the past, for I was now one of the besiegers in the extraordinary siege I am about to describe.

CHAPTER 7

Siege and Taking of Saragossa

On my arrival in camp, I found every one extremely busy improvising shelters under cover. In default of planks, the reeds and canes cultivated by the Aragonese for making fences to their gardens served to build our barracks. The osiers, of which there were plenty on the banks of the Ebro, were also of very great use to us in making the fascines and gabions for all our siege works. It is at such times as these that the united work of any army is an admirable and instructive sight.

It took us about seven days to make our preparations. We had also opened a trench so as to enable us to go down towards the town by zigzag communications screened from the guns of the besieged, across the gardens, olive woods, and broken fields, which were defended step by step by the enemy.

During this interval the leaders in the besieged city did their best to encourage the people, telling them that when the cold rainy season set in, the French would perish of various illnesses in their trenches, and that nothing was needed but sustained courage and steady perseverance. At the same time they urged the inhabitants to complete their preparations for the defence of their houses, the walls of which were loopholed from basement to roof, so that the inmates could fire into the streets.

Further to stimulate public spirit, rough gallows and lofty gibbets were erected in the market place and in the Calle de Cosso on which to hang those who showed any want of courage or who talked of surrendering, and a tribunal was organised for trying and condemning such culprits on the spot without appeal. The priests, moreover, threatened cowards with the Divine anger, whilst the chiefs of the various factions all pointed to the gibbets. Thus hemmed in on every side, the weakest citizens, inspired by fear, simulated an audacity quite wanting to them, and much against their will augmented the roll of the defenders, thus giving to them a power the strength of which it was difficult to estimate.

As for the women, they enrolled themselves into companies, which were divided amongst the different quarters of the town to be defended. The task assigned to them was to carry provisions, ammunition, and any aid needed to the combatants, to look after the wounded in the hospitals, to make cartridges; in a word, to supplement the efforts of the actual fighters wherever and however they could.

The beautiful young Countess Burida, the daughter of one of the highest families of Spain and of a noble character, had scarcely recovered from the fatigues she had incurred during the first siege, before she a second time placed herself at the head of the women of Saragossa, setting them an example of rare energy and devoted courage. The memory of the feats of arms she had already achieved was a spur to the ambition of all the other women, who admired her virtues and her piety, whilst they longed to emulate her heroism. Banded together into several corps, all under the orders of this valiant Amazon, the women of Saragossa also took an oath to perish with their children rather than yield.

Our soldiers meanwhile were full of health, vigour, and gaiety. For some few days they had had no salt, and several had been reduced to use their saltpetred cartridges to give a flavour to their soup. We had expected to get plenty of salt in a district called Salduba in Roman times on account of its salt mines; but we had no native guide to direct us, for every one had fled at our approach, abandoning their homes either for the town or to join guerrilla bands. Captain Ferussat, a very intelligent officer who had studied geology, was sent with a few of his men to try and find the mines, which it so greatly concerned us to discover.

After climbing up steep barren mountains for two whole

days, during which he expected every moment to fall over some precipice or into the hands of insurgents who would strangle their prisoners, he discovered at a little distance from the Ebro, opposite Ulebo and the mouth of the Xalon, a little cave scarcely noticeable from outside, but with the ground without much trodden by visitors. He entered it cautiously and found the remains of the huge mass of rock salt which had perhaps been already worked for some two thousand years. On his return to camp with proofs of his valuable discovery, he was received with the greatest delight.

On the 29th General Junot, Duke of Abrantes, took command of the siege operations in place of Marshal Moncey, whom the Emperor needed elsewhere.

During the night of the 29th or 30th, General Lacoste had the trenches of the first parallel opened on the right bank, completing a great length before daybreak without being noticed by the enemy. For a long time the heat had been extraordinary for the time of year; the snow had melted in the Pyrenees, and the swollen Ebro overflowed its banks, breaking the bridge of boats constructed by us above the town, and some pontoons and debris carried down by the flood, fell upon the bridge of Saragossa. Palafox, governor of the town, was informed of this, and thinking to profit by our forces being divided, he gathered the larger portion of the garrison at the gates, and at eight o'clock in the morning of the 31st he made a formidable sortie with seven or eight columns under gallant leaders, attacking us all along our line on the right bank. But in spite of the boldness and impetuosity of their charge they were driven back at the point of the bayonet. An hour later they returned to the charge, directing their most persevering efforts on the parallel of the false attack opposite the Castillo of the Inquisition. They were unable to break in at that point. Their cavalry, however, was more successful, and falling upon one of our isolated posts which we had neglected to entrench, cut it to pieces. Palafox hastened to exaggerate this partial success with a view to rousing the enthusiasm of the besieged, and with great ceremony distributed to the brave fellows who had taken part in the sortie a number of medals which he had struck in the mint founded in Saragossa many centuries before.

On January 1st, 1809, a well-sustained fire was kept up throughout the day from all the batteries of the place, backed by a sharp fusillade. In the two previous nights our diggers had finished some 2,000 yards of zigzag approaches and trenches, and we could debouch from the right or centre of the parallels so as to advance by means of flying saps. In spite, however, of all these external preparations, no event of any importance occurred until January 10th, when Palafox made a vigorous night attack upon our batteries, succeeding in spiking two of our guns; but he was driven back, leaving sixty men dead in our trenches. On this occasion the General left behind him many copies of the proclamation he had addressed to our soldiers, hoping to induce some of them to desert. This proclamation was written in six languages, and urged those of every nation who had enlisted under our flag, whether "Dalmatians, Italians, Dutch, Poles, or Germans, to abandon a war which was a disgrace to them;" but it provoked nothing but laughter from our troops.

Saragossa is cut in two by the Ebro, which receives two chief affluents, the Gallego from the north and the Huerba from the south, both of which flow through the eastern side of the town and fling themselves at the same elevation into the main stream, forming a kind of cross.

At about four o'clock on the 12th, when the palisades had been sufficiently broken or overthrown by our cannonade for a practicable breach to have been made below the partly destroyed convent of St. Joseph, Lacoste gave the signal for the assault.

Haxo, Lieutenant-Colonel of engineers, immediately dashed out of the trenches with a few companies of infantry and two field pieces, and advanced in such a manner as to drive the enemy behind their covered ways. This bold manoeuvre took the Spanish so completely by surprise that they at once abandoned their outer works and retreated in disorder across the Huerba.

Lieutenant-Colonel Stahl, at the head of a few companies of light infantry, seized this moment to make a vigorous dash for the fort, but he found the ditch so deep that he could not go down into it. Whilst he was getting ready some ladders to make the descent and to reach the breach, Daguenèt, a captain of engineers, managed to get round the fort and to gain a little wooden bridge which the enemy had not had time to cut. By its means he managed to lead his little company of sappers up to the very entrance to the convent, the door of which he tried to break in with blows from hatchets. But the terrible fire from the place mowed down his soldiers from the rear, and he made them lie down flat on their faces on the bridge.

The enemy, thus attacked on every side, defended themselves with fury, and poured down their fire from the windows of every story and every chink or crevice in the walls. The shock of the various discharges brought down the ceilings on the devoted defenders, and many were crushed beneath the ruins. Terror and disorder spread from one group to another, and the fort, now no more than a mass of ruins encumbered with the mutilated remains of the dead, was carried by main force. In the heat of the combat the greater number of the defenders had fallen, and the survivors now either surrendered or escaped by jumping from the windows. The obstinate defence of this convent, and what it had cost us to take it, gave us some idea of all we should have to go through if we were ever to achieve the conquest of Saragossa.

On the other hand, the loss of their Convent of St. Joseph and of other outlying points, with the spread of epidemics within the walls, led the besieged to entertain the most gloomy forebodings as to the future. Palafox's only notion of how to raise their spirits was by the spreading of false reports, and their credulity grew with their danger. He pretended that a messenger from his brother had brought very good news, and he had this news published in the Gazette of January 16th. "General Reding," he said, "had destroyed the French armies in Catalonia, and was advancing to the relief of Saragossa at the head of 60,000 men. The English armies under Sir David Baird and Sir John Moore, with the force under the Marquis de la Romaña, had cut to pieces the army of Napoleon. Ney and Berthier had been killed, and Bonaparte was hemmed in on every side. The troops hastening to the succour of Saragossa were moreover bringing with them from Cadiz a huge convoy of piastres with which to recompense the brave defenders of the town. The Marquis de Lazan was laying France waste, and would bring to Saragossa the spoils of Toulouse."

The people, eager to read every detail of the news, besieged the doors of the printing office in crowds, and took possession of the sheets as they issued from the press. Meanwhile the bells of all the churches were pealing at once: and the noise of the volleys of artillery and musketry, the beating of drums, the sound of all manner of musical instruments, many of them terribly discordant, mingled with shouts and yells of joy, penetrated even to our camp. The noise and the mocking jeers of the enemy, of the cause of which we were in complete ignorance, really almost made us a little uneasy, and we answered the volleys fired in the town with a rapid succession of bombs and bullets, hoping to do something to interrupt the fête; but the general illumination continued till nine o'clock at night, after which nothing broke the silence or relieved the darkness but the fire from our guns.

The state of things in our camp was now beginning to become very critical. Every night signals were fired and bonfires were lit by the peasants on all the mountains overlooking the town, with a view to encouraging the hopes of the besieged. The Spanish organised a general rising in Aragon, and tried to starve us out by cutting off our supplies. General Wathier had been sent by the Tortosa road with some 1,200 infantry and 600 cavalry to reconnoitre the district and procure provisions for us. He was attacked at Belchitte by 5,000 peasants, but he cut most of them down and pursued the rest as far as Alcanitz, where he found other forces assembled in great numbers. After a fierce struggle he took Alcanitz and gave it up to pillage. Nearer us armed bands and the peasants from the Soria mountains constantly threatened our hospitals, bakehouses, and other establishments at Alagon; and even the Pampeluna road, by which our ammunition wagons reached us, was never quite free from the enemy.

Some thousands of peasants who, most fortunately for us,

were badly led, one day suddenly flung themselves upon our outposts and caused a momentary panic; but the same kind of terror seized them a few minutes later on the approach of Marshal Mortier, who put them to flight; whilst Colonel Gasquet, who had been sent out to fetch provisions, met them on his way back, and killed 500 of them. He brought with him several flocks of merino sheep, valuable on account of the fineness of their wool. It did seem a pity to have to kill animals of so pure a breed to feed our troops.

Palafox's brother, the Marquis de Lazan, succeeded in escaping from Saragossa a few days before to try and rouse the provinces and hasten the succour of the besieged town. He at the same time carried off some of the treasures in the Cathedral of Nuestra Señora del Pilar. He embarked with all these valuable objects in a boat on the Ebro, and, under cover of one of the darkest and longest nights of January, he managed to go down the river without being perceived. The English Colonel Doyle made a similar attempt to convey boats laden with muskets &c. to the besieged, fearing that they would run short of weapons and ammunition; but he was not so successful as the Marquis, for our guards seized the boats before daybreak quite close to the town.

Whilst waiting for reinforcements and relief, Palafox held his regular troops in reserve for difficult operations, sending out peasants only as sharpshooters. These peasants were all accustomed to poaching, and very good marksmen; but, either from laziness or want of audacity, they always would wait to get their meals before they attacked us, which gave us breathing time and enabled us to complete our trenches. We, too, wished to spare our men and ammunition, and we therefore replied as little as possible to the fire of the Spanish. The monks did not fail to look upon our silence as a conclusive proof of our weakness, and they united the peasants to harass us as much as possible. It was, in fact always under the leadership of some of the brethren that the peasants, spurred on by their example, roused themselves sufficiently to fire upon us.

One day a tall priest of venerable appearance, with a fine figure and of a dignified bearing, wearing his sacerdotal robes

117

and upholding a crucifix, advanced towards us beyond the entrenchments of the suburbs. His confident manner was that of some inspired prophet who inwardly repeats the words, "O God, in Thee is my trust; bring Thou their evil designs to nought." When near enough to our outposts to make himself heard, he paused, and in a sonorous and confident voice he pronounced an eager exhortation to us to refrain from a useless attack upon a city under the divine protection of the Santísima Señora del Pilar. Again and again we shouted to him to desist from carrying out his courageous resolve; he persevered, and it was not until the sound of several shots fired in the air on every side interrupted him, that he gave up addressing an audience so very little disposed to listen to him. He returned to the town uninjured.

When General Junot, Duke of Abrantes, heard of the approaching arrival of Marshal Lannes, he was unable to conceal the annoyance it caused him. His readily aroused jealousy and excessive arrogance were really the first symptoms of a mental malady which was beginning to get a hold on him, although no one as yet suspected it. He did all he could to press on the taking of the city before another should arrive to deprive him of the glory to be won, and he ordered a general assault for the next day. On hearing of this, General Lacoste hastened to the Duke, and urged on him the imperative necessity of not departing from the orders given by the Emperor to avoid actual assaults with a view to sparing our men, and making more sure of a finally successful result. He represented to him the fact that the town contained no fewer than 100,000 inhabitants, every man amongst them able to carry arms, and therefore to be counted as a combatant, so that there were really at least 50,000 defenders, whilst we had but 16,000 troops opposite the town, the rest of the army being compelled to hold the country. He reminded him also of the skill and industry with which the people of Saragossa had converted their town into one huge fortress, and how eagerly they were now resorting to the same measures which had succeeded so well in the previous siege. He wound up by saying that he thought it his duty formally to oppose an operation which he felt sure would fail. The other leaders expressed their agreement with the opinion of General Lacoste. The Duke then flew into a regular fury, and after using several insulting epithets, he cried, "You are all my enemies, and in reserving the honour of the conquest of the town to the Marshal, you are traitors to me!"

General Lacoste replied with the greatest coolness, "Well, Monsieur le Duc, I hold you responsible for the failure sure to result from your action, and I shall go and tell the Emperor how it came about." This firmness caused D'Abrantes to change his purpose, and the assault was countermanded. It was on this same evening that the illumination of the town I have already described took place.

Several detachments from our army, which had been out to scour the country in search of provisions, returned exhausted with fatigue without having been able to bring anything back with them, for their convoys had been intercepted by the insurgents. Meanwhile Francesco Palafox, the young brother of the General, was trying to rouse the villages and arm the peasants of Valencia and Catalonia against us. Every one of an age to carry a weapon flocked to his banner, and he had soon a great army of half-savage men, all thoroughly inured to fatigue. Smugglers from infancy, used to hard living and sleeping on the ground, and accustomed to a wandering life beset with dangers, they flocked in ready to wage furious war on us. Our soldiers were often without meat and reduced to half-rations of bread. Our hospital at Alagon was already encumbered with sick and wounded, for whom we had neither food nor medicine. The whole country was in fact laid waste for some eight or ten leagues round Saragossa, and we were totally unable to procure any comforts for the sufferers.

Such was the state of things when Marshal Lannes arrived on January 22nd. His presence at once gave the necessary unanimity to our operations, for all felt the influence of his strong and unique personality. He set up his head quarters near the lock, and the very day of his arrival went round the whole of the extensive works already completed.

The Marshal told us that Marshal Victor had just obtained

a great advantage at Ucles over the Duke of Infantado, and to celebrate this victory and the arrival of the new commander a grand volley was fired from all our batteries in the evening. The enemy replied all along the line for a couple of hours, after which complete silence reigned in the town throughout the night. Palafox, however, who had noted the fact that some of our troops had withdrawn, thought the moment favourable for retaking some of the outlying positions he had lost, and was quietly preparing a grand sortie.

At four o'clock in the morning a cannon shot gave the signal, and three strong columns issued from the gates known as the Quemada, Santa Engracia, and Del Partillo, and marched upon us silently and in good order. The first column, which directed its course towards the convent of St. Joseph, surprised the post protecting the little house of Aguilar on the banks of the Huerba. Our men, however, managed to escape, and General Leval, commanding the trench, retook the position, driving the enemy back as far as the town. The second column was more successful; it crossed the Huerba, which was fordable on the right and left of the bridge head, and with extraordinary audacity advanced for some 400 yards along the Monte Torrero road, crossing all our trenches as far as battery No. 5, where they killed our gunners at their posts and spiked their pieces. They were trying to push on yet farther, when the diggers and guards in the trenches, who had now joined forces, cut off their retreat, compelling them to withdraw in disorder. Thirty of the Spanish were killed, and as many others made prisoners. The third column met with such a vigorous resistance that it, as well as the others, returned to the town before daybreak.

Marshal Lannes thought it his duty to begin with an attempt at conciliation, and he sent an aide-de-camp to Palafox with instructions to inform him of the successes recently achieved by the French arms and to exhort him in the name of humanity to stop the bloodshed. He offered the most honourable terms to the town if it would capitulate.

Saint-Marc, the young officer chosen as envoy, was a good-looking young fellow with a fine figure and charming manners.

He wore the brilliant costume in the Hungarian style, gleaming with gold lace and braid, already described, and his approach to the Spanish outposts was announced by the blowing of a trumpet. At first there was great unwillingness to receive him, but after a long delay a body of cavalry came to escort him into the town. His eyes were bandaged, and he was led through all the longest streets, an immense crowd thronging about him everywhere, shouting, "*Ahorcadle! matadle!*" (hang him! kill him!) But now and then the quick ears of the young officer, who was painfully on the alert, caught amongst these ferocious cries the words, "*Buen mozo hermoso!*" (a handsome, graceful fellow). Some of the people were evidently struck with the easy grace of Saint-Marc, whose uniform and richly caparisoned steed set him off to the best advantage. A visiting patrol came in the nick of time to protect the envoy on his way to the interview with Palafox, who received him in the Palace of the Inquisition. He was led in and made to traverse the long winding passages of the gloomy building in solemn and mysterious silence. At last he was allowed to stop, his eyes were uncovered, and he was left alone in a room hung with black, opposite a fine picture, by Velasquez, of *Christ on the Cross*. In view of his funereal surroundings and after all that had just occurred, he began to think that he was to be submitted to the rough tests of free-masonry, or that he might even be in one of the rooms sacred to the Tribunal of the Holy Office itself, which, as is well known, persecuted the brethren and punished with death those who belonged to the Grand Order of Masons.

At last, after a dreary hour of waiting, the whole of which he passed opposite the melancholy *memento mori* in the place from which so many had issued but to go to their execution, Saint-Marc was relieved to see Palafox, the young Governor of Saragossa, come in accompanied by several officers and the members of the *junta*. He presented the letter from the French Marshal, saying that his Excellency had instructed him to beg the Governor to spare the blood of two nations which had every reason to be friends.

Palafox replied that the garrison and the whole population

of Saragossa were at one with him in their determination rather to be buried beneath the ruins of their town than to yield. After this he left the envoy alone again for several hours, Saint-Marc's gloomy reflections making them appear even longer than they were. The fact was that Palafox, though he said nothing of his kind intentions to the young French officer, really detained him till night to save him from the fanatics who clamoured for him to be given up to them. At last, however, a letter for the Marshal was given to him, his eyes were bandaged again, and he was taken under a strong escort back to the outposts.

The despatch ran as follows: "M. le Maréchal, I know the number of troops besieging me, and ten times as many would be required to compel me to yield. My town will glory in her ruins. The General in command does not know what fear is, and will never submit. The enclosed Gazette will make known to you the position in which I am placed." That *Gazette* was a copy of the one the General had had printed on January 16th with a view to raising the spirits of the besieged by the publication of false reports.

Palafox's refusal compelled us to prosecute the siege with vigour, and the Marshal told us once more that he had orders from the Emperor to use every possible despatch, undermining and blowing up the houses so as to intimidate the inhabitants. We therefore prepared to cross the Huerba. The steep banks, entirely exposed on our side, were raked by the artillery and musketry of the place, which was but a little distance off. The descent of the ditch to get down to the bed of the river, and cross it by means of two trestle bridges with epaulments of gabions and fascines, was therefore one of the most perilous operations of the siege. This work, requiring the utmost skill and courage, was, however, soon successfully achieved, but it cost us the lives of several of our best officers.

At another point all was well arranged for facilitating our communications between the two banks of the Ebro. The bridge of boats thrown across the upper Ebro above the town by General Dedon, of the artillery, had been broken on December 30th, but it was already repaired and was strong enough for the passage of our heavy artillery. The other flying bridge across the lower Ebro below the town consisted of two strong boats connected by a platform, over which two twelve-pounders could be dragged at one time. With the aid of these two bridges, therefore, we could easily go right round Saragossa, the blockade of which was complete.

The work of the engineers on the right bank of the river was divided into three assaults, each led by an able man of proved and brilliant valour. Haxo commanded the assault between the Ebro and the Convent of St. Joseph, Prost's forces were in the centre between the Calle Quemada and the Convent of Santa Engracia, whilst Henri led the left wing threatening the Convent of the Trinity and the Inquisition as far as the river.

Sixty pieces of cannon and twelve mortars were directed against the houses which were to be the first attacked, with a view to dislodging the besieged; but in spite of the terrible fire from them, the intrepidity of the Spanish was such that at the very moment when a shell made a breach in the wall of some house, its inhabitants would turn the hole to account as a loophole for firing on their assailants, although a second shell might at any moment bury them beneath the shattered walls of their home; and everywhere we saw barricades being erected amongst the ruins.

Our sentinels were very vigilant, and we were quite at a loss to discover how the besieged got any encouraging news from without. I must just mention here one clever contrivance to which they resorted, though we did not find out about it till long after the siege was over.

Julian Perez, one of the many smugglers of the Pyrenees, who found himself shut up in the besieged town, made his dog the medium of getting news for Palafox. He had a hairy collar made of the same colour as the skin of the dog, and stitched beneath it, in such a manner that it was very difficult to discover the writing, were the words, 'send us some news."

The faithful animal reluctantly submitted to his master's will when one night he sternly ordered him to go home alone. He started, and unnoticed made his way through the French lines, reaching Barbastro in safety, where the wife of Perez lived. Three times the wife placed messages beneath the hairy collar, twice the poor dog, whose very name of Mira meant beware, got safely back to Saragossa, but the third time his thigh was broken by a bullet, and he went to Barbastro no more.

The arrival of the Marshal had acted as a great spur to our energies. Our little body of cavalry behaved splendidly, driving the insurgents harassing us to a distance. Several breaches were apparently becoming practicable, and the fire from our batteries had partly destroyed the Convents of Saints Augustine and Monica on our right, of Santa Engracia in the centre, and of the Capuchins on the left, the last three named abutting upon the ramparts of the outer enceinte. Major Breuille, commanding the miners, now announced that very long mine branches, which it had been most difficult to establish beneath the rampart, had been pushed up to the very foot of the Convent of Santa Engracia, and that huge powder chambers were charged capable of completely demolishing the front of the building. Everything was therefore ready, and the Marshal ordered a grand attack on these three principal points.

General Habert, who was to deliver the assault, assembled his troops in the trenches at daybreak. He gave the command of the first column on the right to Lieutenant-Colonel Stahl, that of the centre to a captain, and that of the left to Colonel Chlopiski. Each column had at the head an engineer officer and sixty sappers. The brigade of General Brun was held in reserve, and the Morlot division was to make a false attack beyond the Del Carmen gate, so as to divide the forces of the besieged or repulse sorties.

At noon, the fog which had partially hidden the town from us having cleared away, the signal was given to fire the mines of Santa Engracia, and our troops dashed into the open to cross the wide rampart and ascend to the assault. All the bells in the town sounded the alarm at once, the people rushed to the points attacked and poured a hail of shot and hand grenades upon us. At the same moment the enemy fired three mines prepared by them beneath the path we had to cross on our way to each of the three breaches, but we passed so rapidly that we escaped the explosions, which hurt none of us. Everywhere we managed to get a footing, although behind each opening the enemy had established batteries which riddled us with grape shot, whilst all the walls bristled with enraged defenders.

After scaling the breach, which really was scarcely practicable, we found ourselves arrested at the top by the wall of a garden rising more than ten feet above the ground on the other side. The neighbouring terraces were covered with troops and artillery which would completely crush us. We had to get out of this altogether untenable position as quickly as possible, and try a second assault on some of the positions occupied by the Spaniards. We flung ourselves forward and charged with the bayonet. In this second assault a Spaniard dealt me a blow with the butt of his musket, which wounded my face and rendered me insensible. A few moments later I regained consciousness, and went to wash away the blood in the water of the Huerba, quickly rejoining the right column, to which I belonged. Meanwhile a footing had been obtained upon the breaches, and several of the neighbouring houses had been taken, the doors and walls having been staved in, though the courts were so raked with the fire of the enemy that they were quite impassable.

In the attack of the centre, the mines laid by Major Breuille under the rampart flung down some half of the walls of the Convent of Santa Engracia. The Poles of the Second Vistula Regiment, commanded by Chlopiski and directed by Rogniat, colonel of engineers, had been divided into several small detachments, which were taken into action one after the other, to avoid confusion. These heads of columns traversed at a run some 200 exposed yards, and dashed impetuously on to the ruins of the first wall of the enclosure, which had been flung down for a considerable length. A second wall behind the first had only been damaged by the breaking open of the breach some eight or ten feet wide, and the guns of the 1,200 defenders of the convent were all pointed on it and pouring forth a hot fire. The first of our brave fellows to arrive, Captain Segond, of the engineers, and Captain Negrodski, flung themselves head foremost upon the breach, and were followed by all the men of the Vistula Regiment, who came on like enraged lions, flung themselves into the opening, and defiled beyond it. A terrible struggle now took place in every part of the convent, monks, soldiers, peasants, even women and children, urging each other on, and disputing every inch of ground, defending themselves from the top to the bottom of the stairs, from corridor to corridor, from room to room, entrenching themselves behind bales of wool or even piles of books, and from every point pouring out a murderous fire. One of the Poles was actually killed on the stairs by a monk with blows from a crucifix. For all that, however, the Spanish were driven back beyond the Capuchin Convent, of which we remained masters. Even six fougasses, which the enemy blew up under our feet, did not arrest us, and we pursued them into the ruins of the adjacent houses, on which also other batteries opened fire, doing us a good deal of damage. We suffered most cruelly from the musket shots fired from the top of the neighbouring belfries, where the best marksmen, who never missed their aim, were stationed.

I was crossing the heaps of ruins resulting from the explosion in the court of the Santa Engracia Convent, with Generals Lacoste and Valazé, on the way to attack the Capuchin Convent, when I was badly wounded in the shoulder by a ricochet ball, which caused a most painful choking sensation. This second wound placed me hors de combat for several days. As I was being supported over the debris of the ruined cloister, my helpers paused for a moment on the scene of carnage, opposite to a white cross rising above a marble group representing the dead Christ in His grave clothes across the knees of His Mother, who was praying at the foot of the cross. Her eyes were uplifted to heaven, but her hands were extended towards the ground, and her grief-stricken expression, with her lips half opened as if to speak, appeared to say, "Almighty God, Thou didst not give life to human creatures for them to destroy each other; oh, appease their homicidal rage, pardon their fatal errors, even as my Son forgave His enemies." A thick cloud of dust and smoke, which had been whirled by the wind round about the statue, formed a kind of aureole, and the figure of the Mother seemed to move. The mist partly hid the dead and dying, whose blood was dropping on the steps of the pedestal; and the sad realities of the awful scene were to me like some sublime and unexpected vision, to which I accorded an involuntary admiration. My weakened brain led me to see the hand of Providence held out to me from the midst of the cloud, and I besought protection from the Almighty. As I did so, Valazé came up, bringing me a few drops of wine in a leather bottle he had found in the ruined convent. The drink restored me, and my wound was not, after all, serious.

The attack on the Trinitarian Convent on the left was even more fierce than that on the centre. Thirty of our carabineers stationed on watch at the entrance to the bridge noticed that the Spanish were running away, and without a moment's hesitation they dashed after them in pursuit, and climbed several of the enemy's entrenchments, getting in through the embrasures. At first they overthrew everything before them, killing the artillerymen at their guns, and rushing along the ramparts shouting, "Forward! forward!" But a hot fire was poured on the brave fellows from every side; many of them were struck down, and their numbers were rapidly diminishing, when a battalion of guards beyond the Huerba, seeing their danger and unable to contain themselves, crossed the river at double-quick pace, and scaling the ramparts flew to the aid of the carabineers, dashing with the flying enemy into the Trinitarian Convent. The Spanish, however, who had yielded to a momentary panic only, now rallied, and hastily turning back spread into the neighbouring houses, from which they opened a murderous fire at close quarters upon our troops, who were exposed all along the rampart. Our ranks were greatly thinned, and our zeal considerably cooled. The enemy saw their advantage. General Mori came up with considerable reinforcements, and we were driven back on to the Trinitarian Convent, which was retaken by the Spanish general. Morlot, commanding our reserve, seeing our disorder, hurried up to our support in the nick of time with two of his battalions. The shock of their onslaught was terrible, and the number of dead piled up on the scene of the conflict was very great. In the end we made more than 600 prisoners, and took fifteen pieces of cannon, which we turned against the besieged from their position on the ramparts. Several officers of great merit lost their lives on both sides, and General Mori was found amongst the dead. Captain Segond, an interesting young French engineer, from whom we had hoped great things, was surprised and killed almost at close quarters by a priest who was hidden behind a pile of stones amongst the ruins of Santa Engracia. He was the son of one of our most distinguished chiefs, and his death was a great grief to his family and to all his brother officers.

It was at the end of this terrible day that a Carmelite monk named San Yago Saas, who had distinguished himself in the previous siege as a brilliant leader and ardent preacher, boasted that he had himself butchered seventeen Frenchmen. Sword in hand, sleeves flung back over the shoulders, leaving the arms bare, robe tucked up, and splashed with blood from head to foot, the furious monk ran to and fro in the ranks saying to each soldier, "Follow my example, and there won't be one of them left." And on the morning of the same day the famous Maid of Saragossa, Augustina Sarzella, reappeared amongst the troops, and by her valour won the appointment of commander of a company of the intrepid women led by Doña Burida. The Maid of Saragossa had long practised pointing cannon and firing muskets, and her skill was only equalled by her intrepidity. During the first siege, which had lasted from June to August in 1808, as she was taking provisions to a battery which was suffering so terribly that the gunners were discouraged, she flung herself amongst the dead and dying, tore a linstock from the hands of an expiring artilleryman, put the match to a twenty-four pounder and springing upon the cannon vowed she would not leave it alive. This heroic deed so encouraged the Spanish that they took fresh heart and opened fire on us with renewed vigour.

We spent the following night in barricading our position with the aid of bales of wool, gabions, and sacks of earth, of which we made traverses. In clearing away the dead bodies of the Spanish which encumbered the ground we came upon the corpse of a young monk still clasping in his hands the pyx containing the sacred wafers he had been courageously carrying to the dying in the midst of the carnage, with a view to encouraging the living to resist to the end by showing them that they would receive spiritual succour at the last.

This arduous day, which had cost us the lives of 600 men, had left us masters of the most important positions on a third of the ramparts, and henceforth we were firmly established in one portion of the city itself. The Spanish general, however, far from being discouraged by the losses he had sustained and by the ill success of the incredible efforts he had made on the 27th, counted all the incidents which had occurred as so many victories.

Meanwhile illness was beginning to weaken the besieged; and to keep up the moral courage of those whom suffering rendered irritable and difficult to lead, the *junta*, which might more justly have been called the Tribunal of Terror, punished the slightest misdemeanour with pitiless severity. Neither age nor rank saved from death those suspected of cowardice, and a single hour witnessed trial, condemnation, and execution. Every morning the people saw fresh victims hanging from the rows of gibbets on the Corso. The heart of Palafox was torn by all these sufferings, but Bazile and the other ferocious leaders of the *junta* were inflexible. The clergy all around by order of that same *junta* organised processions, offered up many prayers, and announced many false miracles, in all of which, however absurd they might be, the people, whose superstition made them incredibly gullible, firmly believed, so that, confident in the visible support of Heaven, their courage and zeal were revived.

The war was now carried on in the very streets of Saragossa, and Lacoste did all in his power to push farther into the town without exposing his troops, knowing full well how discouraging continual losses are. We therefore advanced very slowly but very surely with the aid of the sapper and the miner. As soon as a house was taken, a miner was sent down to the lowest part of the cellars, where he set to work to open a mine beneath the street or under the next house so as to reach the one we meant to attack. This mine was then charged in the most profound silence, and with such skill that the line of least resistance was beneath the condemned house. Directly after the explosion the soldiers, who were held in readiness, flung themselves through the clouds of dust which arose, and took possession of the ruins of the house just thrown down, where to secure possession they quickly barricaded themselves and awaited the night. Then under cover of the darkness they brought in sacks of earth and bales of wool, anything in fact which could serve as epaulments or mantlets, and render more secure our communications in the streets between one block of houses and another.

Every one displayed the greatest eagerness in these dangerous operations, following the example of General Lacoste, whose admirable courage was that of a man of thought as well as action. His talents and amiable character won the esteem and affection of every one, and under his leadership the artillery and engineers worked admirably together, achieving great successes. Unfortunately, however, the army and his personal friends were soon to mourn his loss.

On the 28th the enemy tried without success to retake the Trinitarian Convent. They were also driven back on the 29th, but on these two days our engineers lost six officers and thirty-eight men.

Under the indefatigable Colonel San Genis the Spanish bored holes in every partition and ceiling of their houses, through which to take aim from one story to another. We could hear them breaking up the staircases to use them as barricades, replacing them with ladders, which could be drawn up. Each household in its own particular stronghold laid up stores of hand grenades and shells, which could easily be rolled down on the assailants, with plenty of powder, balls, and stones, whilst priests and women with arms in their hands circulated to and fro beneath a hail of bullets, and even with astonishing audacity headed an attack on our troops in the Capuchin Convent, hoping to drive them out. But all this fury was of no avail against the cooler courage of our seasoned troops, who soon found themselves sheltered behind piles of dead bodies.

Lacoste was very anxious that the works opposite the suburb on the left bank of the Ebro should progress as rapidly as ours were doing in the town itself; but the division under Gazan, which was threatened on every side, had merely established a blockade and had not yet been able to complete the works necessary for the circumvallation of the suburb or for the contravallation of his own position to protect it from attacks from outside. The Marshal therefore went with General Lacoste and myself to push on the works, and the following night (that of January 31st and February 1st) the trenches were opened with a first parallel encircling and threatening the Capuchin Convent. A few days later the fire from twenty pieces of cannon was breaking in its strong fortifications.

On his way back to the town the Marshal gave us fresh cause to admire his wonderful self-possession in the midst of danger. Instead of returning under cover of the deep trenches, he led us across the open within half range of the place, and climbed a mound so as to get a better view of his surroundings. As he was quietly giving us his orders, several shots aimed at his brilliant uniform passed through our cloaks, and one of our officers was wounded. We all at once jumped into the trench, but the Marshal remained motionless and went on speaking to me. It would have been very bad manners on my part to listen to him from a distance, so I climbed up beside him again. It was not until he had said all he wanted to say that he slowly drew back into the trench, where we took the liberty of representing to him that we thought this example of temerity was scarcely needed with troops of such proved courage as ours, and that in thus exposing himself he ran a risk of depriving us of a very able chief at a most critical moment of our undertaking.

In the Gazan camp the fatigue of the troops was extreme. Neither officers nor men were relieved for a single night till they had passed seventy-two hours in the trenches. Food was often very scarce, but in spite of all these drawbacks there was very little illness, as the weather was fine and dry. Most of our soldiers would have preferred fighting twenty battles in the open to working for a single day in the trenches. They were taken there in silence in the dead of the night, with or without their arms, according to circumstances. If they had their weapons they were stacked in piles in some safe place under a strong guard. Picks and spades were then given out to the men by their officers, who placed them in groups at a distance of about three or four feet from each other on a line marked out, and ordered them as they dug to throw the earth out in front without making any noise, or they would provoke the fire of the enemy. When the poor fellows, worn out with several nights passed in this task, were sufficiently protected from the direct fire of the place (and they worked very quickly, so eager were they for rest), they would fling themselves down, their danger and toil at an end at the same moment, and fall into a sleep so deep that even the sound of the firing of cannon did not wake them. They were still, however, exposed to sorties, to the bursting of shells, bombs, grenades, and fireballs, flung amongst them by the enemy with a view to lighting up the place where they were concealed, so as to take proper aim at them. They had also to dread being crushed beneath the showers of stones hurled from the swivel guns of the besieged, but they slept on as peacefully through the hurly-burly of all these plunging fires and death-dealing projectiles as the sailor after a storm upon the waves which threaten to engulf him at any moment; troubling themselves not at all with the thought that for some of them this delicious sleep might be eternal.

Such is, now and then, the life of the infantry soldier during a siege; but for the sapper there is absolutely no break in the dangers to be met at every turn, for he has to work under the direct fire of the enemy in the open as he goes down some counterscarp, and to brave all, manner of vaguely aimed projectiles as he rolls some gabion before him when he is about to open a sap or finish off a trench. Imagine how great must have been the skill and coolness of the engineers who during the last sixteen years had thus taken possession of all the chief strongholds of Europe!

But the example of patient perseverance set by the engineers was quite equalled by that of the artillery officers, whose courage and zeal, directed by thoroughly scientific acumen, never wavered, in spite of the terrible fatigue and privation involved in the task they had undertaken.

The Spanish engineers really seemed to rival our own in their skill, courage, and perseverance. By an unexpected stroke of fate the French and Spanish armies lost in one day two chiefs of engineers, both interesting young fellows, who had done much to contribute, by their eager initiative, to the success of the works on both sides. Just before Colonel San Genis was killed at the Palafox battery, he had said to his officers, "If there is ever any question of capitulation, don't call me to your counsels, for I will find some means of defending you to the death." Whilst availing himself of every resource known in the science of engineering to avert the dangers threatening his fellow citizens, by whom he was loved and respected, he was equally eager to place his mother in safety. His affections were, in fact, divided between his mother and his country, and he was carried when dying to the arms of the parent he loved so well. She wept bitterly over the changed features of her son, but had the melancholy satisfaction of receiving his last sigh. Less fortunate than San Genis, Lacoste, abandoned by the good fortune which had attended him in the assaults of Cairo, Saint Jean d'Acre in Syria, and Gaeta in Italy, was to fall in a foreign land, far from his father and the wife he adored, with no honour but that of having served his country at a distance.

Lacoste had ordered two mines to be charged, each with 2,000 pounds of powder, one in front of Santa Engracia, and the other about a hundred paces from it on the left. To insure the attacks following the explosions being simultaneous, he decided to lead that on the left himself, confiding the other, on the right, to me. As we were going down together from our camp on Monte Torrero, about noon on February 1, he spoke to me of the young wife whom he loved passionately, and told me that though they had been married a year, he had only been able to spend five days with her. He added how much he wished to retire from the Emperor's service and live quietly at home, cheered by the dear presence of his father, his wife, and the children he hoped would be born to him; and whilst calling up a picture of a life full of home joys, we reached the batteries.

Haxo had just taken the Convent of St. Augustine, where several breaches had been opened by our miners before daybreak. At two o'clock in the afternoon, when all had seemed perfectly quiet in that part of the town, the shouts of a vast multitude approaching, with the sound of the tocsin summoning the people to arms, made us hastily resume our weapons. It was Palafox advancing at the head of some eight or ten thousand furious men, eager to retake the houses occupied by us. Their attack was so vigorous that we lost a good deal of ground, but we retained possession of the convent, protected by the entrenchments made by Haxo's orders.

It was just at this juncture that Lacoste and I arrived from Monte Torrero. We first traversed the blood-stained ruins of the convent just taken by Haxo, and then pressed on to join the centre under Prost.

Lacoste, who could not help feeling full of pity for the luckless enemies who were to perish in the explosions, prepared for as described above, tried to drive the Spanish out of the threatened houses, by placing a few mortars behind an epaulment near them and discharging some bombs from them. Just then a ball crossed the bale of wool behind which we were hiding, grazed Lacoste's forehead, and carried off a lock of his fair hair. Laughing at this incident, he said to me, alluding to our talk on the way down from the mountain, "If only that lock of hair had been for her!" and we separated, each to go to his own post.

He had ordered me to set fire to my powder two minutes after I heard the explosion of his, which would be in about a quarter of an hour by our watches, which tallied exactly. My dispositions were made, and we all listened for nearly forty minutes without hearing anything. I sent to inquire the cause of the delay, and my messenger returned to say that all had succeeded admirably, and we were to fire our mine at once. I gave the order immediately; a whole block of ten or twelve houses were precipitated into the air, and a dull muffled sound reached us. As soon as the dust had cleared away sufficiently for us to distinguish objects and recognise each other, Prost flung forward the Poles who were to attack. At this moment Lacoste and Valazé arrived to witness our charge. We climbed through the window of a house near, so as to get under cover amongst the ruins. Our shouts of "Houra! houra!" to urge the Poles forward, aroused the attention of the Spanish, who fired on us through almost invisible holes. General Lacoste and Captain Lalobe, who had followed us, were both mortally wounded in the forehead. The latter died on the spot, and Lacoste survived but a few hours.

This event saddened the whole army, to whom the General was very dear; and the Marshal, who shared the general mourning, announced to the Emperor the great loss sustained in the death of this skilful engineer, who had been full of resource, and whose calm and cheerful demeanour in the midst of the greatest dangers had secured the success of all he undertook. The Marshal appointed Colonel Rogniat to the command of the engineers, vacant by the death of General Lacoste.

All the woodwork and other combustible parts of the houses surrounding us in this attack on the centre were by order of our new colonel smeared with tar and set fire to, and this burning barrier separated us for some days from the Spanish, who were as eager and indomitable as ourselves. They seemed to look upon it as an amusement to practise their skill in taking aim at us, and they were such good marksmen and fired so quickly that the shakos of our soldiers were riddled with bullets directly they appeared above the parapet of the trenches. This made the task of our engineers extremely dangerous, and Haxo, one of our bravest generals, was so worried by the perpetual firing whilst he was at work, that he took exception to my height, and grumbled at me because when I was near him in the trenches I drew down the fire of the enemy, my scarlet helmet, with its gold ornaments and white aigrette, forming a capital mark. The Spanish were so skilful and persevering in this artillery practice, that they actually succeeded in making breaches with it in the walls which they were not otherwise able to injure, and which they thought served as a protection to us. In some parts of the trenches we might have picked up bushelfuls of lead used in this manner.

Rogniat soon found that the houses which had been completely thrown down in the explosions were no real shelter to us, and that our men ran many dangers in crossing the exposed ruins on their way to attack the neighbouring buildings. He therefore had the charges so laid that only the wall next to us was destroyed, in each case leaving the others standing, to serve as a cover to us when we took possession. Heavily charged chambers were henceforth only fired to throw down the walls of the large buildings, which served as something like citadels in the interior of the town.

The experience gained day by day in this extraordinary kind of warfare served to teach us much in every way, and our prudence and method alike grew greater and greater. Directly a house was taken, it was converted into a fortress with the aid of sacks of earth used to wall up the openings on the side of the enemy, whilst we pierced a straight line of interior communications which we could prolong successively into each house occupied. Loopholes were then made opposite those of the enemy, and we soon became nearly as clever in this style of aiming from room to room as were the Spanish themselves.

In the centre our miners were preparing three chambers at the base of the Convent of Jerusalem with a view to blowing it up, when they heard noises beneath them which told them that the enemy was countermining them. They at once charged one of the fourneaux and fired it lest they should be anticipated. The Spanish miners, including one officer and fifteen men, perished miserably, buried beneath the masses of earth which fell on them, and our sappers began making fresh galleries. The courage and calmness with which the military miner braves danger and fatigue are alike admirable. Whilst he is patiently hollowing out the tomb of the enemy's sappers, it often happens that he is separated from them by but the thinnest layer of earth. Whilst some slight noise or movement reveals to him that his enemies are compassing his destruction close beside him, he is not standing up, he cannot confront his enemy in a proud attitude of defiance, the eyes of the army are not upon him to raise his courage and redouble his strength. He is often alone, stretched flat on his face on the ground, or crouching in a cramped position, and he sometimes succumbs, suffocated for want of air. It is often when he is but half alive that he is called to the struggle. What Bayard, what Murat would not find his courage ebb away if he had to submit to being shut up for days in the cold subterranean galleries, where the miners noiselessly creep along to prepare the mine they are to fire? Their disinterestedness was equal to their courage, and in this memorable siege I knew instances of men who, whilst driving horizontal galleries at a depth of some twenty feet underground, broke with their picks antique vases full of gold, silver, and bronze coins, which the Carthaginians, Romans, or Arabs had buried in times of similar calamities. It would have been natural enough if the miner's cupidity had been aroused by the gleam of the metal in the light of his lamp; but not a bit of it he would simply push the treasure and the loosened earth behind him to the next worker, with the words, "Here, pass Peru to the Captain; it will amuse him." Captain Veron-Réville was a connoisseur of coins, and in this way he received a good many very rare medals, several of them found at the foot of an old Roman wall, the hard cement of which bothered our miners a good deal.

Money had been coined in Saragossa for many centuries, and that city owns a most interesting collection of coins. Captain Veron-Réville noticed that the part of the town on which we were working was founded on an old bed of shingle or large pebbles which had been rolled over and over by the Ebro, and was now covered with a layer of from ten to fifteen feet of good alluvial soil. This shingle bed was not without danger to us, although it contained no flint, for it could not be broken up without making a noise which might be heard by the enemy.

Colonel Rogniat found it prudent to make on our line a point of support to meet all contingencies. Between February 2nd and 6th, therefore, he made an epaulment with sacks of earth at the breach in the Capuchin Convent, so as to fortify us in it. Artillery was also stationed there to reply to that massed by the enemy at this point.

In our attack on the right we stretched along the Calle de Quemada almost to the College, crossing the street by means of three subterranean galleries, so as to establish an equal number of chambers under the mines opposite. One of these galleries debouched into an unoccupied cellar, through which our miners and sappers were able to go up into the house above. Once established there they could help us to get into the whole block. (We called any group of houses surrounded by streets a block.)

We crossed the Calle del Medio by a double epaulment of sacks of earth, and established ourselves on the other side in a block of houses which had been undermined in the first siege. In this affair Rogniat had a finger taken off by a bullet, but his wound only kept him out of the trenches for two days, during which I took his place. Morlet, a lieutenant of engineers, who had already performed many brilliant feats of arms, was dangerously wounded at the same moment as Rogniat, whilst Brenne, another lieutenant of engineers, received three bullets.

Every day it became more difficult to protect ourselves from all these shots. The streets of the quarters into which we penetrated grew narrower and narrower, and we were almost at close quarters with the Spanish, who riddled with balls the barricades, planks, doors, windows, and shutters, behind which they thought we might be. In a few moments every protection was pierced with holes like those in lace, and woe betide any one who happened to be on the other side.

In some streets there was not room to place our pieces of cannon and howitzers, and we even had to dismount our little six-inch mortars before we could get them into position. Our artillerymen got over these difficulties with surprising skill and speed, but then the discharge brought the windows, tiles, chimney pots, and sometimes even the walls, down about their heads. These falls of debris worried them dreadfully, and to safeguard themselves against them it was necessary to blind and protect several batteries with beams.

Haxo's skill and unwearying activity, however, daily won us many successes in the attack on the right, and he was already master of nearly all the blocks of houses opposite the Convents of St. Augustine and St. Monica. Two pieces of heavy calibre were pounding a breach in a tower on the Corso, whilst a howitzer at the end of the Calle del Quemada enfiladed the wide opening made by them. All the walls on the enemy's side were loopholed, and covered galleries had been pierced in every story of the houses, and passages or crossings had been established in all the streets between two epaulments. Everything was pressed into the service, and I actually saw sacks of corn, bales of the fine wool in which Saragossa does such a large business in times of peace, and even books from the libraries of the convents piled up in great numbers; the big volumes telling at length the marvellous legends of the martyrs, and the parchment folios were most useful to us. Books can be as easily piled up as bricks; and some on end, others laid down flat, they formed a perfect protection from balls. Many of our men owed their lives to the thickness of the history of some saint, whose piety they would never have dreamt of imitating. Nor was this way of destroying valuable tomes and priceless manuscripts the most distressing sight of the kind we had to witness, for during the night our soldiers, who had no wood to make fires at which to warm themselves, burnt books for the purpose, or tore out the leaves to make torches with which to grope about in the labyrinths of rubbish where they might so easily have hurt themselves. Our cultured officers grieved over this vandalism and tried to prevent it, but wood was not much used in the buildings of Saragossa, and it was often very difficult to get less costly combustibles for the use of the men. It was even more hopeless to make them understand the value of Greek, Latin, Arab, and other antique volumes, which they recklessly tore to pieces to burn. "These musty old books," they would say, "are fit for nothing but lighting fires; we don't understand a word in them." Thus was lost a very valuable collection of manuscripts, including many original historical documents of very great antiquity, of which but a few scattered leaves were recovered.

The attack of the centre, led by Prost, began with a vigorous assault on the Convent of the Nuns of Jerusalem, and Palafox, too much hemmed in by walls to attempt sorties, contented himself, as he had done before, with setting fire to the houses he could no longer defend. In an instant the convent was wrapped in flames, and Prost, taking it for granted that the fire was a proof of the retreat of the Spanish, at once seized the favourable moment to dash through the huge blazing furnace with his sappers and light infantry. He penetrated into the convent, where he came pell-mell upon the enemy, and giving them no time to defend themselves, he pursued them with the greatest intrepidity into every part of the building, of which he finally remained master. During this bloody conflict the flames continued to rage, burning dead and wounded together, and reducing half the convent to cinders.

Never shall I forget the effect produced on me by the appearance of the inside of that convent, of which I caught sight across thick clouds of dust and smoke. The cells of the nuns, once havens of peace and of prayer, were now the scene of an awful struggle. In this hour of desolation the assailants were trampling not only on the rush mats which had been the sole furniture in the retreats of the austere and devoted women, but on all the sacred symbols of their religion, such as rosaries, holy-water vessels, amulets, &c. At every step in the various oratories I came upon implements of penance, such as iron scourges with sharp edges, bearing witness to the severity of the discipline of the nuns, even as the needlework also scattered upon the floors did to the eager charity with which they had laboured for the poor. Some few of these devotees, surprised in their flight, had been detained by the female warriors of the town, and had remained with them amongst the defenders. As we approached we saw them tearing down from the altars the objects of their chaste devotion, in the hope of saving them from desecration. The devoted women, with no thought for themselves and inspired only with religious zeal, took nothing with them but crucifixes and images of the Infant Saviour, which they held closely in their arms as they abandoned with heartrending cries the only homes they had, strewn with tokens of their piety and loving kindness. In all the chapels were numerous pretty little figures in coloured wax representing the infant Jesus, with snow-white lambs all decked with ribbons and various tasty ornaments invented by the childlike imagination of the guileless nuns. Wounded soldiers fell across mangers decked with flowers, evergreens, and moss, or overturned cradles of the Infant Saviour; and the blood of the dying trickled over bunches of immortelles, crowns of roses, and azure blue ribbons.

As soon as we were firmly established in the Convent of the Nuns of Jerusalem, Breuille led his miners towards two huge buildings, the Convent of St. Francis and the Hospital for Foreigners, which still separated us on this side of the town from the Corso. The work of the miners in this protracted siege now became everywhere more formidable and arduous than ever. One day it so happened that two parties of miners—one besieged, the others besiegers—debouched at the same moment from their rival galleries in the same cellar; and there, in a gloom scarcely relieved by the light of their lanterns, they flung themselves upon each other with their tools, their knives, and their sabres, without waiting for any other weapons. It was indeed the war to the knife promised us by Palafox. The furious blows exchanged knocked down around the combatants many of the great stone pitchers used by the Spanish for storing wine and oil, and those who were struck down by pick or matlock were drowned in a mixed flood of wine, oil, and blood. In this subterranean struggle, which left us victors, we only lost two miners.

Another day one of our miners had just made the opening for getting into a cellar to which he had mined his way, and where the silence and peace of the tomb appeared to reign. Already, pistol in hand, he had pushed his head into the gloom, his lamp flinging but a few rays before him; and he was trying to make out his bearings with the aid of his compass, when some Spanish in ambush, who had been watching his proceedings, fell upon him, and killed him in the gallery at the opening he had just made. Fortunately his comrades behind him were able to make their escape in time.

The Spanish miners were able to choose their own ground, and to make their works in advance at the points we were likely to attack. They were therefore less cautious than we were, and their confidence sometimes led them to break the silence we so rigorously observed. Our precautions had the best results for us, and their imprudence lost them many men. Our miners became

141

very skilful in hearing those of the enemy a long way off, and in accurately estimating the position of their mines. They were thus able to avoid them, and we had scarcely ever to deplore a mining catastrophe.

One evening, for instance, near St. Francis and about fifteen feet below the surface of the ground, nine Spaniards, thinking themselves in perfect security, went down into a cellar to prepare a chamber in the path of a gallery we had been excavating, and which was all ready for charging. The noise they made put us on our guard soon enough for us to prepare a similar trap for them; the powder was hastily laid, and our explosion brought the house down upon them, without damaging the cellar in which they were. The unfortunate fellows remained shut up for some hours without daring to make the slightest noise. But at last, when we thought they had all been dead some time, we heard them struggling to free themselves from their terrible position and calling out piteously for help. We all hastened to aid them to climb out of their tomb. They worked from their side and we from ours, and we were already near enough to give them our hands, when the roof of the cellar, shaken by the crash of the explosion, and also, perhaps, deprived of its supports by our efforts to help, fell upon them. Only three were left alive, one of whom was an officer, whom we rescued with the greatest difficulty from under the stones beneath which he was buried.

Whilst we were trying to save the Spaniards, the men in the neighbouring house, never suspecting that we were engaged in a service of rescue, rolled shells and lighted grenades upon us; but for all that, Providence allowed us to accomplish our work of benevolence without shedding the blood of a single member of our party. Our three prisoners were taken to the Duke of Abrantes, and he received them kindly, ordering a good meal to be set before them. From them we learnt to what a deplorable condition the inhabitants of Saragossa were reduced. Although there were so few of us, the blockade was so complete that no news could reach the town. Even the cleverest messengers, who tried to get in under cover of the darkness by roundabout ways, were sure to fall into the hands of our sentries, who were always on the alert to arrest them. Fresh meat and vegetables were altogether exhausted, and there was nothing to eat but fish and salt meat. A chicken was already worth five piastres (about a pound). All the mills on the Ebro were in our hands, and the besieged had no means of grinding the corn of which they still had considerable quantities. True, they had made a few hand mills, but they were altogether inadequate, and the people had to be content with grain merely crushed or bruised. This unwholesome diet did almost as much harm as actual famine would have done, and to these evils was added the terror inspired by the bombardment, which had already lasted three weeks.

Most of the inhabitants had taken refuge in cellars, thinking to be safe there, but in many cases the roofs had been staved in by the fall of bombs. Moreover the air of these damp retreats, far too small for the numbers which crowded into them, was foetid and vitiated in the extreme, so that there was really more danger in breathing it than in sharing in the defence in the open. Already all these evils combined had caused an epidemic, which claimed some 300 victims per day, and had even attacked some members of the garrison. Many were no longer strong enough to remove their dead from their houses, and those corpses which were carried into the streets or to the doors of the churches remained there without burial. Often bombs would burst and shatter the dead to pieces, tearing them from their tattered blood-stained shrouds, so that at every turn the most horrible sights met the eye.

Our prisoners also told us that the irritation of the people under such an accumulation of woes led them to be guilty of many an unjust act. Only the evening before, they said, when beds were sorely needed for the numerous wounded and dying, a bomb had fallen upon the building containing the military stores, and set fire to it. The people who hastened to put out the flames found some thirty unused beds, which had been left, forgotten and covered with dust, in a granary. They at once shouted "Treason!" murdered the keeper of the stores, and then hanged him from one of the gallows on the Corso with this inscription: "Assassin of the human race, who stole ten thousand beds!"

Many women, even more eager in the defence than the men, carried their warlike zeal to extravagance. No conjugal or maternal affection checked their ardour, and they were seen in the midst of the greatest dangers, urging on their husbands and sons, who fell beside them or expired in their arms. The fearless heroism of the Countess Burida was, however, equalled by the generosity of her character. Her hands, too weak to wield a sword, were ever ready to distribute aid to the sufferers, and from her private purse she aided many of the brave fellows whose own resources were exhausted.

On the other hand, the members of the *junta*, such as Fathers Bazile and Consolation, Mossen Sas, and Butron, were all possessed with a spirit of the most pitiless cruelty, and few days passed without their hanging some of those whom they accused of weakness or a desire to capitulate.

Palafox, who was as humane as he was courageous, loathed this system of terror, but he was compelled to yield to the will of these bloodthirsty monks. Prince Pignatelli Fuentes, who was related to Palafox, and also a friend to the French, had received just before the siege the perilous mission of going to persuade the Aragonese to accept Joseph Napoleon as their King. The people wanted to strangle the unwelcome messenger, and Palafox saved his life by feigning severity and detaining him a prisoner in his palace. He did much the same now with some French prisoners in his hands, on whom he lavished in secret as much kindness as he had himself received in France. This generous conduct was very much misunderstood in the town, and there was already a party of ferocious fellows who accused him of weakness, and even suggested treason. His health was beginning to give way under the physical and mental strain. For some time now he had rarely left the cellar in which he had taken refuge from the shells, and whenever he showed himself above ground he was greeted with passionate vociferations from the people, who swore that they would perish rather than submit to a foreign yoke, and the resolution he appears to have formed to put an end to the protracted sufferings of his fellow citizens was again shaken. Had he not already done more for the honour of the country than even the most rigorously interpreted laws of war demanded?

The enemy had tried in vain to retake the Trinitarian Convent. Their last sortie on the 31st, which, as we have seen, was the most vigorous of any, had been as unsuccessful as the rest, and from that date Palafox had given up the attempt. Rogniat was therefore free to call off the engineer officers posted at that point to go with us to the attack on the Convent of St. Francis, which would test our powers to the uttermost.

General Lacoste had intended the attacks on the northern suburb (on the left bank) and those on the town itself to coincide, so as to press the besieged on every side at once, and to intercept their communication by way of the bridge as soon as possible; above all, he was anxious to assault it by a reverse fire all along the edge of the river, hoping thus to harass the besieged so much that they would be compelled to surrender before long. With this end in view most extensive works had been completed under Dode, a colonel of engineers, including the digging of deep trenches with the establishment of many batteries round the Capuchin Convent, and the firing was just about to begin when an unexpected accident delayed the attack. The Gallego, swollen by the rain in a storm which had broken in the mountains, had so increased the volume of water with which we had covered part of the outskirts of the suburb, that the embankment broke, and some half of our works were inundated. We had to construct a batardeau, repair the damage done, and dig fresh trenches.

We had not fired a gun in that direction for some eight days, and the monks came to their windows to look down on us at our work without showing a sign of fear in expression or attitude. We saw them climbing to the top stories of their convent and following every action of ours with inquisitive gaze, chanting places and chatting together just as if we were at peace. They could look straight into our trenches, and to defilade ourselves from them we had to make our ditches deeper and more winding than we need otherwise have done. But for this precaution, good marksmen stationed on the roofs and belfries of the neighbouring buildings could have aimed their wall-pieces at us, and would seldom have missed their mark. The poor monks were, however, very soon to lose their sense of security, for their buildings were totally undefended; not a single earthwork protected this isolated fort, well provided though it was with artillery. The besieged, therefore, when they saw the gabions, fascines, sandbags, and ladders arrive all ready for an immediate attack, suddenly passed from confidence to terror, and hastened to make preparations for defence. They demolished the enclosure wall of the convent, which masked our movements, and began to dig a deep ditch behind where it had been all round the building.

At eight o'clock in the morning of the 8th, twenty-two pieces of cannon opened fire on the convent, bringing down several pieces of the walls in the course of a few hours. The Marshal, eager to learn the results of our cannonade, started with Rogniat and me about noon to the left bank of the river. When he saw how things were going, he ordered the convent to be carried by assault in his presence then and there. Two hundred grenadiers and three hundred light infantry at once flung themselves in several columns from the trenches and dashed into the convent before the monks had been able to get away. Four hundred Spaniards, unnerved by the vigorous cannonade, were unable to defend the building, and ran away at our approach. We took the convent, several guns, a flag, and a few prisoners. One battery, however, stationed by the besieged on the bank of the Ebro, took us in the rear and poured out grape shot upon us. Captain Tissot, of the French infantry, however, did not hesitate to lead his brave fellows up to the enemy's guns and take possession of the battery, but his generous effort had been made independently of his chiefs, and he found himself unsupported. Meanwhile the enemy's gunboats and five or six of their batteries on the right bank of the Ebro opened fire on the little group of Frenchmen, overwhelming them with grape shot. They were all killed or wounded, and Tissot himself was struck down dead just as he had got back to our trenches.

Immediately after the assault of the convent, Colonel Dode constructed communications and epaulments to right and left, to strengthen and cover our troops. He also had loopholes formed in all the walls facing Saragossa. The convent, which was some little distance from the town, had not been disturbed by the bombardment, and the besieged had used it as a hospital. We found all the cells and the church encumbered with the dying. More than 200 dead, still in their clothes, had been piled up in the centre of the convent court, and we thought that they had been brought thither to be burnt. We hastened to set fire to them. The number of the dead of both sexes and all ages, emaciated with fasting, confirmed what our prisoners had told us of the violence of the epidemic and the straits of the besieged.

Though this convent belonged to a Mendicant order, it was very rich in pictures, sculpture, and gilding, but everything had been broken or injured by the cannonade. Darkness soon overtook us, and our only light was the sinister and flickering glow from the fires slowly consuming the bodies of the victims of the epidemic. Groping along and stumbling about amongst the sick, the dead., and the piled-up debris, we made our way through the passages and rooms of the vast building, and presently came to a large library. Its contents were quickly turned to account, as those of others had already been, to dissipate the obscurity, and it was by the light of precious manuscripts that one of our sappers picked up a gold crucifix weighing more than a pound. We made torches of other manuscripts to light us in our exploration of the network of subterranean passages and rooms beneath the convent, and we penetrated into a very remarkable mortuary chamber at a considerable depth, with a roof consisting of one large vault, which appeared even more extensive than it was by the feeble light of our flambeaux. The four walls were pierced with a number of horizontal niches rather like long ovens, arranged in rows one above the other on the models of the catacombs in which the freed men of the Romans were buried near their former masters. The embalmed or otherwise prepared corpses of the monks were introduced feet foremost without coffins, but wrapped in the robes of their order and in winding sheets, after which the orifices were carefully closed and the name of each defunct engraved at the entrance to the cell occupied by him.

We gazed silently at the bodies of the monks who had died or been killed during the siege, when there was no time to bury them, and the sad sight made a deep and mournful impression upon us. No one spoke, and each seemed to be thinking, "Why do we thus trouble the peace of the tomb? Tomorrow, perhaps, we shall all be in like case. . . . Let us rather go and explore the ruins of the convent."

Immediately afterwards Colonel Dode proceeded to establish a third parallel, which had a strong battery planted upon the Ebro, in order to cannonade the town quay, and support our attack from the right bank.

Meanwhile Haxo, on that right bank, seeing himself supported by the works of Colonel Dode on the left, pushed on his attack towards the quay, taking with him his engineer officers and sappers, with a view to cutting off the enemy's communication with the bridge. He worked his way, according to circumstances, by means of sap, demolition, or mining, and had already blown up several blocks of houses in succession. The Spanish defended them with a tenacity which seemed greater every day, and before they deserted them never neglected to smear them over with tar, so as to make it more difficult for us to put out the conflagrations. One day a peasant actually had the temerity to run without cover right up to our outposts and fling some lighted grenades amongst us, a piece of bravado which cost him his life.

In the attack on the centre, the houses adjoining the general hospital had been the scene for several days of a savage conflict. Twice our miners had blown up, with fourneaux charged with some 800 pounds of powder, different portions of a big hotel or private house overlooking the Corso and opposite the Calle del Refugio, and twice our assaults had been repulsed. At last a third attack left the French masters of the burning ruins; but a perfect hail of grape shot, bursting bombs, grenades, and shells made it almost impossible for them to judge of their bearings or to take any measures to defend themselves from being killed, or having to draw back yet again. In all the ruined houses we dashed at once into every story, but our progress was contested step by step with equal fury from cellar to roof, and nothing but the death of the leader on the other side secured us the victory.

Whilst this awful conflict was raging above ground, Breuille had managed to pierce a subterranean gallery from the cellars of the general hospital to the base of the foundations of St. Francis. He was just going to penetrate beneath the belfry with his mines, so that that great building might crush the church and convent beneath it in its fall, when he heard sounds which betrayed to him that the enemy's sappers were close upon him with their countermines, which had indeed already extended several feet beyond his own. The danger was imminent, and there was not an instant to lose. He sent to warn Rogniat at once, and immediately charged his fourneau with 3,000 pounds of powder. The troops who hurried up were ordered to make an end of the struggle with the frantic defenders, and a vigorous simultaneous attack was immediately made upon the same point so as to draw as many of the enemy as possible into the sphere of activity of the volcano which was to bring about their destruction.

The brave Colonel Duperoux with his regiment, and Valezé, a lieutenant-colonel of engineers, with his sappers, placed themselves in ambush in the ruins of the hospital to await the signal. At three o'clock in the afternoon, the time agreed on, Breuille had the charge fired, and the terrible explosion flung to a great height in the air a huge portion of the convent and the cloister, but the belfry, which every one expected to see go over, remained erect. Hardly had the mass of falling debris reached the deep funnel or crater which the explosion had opened, before the Colonel and Valezé at the head of their men flung themselves into the convent and charged the retreating enemy with the bayonet, taking possession of the entire building. The attack was so vigorous that Palafox, imagining at first that we were about to penetrate yet farther into the town, called the whole garrison to arms, and placed the cavalry in order of battle on the Corso and the new market-place, where they waited ready to cut us down. We had hoped that the Spanish would have been intimidated by the magnitude of the disaster, for the explosion had shaken the whole quarter of the town for a considerable distance, but our sudden attack only increased their fury. They contested every inch of the ground, and there was not room to take aim in the desperate struggle. We had to pursue them to the very roofs, where the fighting went on, and those of us who were below saw many fling themselves from the top of walls some eighty feet from the ground rather than yield to their conquerors, who stretched out their hands to try and save them.

The Comte de Fleuri, a French *émigré*, who had led a little troop of peasants along the roofs, penetrated with them into the top of the belfry. In a very few minutes they pierced a number of holes in the roof of the church, through which they poured such a hot fire upon us and so many shells and grenades that on the evening of the 10th we were obliged to abandon the building, but we returned to it the next day, and Fleuri and his men were finally flung from the top of the belfry after selling their lives very dearly.

With a view to being in readiness to direct the arduous attack of February 10th, Prost and I stationed ourselves under cover, close to our troops, in a vaulted gateway in the wall of the hospital. We were, however, in great danger, in the restricted quarters we had chosen, of perishing beneath the falling walls, woodwork, and stones which were showered down upon us. We had not meant to do more than get near enough to watch the awful struggle which we knew to be about to take place, but our eagerness for the success of our enterprise, with our wish to see the effect which would be produced by our attack, was greater than our fear of being crushed to death. Before everything had fallen, therefore, we advanced far enough to be eyewitnesses of the extraordinary and awful catastrophe which occurred. Never, in any war, was there perhaps a more terrible scene than that presented by the ruins of the Convent of St. Francis during and after the assault. Not only did the violent explosion destroy half the building, including even the subterranean cellars in which many families had taken refuge and thought themselves safe, but in it perished more than 400 workmen who were aiding in the defence, with a whole corps of grenadiers belonging to the Valencia Regiment. The Fuentes gardens, the surrounding suburbs, even to the very roofs of the houses, were rendered horrible by the quantities of mutilated human remains with which they were strewn. Not a step could be taken without stumbling over torn limbs, often still palpitating, hands or fragments of arms torn from the bodies to which they had belonged, revealing to us how fearful and widespread had been the catastrophe.

One of the grenadiers who had pursued the Spaniards to the very roof of the church, the wide gutters of which we were searching for hidden or wounded enemies, whom we were now anxious to help, called our attention to two terrible things amongst the ruins, which at any other time would have made us draw back in horror. "Look," he said indignantly, at those hands torn from the arms of the fanatic Spaniards; they are quite black-ened with the powder they fired at us!" and as he pushed them aside with his foot to avoid treading on them, he bent down to raise a mass of remarkably thick and glossy hair. He was examin-ing it curiously, thinking it was a wig which had belonged to some woman, but as he took it up he suddenly dropped it again with an exclamation of horror, for the beautiful ebony masses were still attached to the remains of the head of a young girl with ghastly mutilated features. The grenadier was no less af-fected than we were by this melancholy sight, and presently ex-claimed in an excited voice, "Look at that stream of blood! Look at the lamentable results of obstinacy and rage!" We looked and saw the blood of a number of Aragonese flowing beneath our feet into the gutters of the roofs, whence it poured through the prominent Gothic gargoyles, representing dragons, vultures, and winged monsters. For some eight centuries nothing but rain water had flowed from these gutters and spouts; but now, by a horrible contrast, they vomited forth upon the assailants below torrents of human gore.

The explosion had made a wide opening in one wall near the chief entrance, and torn up all the pavement of the nave and cloisters. In this upheaval everything had been turned topsy-turvy. The cornice of the nave, the pulpit, the altars of the side chapels, had all been flung down and were partly buried, whilst the bodies of the dead, which had been shut up in the crypts for centuries, had been wrenched from their resting-places and flung upon the surface of the ground. Then we entered the breach the Spanish were already returning to the church through the sacristy. They barricaded themselves in the midst of the ruins, behind benches, chairs, and overturned confessionals. Even reliquaries and fragments of the exhumed coffins from the crypts were pressed into the service to make a cover from behind which to fire at us. A shower of balls fell on us from every side, the most murderous coming from the galleries above us, especially through some small openings in one of the big pillars beside the choir, in which were the steps leading up to the belfry. Fortunately the breach in the wall of the church was a very wide one, and our column entered easily through it, quickly invading the whole building. The defenders were driven from their entrenchments and from the lateral chapels by a tremendous bayonet charge, and pursued by our men up the narrow and dangerous spiral staircase in the big pillar even to the roof, great numbers of them falling beneath our blows.

The struggle in the beautiful but sombre Gothic building was a truly remarkable sight. Through the broken stained-glass windows, with their subdued colouring, a ray of light shot here and there, touching with a celestial glory some group of furious combatants, or the clouds of bluish smoke from the burning powder which was almost suffocating us. Rising up from amidst the gloom and clearly outlined against the east window, was the high altar of brown marble, approached by eight steps and surmounted by a splendid canopy, originally upheld by eight Corinthian columns, and adorned with numerous angels wearing crowns on their heads. Several of the columns had been broken in the explosion, and some were now standing, whilst others lay on the ground, producing an irregularity of effect which might have been taken for the result of a happy inspiration on the part of their artist. In the nave, which was some 150 or 160 yards long, all was wrapt in gloom from the choir to the breach near the great doorway, and it was here, amidst coffins, bones, and broken marbles, that the hottest struggle took place.

From one of the old broken coffins protruded the livid shrivelled features and part of the body of a bishop still wrapped in his sacerdotal robes. His dried and bony arms seemed to be pointing at us; his dark eyes set in their deep sockets, and his mouth with its terrible expression, combined to give him the appearance of some such phantom as that of Samuel called from the grave by Saul, and we seemed to hear him cry, "Saul! Saul! why hast thou disquieted me to bring me up?" The terrible confusion, the carnage going on amongst the bones of the long since dead, with the mitred spectre swaying to and fro beneath our feet, combined to make up a picture which to our astonished eyes appeared the very acme of desolation.

A little later, when I went down after the enemy had been driven from every part of the church, the effects of light were still admirable, but the scene had completely changed. Here the exhumed remains of monks and prelates, given up to the tender mercies of the soldiers, were being stripped of the rich vestments in which many of them were still wrapped; there a group of weary, saddened, and exhausted combatants, worn out with the perpetual fighting, were eagerly seeking consolation in long draughts of the choice wine left behind by the unlucky Recollet friars, and presently, when the goatskin bottles in which the precious liquid had been stored were empty, they blew them out, and fell to playing at ball with them like a parcel of children. There, too, were many of our brave army doctors caring with equal solicitude for Spanish and French, and it was impossible not to admire the calm courage with which they faced all manner of dangers to come to our help. Unfortunately, however, their efforts were unavailing to restore two engineer officers of great merit, Captains Vierveaux and Jencesse, whom we lost on that terrible day in the attacks of the centre and the right.

We took possession of the two chapels and of the houses adjoining the Convent of St. Francis which skirted the Corso, here some hundred feet wide; and to harass with our fire as much as possible every one who passed along that important thoroughfare, we placed good marksmen in the belfry, in the very positions where the Spanish had but recently met death rather than yield. From the top of the tower we looked down upon streets full of barricades and traverses prepared for the further struggle, and also of gibbets laden with victims. All these menacing preparations and ominous-looking objects showed us that the leaders of the people were in anything but a pacific mood. For all that, however, the melancholy way in which the inhabitants crept along in the streets and squares strewn with the dead, seemed to suggest that discouragement was at last setting in, and that it had been with the fury of despair that the Spanish had fought during the preceding day and night. The town was now but a hemmed-in cemetery. The dead everywhere encumbered the ground, and the besieged no longer had the strength to bury or even to remove them. There was really no longer any room left for interment, and the indifference of the passers-by had become such that they would push a body out of their way with the foot as coolly as they would a stone or any other obstacle. Judging from the brisk way in which they moved about amongst the crowds, the women and the monks were the only people who retained their original zeal.

One day we had just gone down into a cellar where some of our Poles were on watch, when they saw through the grating a Spaniard picking up the lead of some exploded balls in a little garden. They fired at and killed him. He had scarcely fallen when his wife, weeping and pouring forth imprecations upon his murderers in a despairing voice, flung herself upon the body. Our soldiers, whose feelings of humanity had kept them motionless in face of the broken-hearted widow, would have generously respected her grief had she not, muttering curses on us the while, torn off her husband's cloak, cartridge case and musket, to take them away with her. This was too much; a bullet at once stretched her lifeless across the dead she wished to avenge. A few minutes later a young girl of about fifteen or sixteen years old rushed into the garden, uttering heartrending cries of *"Mi padre! mi padre! Alma de mi madre!"* She seemed to be in the grasp of the most agonised grief, and tore her hair as she convulsively embraced the dead bodies, trying to recall them to life, and entreating us to kill her too and put an end to her sufferings. Not one of our men was cruel enough to shed the blood of the orphan on the bodies of her parents, but she in her turn had the temerity to provoke us. After several fruitless efforts to carry away her mother's body, she wrapped it in her father's cloak and tried to drag it along with the cartridge box and musket which had cost that mother so dear, urged to this action as much by the imperative necessity of vengeance as by her filial piety. We could not blame the poor child for her hatred of the murderers of her parents, and we heard our Poles call out to her, first in their own Sarmatian language and then in Spanish, "*Malenka nie cekay sien! Chiquita, no ten miedo!*" (Don't be afraid, little one.) Few days passed without something of this kind occurring.

In spite of the great fatigue of our troops, there was less suffering in our camp than in the town. The sky was clear and the sun bright and warm in Spain that year, and though it was as yet only February we enjoyed the mild temperature and all the other delights of an early spring. Strawberries were already red and ripe, laurels, rose and fruit trees were in flower, the air was full of the scent of lavender, rosemary, violets, and narcissi, invigorating our men and saving them from epidemics.

To shield themselves from the freshness of the temperature at night, the soldiers had carried off to the camp all the pictures they could from the churches and convents, and the painted varnished canvases proved a first-rate protection alike from the sun, the rain, the cold, and the damp. In default of straw they used the parchments of old manuscripts to make their beds, which, if not less hard, were much drier than the bare ground. Under any other circumstances one would have said, "Better suffer than destroy;" but now it was a case of life or death, and the largest books were used to sleep on, the decorations of altars, the statues of saints, and the gilded carvings in wood to make camp fires, whilst pictures from the church served to cover in huts.

A visit to the camp was quite a treat to us, and the exhibition there was really not unlike that once held in the Place Dauphine, opposite the Palais de Justice, in Paris, in 1792, when young artists had not yet been admitted to the honour of showing their pictures in the Louvre. The Poles, who are

Catholics and generally very pious, were particularly pleased with the sacred pictures. Little accustomed in their own land to find anything equal in merit to the canvases from the sacred buildings of Spain, they were found eagerly gazing at the subjects taken from the Bible or the lives of the martyrs. Generally quiet and self-possessed enough, their imagination was kindled by the sight of these sublime conceptions, and they were inspired by the contemplation of the generous devotion of the martyrs and the palms of victory bestowed on them by Heaven. The desire to imitate their noble example gave them strength to persevere in their arduous tasks, and the hope of an eternal recompense sustained them as nothing else could have done in all they had to go through. Their bearing, full as it was of resignation, showed us that their powers of endurance were very far from being exhausted as yet. The French, on the other hand, who were by nature more high-spirited and volatile, stood privations and fatigue with far less patience.

One day the Marshal was passing near a group of soldiers looking at a picture, and to his surprise overheard these words: "The draught of water the good Lord is going to let the old fellow drink is rather like the booty our Marshal has promised us!" The Marshal went up to the men, and saw that they were admiring a picture by Murillo representing Jesus bidding Peter come to Him on the water. "Well, my friends," said the Marshal, "God is speaking to St. Peter here very much as I do to you. God says to Peter, 'O thou of little faith, wherefore didst thou doubt?' That is to say, 'If thou hadst had faith in my words, thou wouldst not have sunk'; which means for you, if you have confidence in me, hope will sustain your courage, and perseverance will overcome all obstacles. Yes, my friends, in a few days, you to whom I speak will take Saragossa!" The soldiers all listened quietly, and their faces, on which no smile had been seen for days, brightened up with one accord, whilst the cheers with which they escorted the Marshal when he ceased speaking showed what faith they placed in his promises.

The Marshal was not wrong in his prophecies. The besieged were reduced to a state of the greatest misery, and the cruel measures of repression of the *junta* could do no more. For a time they had been able to rule by terror, but now every one with any sense, such as merchants, shopkeepers, and rich men with anything left to lose, seeing that it was no good to hope for the long-expected succour, were anxious to capitulate. Others, weakened by famine, fatigue, and anxiety, had had nothing to save them from starvation but a few ears of corn, which they could not even grind, whilst some were so maddened and brutalised by their fury that they were no longer capable of reasonable action. They blindly followed the orders of the monk-ridden *junta*, whose greatest fear was that the French, so soon as they were masters of Saragossa, would suppress the convents of Spain, as they had already done those of France.

Some hundred wretched peasants, men, women, and children, deserted one morning *en masse* in the direction of the Castillo del Algaferia, and entreated our outposts, who tried to drive them back, to kill them rather than compel them to return to the town. The captain of the guard, too generous to do anything so cruel, took them to the Marshal, who received them with an air of severity, reproaching them in a stern voice for having shed so much French blood by their determined obstinacy. "You ask to be allowed to return to your homes," he said; "you deserve nothing of the sort." He then ordered guards to surround the poor wretches, who thought they were to be led to execution, and added, "Here, take them away, give them something to eat and drink, and when they have recovered a little give each of them two francs and a couple of loaves and take them back to Saragossa. I wish the people in the town to know that we have plenty of provisions, and what they may expect from my generosity." Henri IV., whose position and noble nature alike compelled him to try and win the hearts of his people, treated them with no greater magnanimity at the gates of Paris than did the Duke of Montebello these strangers of an alien race outside Saragossa.

The Swiss troops in the town, who had hitherto fought with unabated courage, were now no longer proof against the terrible tests to which their fidelity was subjected; they began to desert at intervals, and on February 14th a complete company of some fifty Swiss guards, headed by their officers and bringing their arms and baggage, joined our ranks on the rampart near the Capuchin Convent of Jesus.

On the way from the portion of the town occupied by us to the camp, we had to pass a great many sentinels and vedettes stationed amongst the masses of melancholy-looking ruins, encumbered with the dead bodies of the Spanish and all manner of rubbish. These sentinels kept careful watch on the inhabitants of the still unconquered districts, and reported at once everything that occurred amongst the besieged. The Poles of the three regiments from the Vistula acquired incredible skill in this service. They would at once notice every little opening made by the enemy in the walls, even if it were no bigger than a penny piece, and would point it out to any of us who happened to approach it, warning us to be on our guard. These warnings were generally given by signs, as very few of us understood Polish, and they were not only very valuable but also often quite comic on account of the quaint pantomime with which our eagerly benevolent friends enforced them. Looking at us with eyes full of meaning, they would point to the dangerous little hole or hidden loop-hole with one hand, whilst they placed a finger of the other on their lips to enjoin silence; any one who neglected to obey these expressive signals was sure to be immediately shot down, for the apparently insignificant little holes were so close to us that every bullet from them found its billet. Equally well guarded against surprise were the many galleries we had had to pierce in all the different houses belonging to the block. We often had to pass from one block to another by way of narrow streets, where we had not thought it necessary to make traverses. In such cases we made breaches or openings opposite to each other, and the officer when he went on his rounds had to jump from one side to the other of the street; and if he was not quite agile enough to achieve the crossing in a single bound, well-aimed shots would be sure to bring him down dead midway. We lost many officers in this way, but the skill and unwearied watchfulness of our Poles saved the lives of a good many Frenchmen, who were too much disposed to despise the caution which they thought detracted from their courage. I myself twice owed my life to our Poles, and I am very certain that but for them our loss would have been very much greater.

The victims of the epidemic were now so numerous that we found their bodies abandoned, in the clothes they had worn when alive, in every street and house of which we took possession. Happily for us the air was still so sharp and cold that the corpses dried quickly, and there was nothing repulsive in their appearance, nor was there any bad smell from them. They were very light and easy to lift too, and looked like pasteboard figures covered with dust. I can still see one room in the second story of a house which had been broken into and partially destroyed from the bottom to the top. An explosion had surprised a father and daughter just as they were taking their siesta after their meal by a little round table, on which a few drinking vessels still remained. The old man, who was pretty well dressed and partly wrapped in his cloak, was seated in a big black wooden armchair, and his daughter, also completely dressed, was stretched on a rush mat at his feet. There was nothing in their features to betray what they had suffered, and during the few minutes I spent near the motionless group I really wondered whether the bodies were real or made of wax.

So far the hopes Palafox had founded on the rainy season which was to inundate us, and compel us to abandon our trenches, had not been realised, but our army was dwindling day by day through the continual fighting and from illness. We no longer had troops enough to make our attacks at the most favourable moment, and Roginat was obliged to abandon all idea of gaining more ground towards the left of St. Francis. If Palafox had now been able to realise all the advantages he might have gained by flinging himself with a strong force of his men, say a column of 20,000 determined troops, on to one or the other bank of the river, our position would soon have become very critical, but that General was ill and in his turn suffering from the epidemic. His energy seemed to be declining with his health, and he may perhaps also have been rather afraid to risk leading men out to fight, who, though they were brave enough within walls, had failed in courage before our forces in the plains of Tudela.

Rogniat, compelled to concentrate his forces, now had all the houses near St. Francis blown up by mines, so as to prevent the enemy from approaching except by the open. He next gained a little ground on the right, and there established a blinded battery, in which was placed a howitzer, with which the Corso could be raked; a little farther still on the right a twelve-pounder was placed in another blinded battery, and this greatly harassed the besieged, enfilading as it did the whole of the Calle of San Giles, which led to the bridge in the centre of the town.

Whilst these works were being constructed, our sappers were undermining the Corso in several parts; under Prost they were advancing by six galleries, the first two of which had already reached the other side beneath the theatre and the adjoining house, whilst under Haxo two galleries were being pushed on in the direction of the University.

One day, as Marshal Lannes was going round the lines of the suburb, a Spaniard, hidden amongst the ruins, fired at him at such close quarters that the inside of his cloak was singed. Irritated at this audacity, Lannes climbed on to the ruins of the Convent of Jesus, and himself fired a dozen shots. The enemy then directed a howitzer on the gap from which the shots proceeded, and one of the shells cut in two Captain Lepot, of the engineers, who was looking over the Marshal's shoulder.

In the town operations were rapidly proceeding; but Haxo, who had nearly reached the Puerta del Sol, found that his position was too much exposed. He could not advance farther without running the danger of having the enemy behind him in the entrenchments he was occupying, besides which our troops were now too few for extended or repeated attacks, so that there was nothing for it but to try surprises. It was of the utmost importance that the suburb on the left bank of the Ebro should be taken at once, so as to place what was called the Tanners' Quarter between two fires.

The Marshal therefore ordered a simultaneous and general attack upon the town and suburb for the morrow, and at the same time gave instructions that epaulments should be erected during the night on the roads by which he feared the enemy might escape us.

In the attack on the town we availed ourselves of the position we already occupied, blew up a house, and opened a breach with a petard. The Poles at once flung themselves into the gap and dashed across the fire, pursuing the enemy by way of their own communications. The Spanish were compelled to abandon their circular battery and covered way on the quay, which were taken in reverse.

The next day our miners set fire to the two chambers, charged with 1,500 lbs. of powder, beneath the University, and the explosion tore open two great breaches, through which we flung two columns of troops, who took possession of the great building. The enemy were now driven to abandon the Corso.

At the same time the Marshal ordered the Gazan division to attack the suburb opposite to him. Ever since daybreak all the siege artillery had been playing upon the approaches to the bridge, with a view to intercepting communications, and all the parapets were already thrown down. The aim of our principal attack was to get possession of the convent near the San Lazaro bridge, which commanded that one connecting link between the town and its suburb.

About noon a practicable breach had been made at San Lazaro, and our fire with that of the enemy redoubled at every point. In the plains the noise of the detonations of artillery died away in the distance, but in the streets of the town the roar resounded from every wall, and the crashing of the roofs beneath the bursting bombs, the crackling of numerous fires all blazing away at once, the ringing of the tocsin from every belfry, the hissing and whistling of bullets, bombs, and grape shot, the shrill rattle of the mortars, all jumbled together in one, and supplemented by the echoes flung back from the roofs of the churches, which shook so much that the pictures on the walls were flung upon the heads of the combatants, combined to make up a military music which must have struck terror into the hearts of the besieged, though it filled our troops with delirious joy.

The enemy had nearly 7,000 defenders in the suburb, when this terrible hail of projectiles cut off their communication with the town. The discharge from our guns made openings here and there in the enclosures of the gardens, and each bullet hole was at once turned to account by the Spanish as a loophole from which to fire at us.

The walls were, however, everywhere falling before us, and the defenders presently withdrew into the Convents of San Lazaro and Santa Isabel, which we were breaching. Our cannonade had overthrown the big gate of a stable yard in the latter building, and we were just going to dash in, when some peasants on the other side lifted up the gate and held it in position by main force. Twice it was flung down, and twice replaced in the same manner, and we were obliged to knock over the pillars that supported it with our artillery, so as to destroy there with the door, before we could avail ourselves of the breach. A little later, when we did enter, we found a number of Spaniards lying crushed beneath the door, having bravely sacrificed their lives in the struggle to keep it closed.

On the first rumour of the general attack to be made, the commandant of the suburb had rushed to his post to defend his position, but he was killed in crossing the bridge. The news of his death quickly spread amongst the defenders, and threw them into some confusion, of which the Marshal, who noticed it directly, was not slow to avail himself, for he immediately ordered the attack to begin.

The sharpshooters at once debouched from the trenches and advanced in skirmishing order, so as to suffer less from the grape shot poured on them from the Spanish batteries on the right bank and the gunboats on the river. Three columns supported this movement, and an oil store was soon broken into and at once became strewn with the dead. We then pushed on through narrow passages into several houses, which were vigorously defended, and where every one was put to the sword. Into one of these houses, where our advance had been checked for an hour by the courageous resistance of the Spaniards, Captain Gallard managed to penetrate with his company by way of the roof, and climbed down through the granary, taking the defenders in the rear and putting them to flight. Every one who dared to resist was struck down. Presently, in the midst of the cries of distress of those he had overwhelmed, and surrounded by a smoke so dense that he could see nothing before him, the French captain, who imagined he was finishing off the last of his enemies, was in his turn taken by surprise. He redoubled his efforts, flung himself upon those who were entering the house from below, and fell gloriously, covered with wounds; but, alas! it was by the bayonets of Frenchmen that he was struck down, for Captain Clerget, another officer of the same regiment, had broken in the door of the house just at the same time as Captain Gallard got in at the roof, and it was not until too late that the former discovered his fatal mistake, realising that he had had the misfortune to slay a brave brother officer and many of his men.

As soon as they got a footing in the houses adjoining San Lazaro, our troops were able to penetrate into the court of that convent. They then broke into the wall of the church with the aid of a charge, the monks making a desperate defence. Behind them was a mass of men, women, and children, who, not having dared to cross the bridge, had taken refuge at the foot of the altar, and now pleaded piteously for mercy. The smoke was, however, too dense for our troops to see the victims whom they would willingly have spared, everything was sacked, and not until all were dead did the cries cease and silence once more reign in the sanctuary. Meanwhile the wide staircase, the cells, and the passages of the convent were the scene of an equally bloody and obstinate struggle. The convent was completely taken, and from every window monks and soldiers, who had aided in its defence, flung themselves into the Ebro beneath. Our fire was now immediately turned upon the entrance to the bridge, to prevent those still in the suburb from getting back to the town.

The inhabitants of the suburb were overwhelmed with consternation when they lost their chief at the very moment of the discovery that their retreat was cut off. They gave up any attempt to defend the bridge head or the houses, and wandered aimlessly about in scattered parties, trying to escape, but not knowing which way to turn, when they found every way out closed by our troops. Three hundred of them, more courageous than the rest, led by one Fernando Gonzales, dauntlessly braved our fusillade and managed to make their way back into the town by forcing a passage across the bridge in the midst of a hail of bullets from the Convent of San Lazaro. The smoke from this fusillade soon wrapped them in so dense a cloud that they were hidden from our view. Very few were wounded in the brief transit, and their chief was fortunate enough to take with him into Saragossa nearly all who had had the pluck to follow him. Some also escaped with the aid of boats, yet others swam across the river, but very many were drowned. Another party, numbering about 3,000, tried to flee up country by way of the banks of the Ebro, but General Gazan promptly sent a regiment of cavalry to bar their passage. Their position was desperate, and their strength exhausted from the privations and fatigues of the protracted siege, so they laid down their arms and were taken prisoners.

The commandant of the suburb, whose death had so discouraged the defenders as to lead to their defeat, had been the French *émigré* Baron de Versage, who had thus died fighting against his fellow countrymen.

Although Palafox was so ill that he was scarcely able to stand, he undertook to go to the succour of the suburb with General Philippe de Saint-Mart. Three times that general tried in vain to debouch from the bridge at the head of his troops. A few hundred men did succeed in getting over, but our batteries on the left bank swept so many on the approaches to the quay, that the main body decided that it would be impossible to cross the whole length of the bridge without cover, although the broken-down parapets had been replaced by epaulments of sand-bags and bales of wool. The rest of the Spanish troops therefore remained in the town, and were unable even to prevent us from taking the University buildings on that side.

We remained masters of the position, and were now able to bombard that part of the town which had hitherto suffered least. We had taken seventeen pieces of cannon and 3,000 prisoners, whilst nearly as many more of the defenders had fallen beneath our fire. This brilliant victory, won in the open by a small division, of which only 600 men took part in the actual conflict against determined and well-entrenched troops, did wonders to raise the spirits of the besiegers, and cost Gazan not more than fifty of his men.

During the confusion of the attack on the suburb, in the midst of a cross fusillade from every side, a nun of the Convent of Saint Elizabeth, whose great age prevented her from running away as quickly as her companions, drew all eyes upon her, as with tottering yet dignified steps she made her way across a square strewn with the dead and wounded. Her disordered robes, and her uncovered head with its thin hair, showed that she had been called to escape from danger in a time of trouble. But the noble expression of her features bore witness to the calmness of her spirit, and she passed through the clouds of white smoke and amidst the clash of arms without showing a sign of fear. She looked like some such ministering angel as appears in dreams, slowly descending from above in a celestial glory, upheld on the wings of hope, and sent from heaven to bring peace to afflicted mortals when their souls are torn by their violent emotions. In the midst of the awful struggle she seemed to be saying, "Almighty God, I have done no wrong; I am beneath Thy shield, and will fear no evil." Her sweet, benevolent old face, and the unruffled calm which radiated from her whole person in the horrible uproar going on about her, aroused the astonishment and interest of every one who saw her pass by; all dreaded every moment to see her fall, and would have liked to save her, but it could only be done at the risk of life, for to reach her it would be necessary to cross the open square exposed to the fusillade of the Aragonese. But such a grand chance of protecting the weak could not long appeal in vain to Frenchmen. An officer and several men dashed forwards without orders, seized the old woman by the hands, and, supporting her with their arms, quickly dragged her out of danger. They were trying in broken Spanish to set her mind at rest by explaining why they had treated her with such scant ceremony, when, to their great surprise, she replied with a sweet smile and in a feeble voice in excellent French, "Generous soldiers, I too am French, and your weapons have no terrors for me. It is fifty years since I entered this convent, and I entreat you to let me join my old companions, that I may pray and die with them." Touched by her noble confidence in him, the young officer overwhelmed her with attentions and had her taken to General Gazan. He too took the greatest interest in the sainted woman; she was treated with every care and respect, and a few days later she was able to resume her pious occupations. She turned out to be the sister of the celebrated actor Grandménil and to have been born at Bordeaux.

As soon as I got back to the town after the expedition to the suburb, I went to have a look at the University buildings, of which we had just taken possession. At three o'clock, when the struggle in the suburb was at its hottest, the three great mines under the University, each charged with 1,500 pounds of powder, were fired at once. Five hundred picked men, some French, others Poles, divided into two columns, flung themselves into the buildings in spite of the fire from the Puerta del Sol and the neighbouring houses. The Spanish, who were beginning to be discouraged by all their misfortunes, offered, however, but a feeble resistance. We took the University, and in our pursuit of the defenders we dashed pell-mell with them, by way of the Calle del Sepulcro, right up to the Church of the Trinity, which still remained in the hands of the besieged. Another column penetrated at nightfall, without striking a blow, into a house at a corner of the Corso, at which no less than ten previous assaults had been repulsed. At the same time Prost took possession of part of the Palacio Fuentes, which he set on fire with a view to isolating his left flank and guarding against surprise.

Officers and men were now alike excessively fatigued. The epidemic was beginning to affect us, and the hospital at Alagon was crowded with the sick and wounded. We were short of doctors, of nurses, of beds, of food, of linen, in fact, of everything, and the victory of the 18th came in the nick of time to raise the spirits of the troops, and restore all their original energy, whilst it at the same time greatly discouraged the besieged. Harassed and exhausted, shut up within their walls, and no longer able even to walk on the quay, the luckless defenders were actually within sight and earshot of the surrender of the 3,000 men who laid down their arms on the other side of the river. The news quickly spread through the town, and neither Palafox nor the *junta* tried to deny it.

The struggle became more bloody as the defence grew more concentrated. The population decreased in a most alarming manner, and every day ten times as many perished from typhus as the day before. This terrible scourge especially attacked the peasants, refugees from the country, and wounded soldiers without fixed homes or relations to help them. There were no longer any regular hospital attendants; the medicines for the sick were exhausted, and rice water was all that was left to assuage their sufferings. The unfortunate invalids had nothing but a little straw on which to rest on the pavements of the long, cold, vaulted passages which form the entrances to all the houses of Saragossa. There they died of hunger or were consumed by the fever, without a hand to give them a cooling draught. The Countess Burida and the women who had devoted themselves to succouring the wounded were now either dead themselves or scarcely able to drag themselves to the side of their nearest relations. Gangrene set in rapidly on the slightest wound; the few sentinels whom the fear of being murdered, or some little remnant of courage, still kept at their posts, were struck suddenly down by fever. They were to be seen sitting shivering on the stone benches wrapped in their cloaks, their weapons dropping from hands no longer strong enough to hold them, and many actually died before they could be relieved.

Palafox himself, attacked by the epidemic, but harassed still more by the cruel demands of the monks and the harsh measures of the intriguing *junta*, to which he was compelled to lend his name, found himself no longer able to bear the burdens of government, and his orders with those of the other military chiefs were already set at defiance. It was feared that Palafox and his colleagues would leave, as they had done in the previous siege, under the pretext of hastening the arrival of succour; and, to guard against this, those of the inhabitants who still rejected all idea of capitulation kept a very careful watch on the gunboats, which might facilitate an escape. Of the leading fanatics of the town, many had, however, now succumbed, and in losing their support, Bazile, chief of the *junta*, also lost his own power and credit. The clergy and the populace were at last beginning to give up counting on the miraculous protection of Nuestra Señora del Pilar, when they found that she disdained to preserve her own church from destruction. The garrison thought that they had now done enough for the glory of the Spanish name, and many influential men amongst the inhabitants, finding themselves compelled to yield to necessity, now at last dared to say that the hour had come to leave off fighting. They went to Palafox, whom they found still full of energy, but too ill to retain any more hope of winning the obsidional crown. He had heard, too, of our successes all over the Peninsula, but he meant to risk one more attempt, which might perhaps enable him to gain time, and to carry out certain generous intentions. He was exceedingly anxious to do something to ameliorate the terrible condition of those of the Aragonese who had survived all their awful sufferings. Too proud, however, to take a step in open daylight which would be sure not to be approved of by the general public, he waited till night to send an envoy to the French Marshal.

Hoping to get the best possible terms in the deplorable and humiliating position in which he found himself, Palafox instructed his aide-de-camp, Gassellas, to seek the Marshal and ask for a truce of three days, during which he wished his messenger to be allowed to go and verify the state of affairs in the Peninsula, adding that if the moment for capitulation had indeed arrived, he demanded the same advantages that the Marshal had offered on January 24th; moreover he asked that the garrison should be allowed to join the Spanish army, taking with them their covered wagons.

The state of things was, however, very different now from what it had been a month before, and the Marshal's reply contained the following words:

General, I have had you informed of what is passing in Spain. When a man of honour gives his word, it should be looked upon as sacred. With this letter I send you the capitulation of Ferrol and of Coruña. I swear to you upon my honour that you have no succour to hope for. There are no longer any Spanish armies: all are destroyed. King Joseph has entered Madrid. All the towns have sent deputations to him, and many Spanish regiments have entered his service. Such, General, is the unvarnished truth. It is permitted to no one in this world to doubt the loyalty and generosity of the French nation. I am ready to grant a general pardon to all the inhabitants of Saragossa, and I promise to respect their lives and property.

Dictated by the Duke of Montebello, in the trenches before Saragossa, February 19, 1809, and signed "Lannes," Marshal.

As soon as the envoy had started with this communication, the firing recommenced.

Much hurt at this refusal and worn out by a consuming fever, the noble and chivalrous Castilian, General Palafox, wishing to evade the shame of signing a capitulation, resigned the command to Count Philippe de Saint-Marc; but as a foreigner that general could not hope to win the confidence of the people who had wanted to hang him six weeks before, and he hastened to transfer his temporary authority to the hands of a new *junta*, consisting of thirty men chosen from amongst the notables of the town, including several ecclesiastics of high rank, magistrates, and officers of the army, under the presidency of Don Pedro Maria Rio, who was named regent. The *junta* passed the night in deliberating on the measures to be taken.

In the morning, from a kind of observatory in which I was stationed with some other engineer officers, we saw a great crowd of people assembling in the cathedral square. They all seemed so animated that we thought at first they were consulting as to how best to prevent the walls of that quarter from coming down. Anyhow, they were gathering together because something of the gravest importance was about to occur, and were all very much agitated. There were no women or monks amongst them this time, and the men, who seemed to differ greatly in opinion, were disputing hotly. It was now easy to see from their behaviour that the question of the capitulation was being discussed, and that the siege was drawing to a close. Whilst the eager discussion was going on, a sharp fire from the fifty pieces of cannon in the batteries was making a most horrible din, and several mines near by exploded. Six new galleries had now reached the other side of the Corso, one under the Law Courts known as La Audiencia, another beneath the theatre, and the other four beneath the biggest hotels. Each chamber had been charged by Breuilie's orders with 3,000 pounds of powder. Everything was prepared for the various explosions to take place simultaneously the following morning, and we were stationed so as to be able to cross the Corso as soon as the most beautiful quarter of Saragossa had been thrown down.

Our great desire to have done with it all produced in us a kind of feverish agitation, and the moment fixed seemed still very far off, when at about three o'clock in the morning we saw rise up from the midst of the crowd of irritated men several swords, from which floated white handkerchiefs, as a sign of a desire for peace and a request for a parley. Nothing could possibly have been more interesting to us than these demonstrations, and we hastened in our turn to hold up our handkerchiefs to show that we were favourably disposed to listen. A messenger was at once sent to the Marshal to inform him of what was going on, and we stopped the firing near us for a moment. The Spaniards then advanced into the open, and we called out to them to have confidence in us, and to surrender. At the word 'surrender!', the anger of some of them once more got the better of them, and they began to fight amongst themselves with renewed rage. To bring them to reason we had to resort to the brutal argument of the cannon, that *ultima ratio regum*, and the whiz of two balls fired over their heads at last decided them to treat definitely with us. One of their officers climbed over a wall with the aid of a ladder, and presenting himself before us asked that the Marshal should send the same envoy to them as he had done a month previously.

At four o'clock the order to cease firing all along the line was given, and Saint-Marc, aide-de-camp to the Marshal (who had acted as envoy in the earlier portion of the siege), presented himself at the outposts near the Puerta del Carmen. His eyes were bandaged, and he was taken to the *junta*, then in session at the palace occupied by General Palafox near the Portillo, in the least injured quarter of the town.

Saint-Marc was compelled to cross the whole of the town, and everywhere insulting remarks about the French were shouted in his ears, till he felt that his life was in the greatest danger amongst the furious fanatics. Arrived at the palace of the *junta*, the bandage was removed from his eyes, and he found himself in the presence of forty men whose worn and livid features and angry eyes expressed alike suffering and rage. The new *junta* consisted of Palafox, visibly weakened by illness, the *émigré* Philippe de Saint-Marc, and several officers, citizens, and ecclesiastics, including Bazile of the old *junta*. The new members were self-controlled and moderate compared with those of the former *junta*, in which had figured the redoubtable *curé* of the Church of San Gil, the intrepid Sorgo, Marino, Lios, and Benito; the ferocious George Arcos, keeper of the big café on the Corso, with several others who had now been carried off by typhus, killed in the struggle, or blown up in the explosions.

In a very short speech Saint-Marc congratulated the assembled members on the admirable courage and devotion which would make the people and garrison of Saragossa forever famous, and on the fact that they had at last brought themselves to listen to the pleadings of humanity and were about to stop the streams of blood which had been ceaselessly flowing for the last two months. Don Pedro Maria Rio then took up the word, and, speaking in the name of Palafox, he pronounced a pompous eulogy on the heroic conduct of the troops and the inhabitants, and demanded for them honourable terms of capitulation. Saint-Marc answered that every confidence might be placed in the generosity of the Marshal, but that he had orders to demand the surrender of the town at discretion. A cry of indignation burst from the assembly, and it seemed as if there was little hope of a pacific arrangement. The envoy had the greatest trouble to calm the storm and make his voice heard again, but at last his sang-froid and courteous language succeeded in appeasing a few members of the *junta*, who tried to calm the others; and the discussion was again taking a favourable turn, Palafox was even saying that he only wished to treat for the garrison, and that he and the *junta* would do all in their power to get the inhabitants to send deputies on their own account to the Marshal, when an unforeseen incident placed the life of Saint-Marc in the very greatest danger.

The news of the armistice had rapidly spread amongst the people, and they had all hastened to avail themselves of it to issue from their cellars and from behind their defences to breathe in the open air without fear of being shot down. Unfortunately, however, Breuille and Prost, occupied in subterranean passages a good distance off, did not hear of the cessation of hostilities in time, and they fired a mine at a most inopportune moment. The explosion produced a lofty jet of stones, forming a regular pyramid or obelisk in the air, extending to a great height, and visible to the whole population of the town, who, already full of distrust, at once suspected treason. Crowds rushed to the *junta*, joining those already round the palace. Shouts for vengeance and death resounded on every side, and all were eager to tear the treacherous envoy to pieces. Palafox, ill as he was, was scarcely able to protect Saint-Marc, whose good faith he never suspected for a moment; whilst General Philippe de Saint-Marc, who but a little time ago had himself been saved by Palafox from the same furious multitude, was powerless to interfere on his fellow-countryman's behalf. The tumult increased, and the cries of "Death to the traitor!" drowned everything else. The issue of the crisis appeared extremely doubtful, and the envoy could not help feeling great anxiety, when the door of the council chamber was flung violently open, and a number of Spanish officers with eager faces and holding their drawn swords in their hands rushed towards Saint-Marc, exclaiming that they would not suffer the rights of envoys to be violated in his person. They then closed round him, and with generous devotion swore that they would protect him with their own bodies till the incident which had so roused the fury of the populace could be explained.

The Marshal had seen the explosion, and, guessing at once the critical position in which it would place Saint-Marc, he immediately sent an officer to explain how it had come about, and to express his regret. It had been extremely difficult to send the order to cease firing to all the French leaders at once, on account of the great extent and the winding of our trenches. The officer's explanations were favourably received by the people, who soon calmed down; and the deputies chosen by the *junta* prepared to accompany Saint-Marc to the Marshal, who, with the other chiefs of the army, was awaiting them at the lock.

The deputies dared not openly cross the town in full view of those few obstinate men who, still full of energy, wished to prolong the defence, and held in awe those whose strength and courage were alike exhausted by the protracted struggle. Fearing lest these fanatics should be guilty of some fresh excess which would yet further aggravate the sad position of the town, the deputies waited for the night and arrived at the lock with the envoy about seven o'clock the next morning. Saint-Marc, hoping to reach safety more quickly, directed his escort to go to the gate of the town by which he had entered it, where his friend Captain Labédoyère awaited him with a squadron of lancers, all no less impatient than their chief to fly to the succour of the envoy.

The Marshal, surrounded by his staff, received the deputies with great respect, but with assumed severity, demanding at first that the town should surrender at discretion. In his own heart he really wished to grant honourable terms of capitulation to troops whose courage he admired, and he was also most anxious for every reason to complete his enterprise, as his army was weakened by sickness and fatigue, and the ammunition, indispensable for the successful prosecution of the siege, was beginning to run short. It must be remembered that all the powder, projectiles, and other war material was brought to Saragossa by way of Pampeluna and Bayonne under the greatest difficulties. The Marshal, therefore, feigning to yield to the urgent entreaties addressed to him not to reduce to the last extremities the unhappy people who would rather die than submit to the shameful yoke to which their representatives would have been forced to submit, consented to grant a capitulation.

The deputies then made an attempt to exact certain conditions. Amongst the requests they made were these: the clergy were to retain their offices, and their ecclesiastical revenues were to be guaranteed; Ferdinand VII. was to be recognised; and other equally inadmissible claims were put forward. The Marshal's reply was to have the plan of the siege unrolled before them, that they might realise how little hope there was left; he pointed out the position of six huge mine chambers under the town, adding that they were quite ready for firing, and that each one contained a charge of 3,000 pounds of powder. At these words, which appeared to make on them a profound impression of terror, all the deputies crossed themselves, and one of them, who, like the rest, had followed with the greatest attention all that the Marshal had said whilst pointing to the plan, cried in accents of the greatest grief, as he crossed himself with his thumb on his forehead and mouth five or six times: "*Ah la casa Ciscala!*" It was his own home. From the exclamations of the deputies we learnt the names of the different buildings threatened, including the Ducal Palace of Villa Vermosa, the Olivar and Cerezo hotels, the theatre, &c.

The deputies, trembling with anxiety, now hastened to submit, to prevent all these fresh disasters, and signed the following articles:

"A general pardon is granted to the town of Saragossa; the garrison is to go out with the honours of war; they will pile their arms 200 paces from the Puerta del Portillo; the officers will retain their swords, the soldiers their knapsacks; they will be taken to France, where they will remain as prisoners of war; private property will be guaranteed; religion will be maintained and respected; the peasants will return home without molestation; the officials will take the oath of allegiance to King Joseph."

The terms being thus settled, the deputies, accompanied by two of the Marshal's officers, left the head quarters at ten o'clock at night, and not daring to face the furious and anxious populace waiting en masse in the streets of Saragossa, they went to the Palace of the Inquisition, outside the town, where they made known to Palafox and the *junta* the result of their mission. Bazile and a few other members of the *junta* were very much grieved at the capitulation, but the whole assembly submitted in silence to conditions better than they had dared to hope for; and to insure the prompt execution of the terms agreed on, they at once ordered the commandant of the guards surrounding the Castillo d'Aljaferia to give up the posts under him to the French troops, who occupied them at once.

The news, which we had wished to keep secret till the morning, was quickly known all over the town. Many infuriated fellows had not even waited for the return of the deputies to resort to violent excesses. They had seized some of the artillery with a view to prolonging the defence, and doubled the guards near the boats to prevent the escape of the members of the *junta* who had excited their suspicions. There were but very few of these unreasonable agitators, still they were so excited and menacing that it was likely to be very difficult to make them submit to the terms of the capitulation. They shouted "Treason!" and ran about the streets calling for death to the deputies, and even wanted to murder those who were less fanatic than themselves. Colonel Marco del Pon, commander of a corps of Aragonese grenadiers, who had not only to watch the movements of the enemy outside, but also to put down the rising of the people within the walls, passed a night of the greatest anxiety amongst the mutineers. But the mass of the people, too exhausted and suffering to keep up their violent opposition long, soon separated themselves from the agitators, and applauded the decision arrived at by the *junta*. The fierce minority, finding themselves unsupported, gave up their resistance, and this long night, full of tumults, of hopes and fears, was by no means one of the least painful passed through by the unfortunate besieged.

As soon as ever our guards were posted round and within the Palace of the Inquisition, we lit torches and set off to the rescue of the luckless Prince Pignatelli, Marquis de Fuentes, a grandee of Spain, with whom we had been intimate during his many years' residence in Paris, and to whom we were much attached on account of his many estimable qualities. The Emperor had sent him the year before to Saragossa on a mission of conciliation, and he had ever since been languishing in the dungeons of the Inquisition in spite of all Palafox's efforts to alleviate his lot. The poor Aragonese nobleman had nearly lost his reason in consequence of the cruel treatment to which he had been subjected by order of the *junta*. When he heard our loud shouts as we approached his prison and saw the glare of our torches, he thought that his enemies were coming to drag him to execution, but when he felt our arms about him he recognised us and called us nearly all by our own names. Alas! when he found himself free to breathe in the fresh air, once more, his surprise and joy were so great that he was unable to bear the excitement, and a few hours later he expired. General Guillielmi, formerly Captain-General of Aragon, but replaced by Palafox, and several other persons, who had been imprisoned since the beginning of the siege because they were suspected of being favourable to the French, were also now set at liberty and taken to the Marshal.

At daybreak on the 21st all the posts outside the town were occupied by the French. At noon our troops, few in numbers but imposing from their soldierly bearing, were drawn up in order of battle with lighted matches, facing the Ebro in the Aragon road, with reserves placed in suitable positions to guard against all contingencies. The Spanish column soon came out in good order, carrying their flags and their arms. Never perhaps had any of us before gazed on a sadder or more touching spectacle. Thirteen thousand sickly-looking men, bearing in their bodies the seeds of disease, all frightfully emaciated, with long black matted beards, and scarcely able to hold their weapons, dragged themselves slowly along to the sound of the drum. Their clothes were dirty and disordered; in a word, everything about them bore witness to their terrible misery; but in spite of their livid faces, blackened with the smoke of powder, and scarred with the deep traces of rage and grief, their whole bearing still radiated forth an indescribable dignity and pride. The bright-coloured Spanish sashes set off their figures, the large round hats surmounted by a few black cock or vulture feathers shaded their foreheads, and the brown cloak or horse blanket flung negligently over the varied costumes of Aragon, Catalonia, or Valencia, gave a certain grace, perhaps even elegance, to the torn garments and tattered rags reduced to their present condition in a struggle so noble, and new covering mere living spectres. The weeping wives and children of the poor fellows, who encumbered the ranks, constantly turned towards the Madonna, to whom they still prayed. When the moment came for the gallant troops to pile their arms and deliver up their flags to us, many of them gave violent expression to their despair. Their eyes gleamed with rage, and their savage looks seemed to say that they had counted our troops, and deeply regretted having yielded to such a small number of enemies. They started for France, and Saragossa was conquered!

Thus ended this memorable siege.

CHAPTER 8

The War in Austria in 1809

I was impatient to carry the news of the taking of Saragossa to Napoleon, so I started on the very night of the capitulation (February 21) at full speed for Bayonne, where I had left my carriage. Fearing to be hindered by the escort I ought to have taken with me, I braved the danger of crossing, accompanied by one postillion only, a country where guerilla bands were waging war to the death with the French. Those who were taken by our soldiers with arms in their hands were hung immediately from the olive trees bordering the roads. In one of the narrow lanes I had to go through, a mutilated corpse, hanging from a branch, swaying about like a flag in the wind, barred my passage; and as it touched me and I was about to push it aside, I had the curiosity to examine it. The body was dried up, but the features were not disfigured, and I saw that it was the corpse of a white-haired peasant with a grey beard, still wearing all his clothes. I was greatly surprised to find that it weighed no more than a pasteboard figure would have done.

I arrived without mishap at the Tuileries on February 27, where I was received by the Emperor. I found him sitting at a small table, with a pretty child of three years old on his knee. They were very happily eating their breakfast out of one plate. The Emperor congratulated me on there being no trace of the wound which he had been told had disfigured me, and listened with great interest to every detail of the siege and surrender of Saragossa. He asked about the health of the Marshal and the state of the army, and expressed a regret which did him honour at the loss of his aide-de-camp, Lacoste. He even instructed me to convey a message of sympathy from him to the widow, and to tell her that he should continue to her the annuity of fifty thousand francs he had given to her husband.

During our conversation the Emperor fondled the child on his knee a good deal. It was the eldest son of his brother Louis, King of Holland, who had married Marie Hortense de Beauharnais, daughter of the Empress Josephine. The marked tenderness shown for this little nephew, who was a graceful looking boy, led us to think that Napoleon intended him to inherit the throne he had founded; at least there was a rumour to that effect in Paris at this time. After his frugal repast the Emperor, as was his custom, took some coffee without sugar, and the child stretched out his pretty little hands to seize the cup and drink some coffee too, but he pushed it away with a wry face when he found how bitter the contents were. The Emperor said to him, laughing, "Ah, your education is not complete yet; you don't know how to disguise your feelings." I thought these words significant.

The Emperor promoted me to be Colonel of Engineers, and I took the oath of allegiance according to the form then adopted. Great éclat was always given to the ceremony of taking the oath, with a view to binding more closely together the officers of the army and the chief of the great empire they had aided in founding. Those newly promoted were summoned one by one to the throne room, where the great officers of the Crown were grouped about the Emperor. As we entered we saluted three times in the style taught us by M. Gardel, superintendent of the opera ballets, to whom we had been sent to take a lesson beforehand. This lesson had amused us very much, but it failed to give the supple grace of courtiers to most of us, who remained rough soldiers and republicans to boot to the last. When we had learnt to draw back the right foot gracefully, as we respectfully bowed the head and shoulders, we entered the Tuileries and marched proudly into the throne room towards the noble and dignified assembly, to take, in presence of the Emperor, the oath of fidelity to him, which was read out to us by the Duke of Bassano. The clumsiness of some of us in making a salute to which we were little accustomed, made it difficult for the solemn audience to keep from bursting out laughing, which would have been very prejudicial to the dignity of the ceremony.

The succeeding days were passed in brilliant festivities. The Emperor, often weary of living in state, was very fond of disguising himself with a black domino at masked balls, and sometimes he had the pleasure of not being recognised. The Arch-Chancellor, who was always anxious to please his sovereign, gave a good many of these fêtes, at which his pretty niece, Mlle. Busterèche, who later became Mme. Lavollée, helped him to do the honours. These balls, at which everything was on a scale of imperial lavishness, were full of the most piquant attractions for the young, and made up to a great extent for all the privations and losses of the war.

The Empress Josephine, who was losing hope of giving the Emperor a son, had now laid aside the rôle of a young and pretty woman, to take up that of grandmother to the sweet child the Emperor was so fond of. Few women excelled her in that grace which many prefer to beauty, because it is far more durable. The Empress knew only too well how difficult it would be for her to retain the affections of a husband younger than herself, and she spared no pains to make his home attractive to him by constantly varying such pleasures as were likely to bind him to it. Far from betraying any jealousy, she gracefully sacrificed her own *amour-propre*, and surrounded herself with the most remarkable young women of the day. She summoned the most famous artists of the day to the concerts at Malmaison, including the celebrated Mme. Grassini, as much admired for her beauty of form and face, and for her wit, as for her fine contralto voice; and the great soprano, Crescentini, with other stars of the Italian Theatre. Inspired, no doubt, by their brilliant audience, these talented musicians excelled themselves in the force and beauty of their renderings of their beautiful themes, and Zingarelli's touching music was never more greatly appreciated by the public than in the scenes of despair between Romeo and Juliet, which were represented before the Court by most skilful actors. Talma, who wore, like the rest of us, the

Court costume of the time, gave, with the help of his wife, a few scenes from "Othello," filling us with terror, and impressing us with all the greater horror because they were acted without any of the paraphernalia of a theatre, which would have given them something of unreality. They were rendered with such truth to nature, in the very midst of us, that each one felt as if he were looking on at an actual tragedy, and we were all deeply affected. Then we were allowed to breathe freely again, for we repaired to the dancing rooms, whilst later the most recherché supper renewed our ardour, making us forget in the delights of the dance and of the table the fact that the sun had risen some hours before. Just a few whist tables were scattered about at these gatherings, but I never saw any one use them, except a few of the elder and more distinguished diplomatists, such as the Austrian Envoy, Von Cobenzel; the Baden Ambassador, Von Terret; the Marquis de Suchesini, representative of Italy, and Prince Talleyrand.

During one of the evenings I passed at Malmaison the Empress begged me in a very gracious and touching manner to make a copy for her of my picture of the Bivouac at Austerlitz, which had attracted crowds at the Salon, and had been placed in the Diana Gallery of the Tuileries by the Emperor. The Empress already foresaw the coming divorce, and though of course she did not confide her premonition to me, it was evident that she wished in her future isolation to have about her any portraits and souvenirs she could collect of the husband she loved. I promised to make the copy, but the new war prevented me from having time to do it.

In the beautiful palace, later the residence of the celebrated banker and politician Lafitti, but at this time occupied by Queen Hortense, that lady gave to all the festivities a character at once piquant and refined. The charming grace of the mistress of the house pervaded everything; rather fascinating than beautiful, and secure of pleasing all who were brought under her influence, she gathered about her a delightful circle. The leaders of the army, the ministers and indeed all the chief men of the Empire, had married young and beautiful women who formed part of the Court of the Empress. The beauty of these young brides and the richness of their toilettes added fresh lustre to the brilliant fêtes presided over by Queen Hortense, and it was a delight to meet at them such ladies as the Duchesses of Bassano, Vicenza, Montebello, Elchingen, Abrantes, and Rovigo, with the Countesses of Duchatel, Reille, Barral, Saint-Martin, Renaud-de-Saint-Jean d'Angely, Visconti, Lambert, Mathieu, Favier, Mathis, Pélaprat, Gazani, &c.

Amongst those who added fresh lustre to the circle of Queen Hortense, I must mention specially the graceful young bride of General de Broc. This interesting and remarkable couple were, alas! fated to have but a short life. It might well have been said of their home that it was one of those rare spots on this earth of ours in which the joys of the innocent and the pure could still be enjoyed. General de Broc was killed in battle, and Queen Hortense was devoted to his young widow, but her friend was torn from her one day in a most tragic manner when they were out walking together. The two ladies were crossing a plank spanning the Cascade de Grézy in Savoy, and the Queen went boldly over without accident, quite undisturbed by the noise of the rushing water beneath. Madame de Broc, however, in following her, hesitated, her foot slipped, and she fell into the gulf below and was in an instant lost to sight. In her despair the Queen ran back and was ready to fling herself over after her. Efforts were made with pitchforks to rescue the victim of the terrible accident, but the fear of wounding her was so great that nothing resulted but the tearing of her clothes, and the body was not recovered until life had long been extinct. Full of sorrowful regret, the Queen founded a hospital and erected a tomb near the scene of the catastrophe in memory of her friend, inscribing on it: "Here Madame la Baronne de Broc, aged twenty-five years, perished in sight of her friend. Oh all you who visit this spot, think of those who love you and be careful how you attempt to cross this abyss!" When the misfortune happened, all Paris was deeply afflicted; but such is the life of great cities that only a few hearts continued to grieve, pleasures of one kind or another soon consoled the rest.

Meanwhile the Emperor of Austria had ordered the calling out of so many men, that the army of the Archduke Charles was raised to a strength of 300,000, and its organisation had been completed by the promotion of a great many generals. The news from Germany was becoming urgent, but the Emperor, anxious to throw the odium of beginning the hostilities, which would break the peace so useful to Europe, upon Austria, gave no orders to his own troops in Germany, which would have betrayed his desire to be ready to recommence the war; on the contrary, he did everything in his power to encourage his enemies to suppose that we were living in perfect security, and that it would be quite easy to surprise us.

The Austrian Ambassador, Prince Metternich, continued to treat with us as if we were at peace; but the Emperor, true to his policy of forcing the Court of Vienna to take the initiative, never relaxed his vigilance, and was often found bending over his maps studying the chances of the war he knew to be about to break out.

On the very day when Marshal Victor brought the news of the victory of Ciudad Real, the Emperor was exercising at Paris that best of all royal prerogatives, the remission of capital sentences. The laws of the Republic condemned to death emigrants taken with arms in their hands fighting against France, and a French lieutenant-general, the Comte de Saint-Simon, had been made prisoner leading Spanish troops in a fight near Madrid. He was dragged before a court-martial, and the sentence of death was about to be carried out. The more generous the Emperor had been in allowing emigrants to return, the more severely had he punished those who added to his difficulties in pacifying France by joining those who were fighting against her.

It really did seem necessary in this case to make an emphatic example. For several days the Emperor resisted all appeals on behalf of the condemned, but at last, having decided to remit the sentence, he allowed the Empress Josephine, the protectress of all the unfortunate, to present to him the daughter of the condemned Count. The young girl flung herself at the feet of the Emperor, and bathed with her tears the hands stretched out to raise her, when her petition for the life of her father was granted. This act of clemency had a far better effect in France than the carrying out of the punishment would have had.

I was now occupied all day at Prince Berthier's quarters in marking with pins on our maps the position of all the troops we had in Germany, and of the reinforcements on their way to join them, with that of the stores of provisions, forage, shoes, &c., the parks of artillery and transport wagons, and even those movements of the enemy which we had been able to ascertain. The various corps represented by movable pins with different-coloured heads on the maps of Germany, the Tyrol and Italy, looked very like the chessmen on a board whose movements we could combine as they took it in turn to play. This guess-work prepared us for the more serious operations we were presently to undertake on the ground represented on our maps.

There was no time now for me to go on with my painting and fix on canvas my memories of the army, but my enthusiasm for the art was kept up by constant visits to the chief French painters of the day, such as Regnaud, Vincent, David, and the worthy pupils of the last-named, my friends Gorodet, Gros, and Gerard, whose work did so much to spread the renown of the great deeds of the Empire. Gerard, whose business capacity was equal to his talent, had already made his fortune, and he and his wife, the pretty fascinating Roman girl he had married when a student in her native city, entertained at their dinners and receptions the chief celebrities of the day, including Corvisart, the Emperor's skilful physician; the clever chemists Fourier and Berthollet; Cuvier, whose name alone means more than any adjective we could use in connection with it; Monge, the profound geometrician; Von Humboldt, the illustrious traveller; Guérin, the sympathetic painter of "Aeneas and Dido;" Talma; Mlle. Georges, Mlle. Mars, with many others.

My friendship with the great artists of the day and the good advice they were generous enough to give me were of service to me in helping me to remove the chief defects of my early works, and render them more worthy of being offered to the public. They themselves, indeed, welcomed a brother artist who had been able, without exposing them to any of the dangers of war, to give them in his painting some idea of the many interesting scenes he had witnessed.

The weather was now dreadfully bad, a continuous downpour of rain had damaged all the roads by which we had to return to the campaign, and swollen the Danube to such an extent that the ravages made by its waters were greater than had been known for more than a century. All this had doubtless delayed the Austrians from assuming the aggressive. But the decisive moment was approaching, and the Emperor was watching for it in the Tuileries. A series of signals arranged by Guillerninot from Passau and Munich to the telegraph office at Strasburg, were to announce to him in a few hours that the time had arrived for him to leave Paris and place himself at the head of the army.

The chief French corps were those under Marshal Davout, occupying Würzburg, Bamberg, Nuremberg, and Ratisbon, and the Emperor stationed the Bavarian army around and beyond Munich, giving the command to Marshal Lefebvre. Marshal Masséna started for Ulm and Augsburg with 40,000 men, Marshal Bernadotte took command at Dresden of the Saxon army, joining it to the troops under General Dupas, the Würtembergers gathered together at Elwingen, and the Polish army under Prince Poniatowski was to threaten Cracow, whilst the Russian division under Suvoroff (son of the great general who had aided the Austrians against the French in Italy in 1799) was also to enter Galicia.

Having thus made every preparation for a brilliant attack all along the Danube, the Emperor gave his final orders on March 31 to the Prince of Neuchâtel, sending him to take command of the army till he arrived to do so in person. The Prince took me with him in his carriage, and also his two secretaries, the estimable Baron Leduc and the indefatigable Salomon, whose special business it was to look after the movements of the troops, and who, though he had been badly wounded and still had a ball in his thigh, never remitted his arduous efforts by day or by night.

The roads were not then what they are now, smooth and easy to drive over, but very irregular paving stones inflicted positive torture on travellers whose carriages had not easy springs, and the best constructed vehicles were often broken. This was in fact our fate at the gates of Epernay; for though we had paid our post-boys very highly to make our carriage dash over the ground at furious speed, it was broken close to the charming source of the Sillery, and much to our regret we had time whilst our vehicle was being repaired to breakfast at Epernay and taste the wine of the district.

At Metz the Prince reviewed the troops which were on their way to Germany, and on the third day we arrived at Strasburg. In 1788, when I was a child, it had taken the Marshal de Contades, then Governor of Alsace, eight days to post the 100 leagues between Paris and Strasburg, and now in 1843 I can do the 200 leagues between Paris and Toulouse with the mails in forty-four hours without being jolted or meeting with any obstacles. This difference, with the way in which distances have been everywhere bridged over, shows the wisdom of the immense expense incurred by the State in the improvement of every branch of the public service.

The Levis, Jewish merchants at Strasburg, made me pay a very high price for the six horses and the carriages I was obliged to buy for the campaign. I directed my servants to go to Ratisbon with those of the Prince and of his staff, whilst I myself accompanied him in his inspection of the fortifications of Kehl and of the troops on their way to join the army. On the ninth day these preliminary tasks were all achieved, and the Commander-in-Chief let me rejoin him in his carriage to go with him to Donauwerth on the Danube.

Prince Berthier now found himself placed for several days in a position of most onerous responsibility, for he was provisional Commander-in-Chief with precise contingent orders, which did not as yet apply to the state of things in the districts in which he found himself.

His first care was to press on the march of the troops and of the convoys, and to ensure their reaching their destination without hindrance. This important work detained him at Strasburg till April 11th, and everything indicated that the enemy, drawn up between Passau, Branau, and Salzburg on the other side of the Inn, was ready to cross that river.

In fact, the Prince heard on the way that on the 10th the Court of Bavaria and Marshal Lefebvre had received from the Archduke Charles the following letter, dated from head quarters, April 9th, 1809:

> In accordance with a declaration from his Majesty the Emperor of Austria to the Emperor Napoleon, I beg to inform the Commander-in-Chief of the French army that I have orders to advance with the troops under my orders, and that I shall treat as enemies all who offer me any resistance.
>
> (Signed) *Charles*

Several proclamations addressed to the Bavarians urging then to join the Austrian army accompanied this letter. After sending this simple notice by one of his aides-de-camp, the Archduke crossed the Inn. On the approach of his army the Bavarian troops drew back upon Munich, whilst the whole of the Royal Family left that city and retired beyond the Danube. On the 13th we arrived at Döllingen at the same time as the King and Queen of Bavaria. The Royal Family and their Court were alike grieved and anxious, and Prince Berthier had to do his best to reassure them, telling them from the Emperor that he promised to avenge the aggression, and very soon to make the King of Bavaria, at the expense of Austria, more powerful than he had ever been before.

The Archduke, uncertain as to his plan of campaign, which he had had to modify several times against his will, only advanced some six leagues in six days in a hesitating manner by way of the right bank of the Danube opposite the Bavarians, whilst on the left bank his advanced posts from Bohemia met the French on the 13th at Amberg and Hirshem. Our divisions had orders to fall back upon Ingolstadt and Kelheim, leaving at Ratisbon only one division of infantry and one corps of cavalry as advance guards to the army on the two banks. They would thus be able to retire in case of need on one side or the other according to circumstances. When he arrived at Donauwerth on the 14th, Prince Berthier heard at the same time of the advance of the Austrians by way of Bohemia, and of the attack on the Bavarians. In the intense anxiety which these movements caused him, the Marshal feared that we might lose the advantages offered to us by the Ingolstadt and Ratisbon bridges, and he ordered Marshal Davout and General Oudinot to support each other in bearing down upon Ratisbon by both banks, so as to retain that town and command these two passages across the Danube as bases for the later operations of the Emperor. This manoeuvre was not without inconvenience, since it laid bare our left wing on one side of the Tyrol, and destroyed the parallelism of our order of battle with that of the enemy.

On the 15th, however, Prince Berthier went to Augsburg to confer with Marshal Masséna, returning to Donauwerth on the 16th. On the same day Jellachich entered Munich and attacked Masséna's right. The anxiety of Prince Berthier now became greater than ever, and it grieved me very much to see a man who was always so calm and courageous under fire, and whom no personal danger could intimidate, trembling and sinking beneath the weight of responsibility thrown on him now. It was not the enemy he feared; he would rather have been killed than compromise the position of his General, whom he might be exposing to the risk of the loss of a battle by hazarding combinations of which he was not sure the Emperor would approve. In this harassing perplexity we had during four days and nights to go constantly backwards and forwards between Ingolstadt and Donauwerth, so as to be always on the spot where the danger was greatest.

Fortunately the Archduke Charles, expecting to meet a very formidable enemy, hesitated as much as we did, advancing slowly and settling on no definite plan, thus giving time for our troops to come up and the Emperor to arrive.

The Emperor, informed in Paris on the evening of April 12 of what was going on, started that same night with the Empress Josephine, and leaving her at Strasburg reached Donauwerth on the 18th. The position of Prince Berthier was immediately changed. The army had no longer for its head a man overwhelmed with powers too great for him, acting for another whose combinations he was afraid of upsetting, but it was commanded by the Emperor himself, that skilful generalissimo, who resumed the leadership of an army ready for battle, who in a moment detected the weak and strong points of his adversary, and did not hesitate to begin the attack. A great struggle between two illustrious chiefs was now to begin.

The campaign of 1809 was indeed the grandest spectacle offered to the world during the all too short duration of the Empire, and I count myself fortunate not only to have been one of the actors in the fine drama, but also to have survived to record with the brush and with the pen what I witnessed.

On April 18th several volleys of artillery announced to the army the arrival of the Emperor, who greeted his troops in the following finely conceived and inspiring proclamation:

'Soldiers! the territory of the Confederation has been violated. The Austrian General would like us to fly at the mere sight of his army, and to abandon our allies. I have come to you with lightning speed.

'Soldiers! you were around me when the sovereign of Austria came to my bivouac in Moravia; you heard him implore my clemency and swear eternal friendship with me. We have conquered in three wars: Austria owes everything to our generosity: she is three times perjured!

'Our past successes are a sure guarantee of the victory awaiting us,

'Let us march, then, and let our bearing be such that the enemy will recognise their conquerors.'

The news of the commencement of the war and of this brief address electrified the French and our allies, while the Austrians, who heard the volleys from our cannon, understood the cause of the demonstration, and were as much intimidated by the arrival of the Emperor as they had been encouraged by his prolonged absence.

It was his soldiers' eager devotion to him which enabled

Napoleon to get them to make the long rapid marches which brought his forces punctually to the very points where the enemy least expected to meet them. In twenty-four hours from his arrival, the Emperor was thus in his turn ready to take the offensive. Directly he reached Donauwerth on the evening of the 18th, the Emperor had written the following urgent lines to Marshal Masséna, and they were not without effect:

"One word will be enough to make you understand the position. The Archduke Charles has debouched from Landshut upon Ratisbon with three corps, estimated as 80,000 strong. Davout, leaving Ratisbon, is marching towards Neustadt. That Marshal will act against the Austrian army, but the enemy is lost if your corps, debouching before daybreak by way of Pfaffenhoffen, falls upon the rear of Prince Charles. Between the 18th, 19th, and 20th, therefore, all the affairs of Germany will be settled...." The Emperor added with his own hand at the bottom of this letter: "Activity! activity! speed! I rely on you."

After ordering his other generals to be at Ingolstadt as soon as they heard the cannon, he started with Prince Berthier for that town, where their carriages awaited them. Not nearly so well served in that respect as the Emperor and Major-General, I only found three of the horses I had sent from Strasburg, but fortunately I was able to secure several others, though at a very high price.

On the 19th, then, the Emperor was at Ingolstadt, and on the same day Marshal Davout, in accordance with the orders he had received, left but one regiment at Ratisbon to retain possession of that great town, relying upon the power of the colonel in command to hold it somehow for forty-eight hours at least. Unfortunately that officer was guilty of the imprudence of using up all his cartridges the first day in a fusillade he could have avoided if he had burnt the bridge, but he was afraid to take upon himself the responsibility of destroying that important communication, which he had orders to guard against the Austrians. Either from weakness or out of pity for the inhabitants, he did not draw upon the resources of the town to replace his exhausted stores, and although he might certainly have waited until the loopholed doors and windows behind which he and his men were stationed had been shattered by the cannonade of the enemy, he was actually guilty of capitulating, of allowing himself to be disarmed, and of giving up the town in obedience to the reiterated and almost simultaneous summonses to do so from General Kolovrath on the left bank, and the Prince of Lichtenstein on the right. This prompt defection detracted from the brilliant results the Emperor expected to achieve the next day, but for all that it only delayed for forty-eight hours the defeat of the enemy, on whom we were about to take a signal revenge. It was merely for the sake of concentrating as large a force as possible upon the point indicated by the Emperor, that the Marshal had left so few men at Ratisbon. When, however, he turned his back on that town and on the Austrian army, to place his troops in line on the left of the other corps the Emperor had ordered to advance, the enemy thought he was in retreat, and were encouraged to attack with superior forces the St. Hilaire and Friant divisions at the village of Peissing. Two French regiments were hotly engaged there, and the 52nd, bringing up the rear, had to repulse the successive charges of six regiments, driving them back one after another, and by this heroic resistance covering the movements of the advance corps. A little later, at about two o'clock, General Morand defeated an Austrian division, driving it on to the corps under Marshal Lefebvre, a whole regiment of the enemy's dragoons being cut down by the Bavarian cavalry. In this struggle, known as the battle of Thann, the Austrian loss was very great. It was after this affair that Davout's corps was able to take up its position in line with the other corps of the army.

On the 20th the Emperor arrived at Vobourg, where he learnt that the Archduke's forces, numbering 80,000 men, were advancing upon Abensberg to give him battle. He mounted at once, and we accompanied him in the reconnaissance he made of the line of his own outposts and the position of the enemy. He returned to Vobourg in the evening to issue his orders, after which he informed his generals that the next day would be a second Jena.

On the 21st the Emperor went to the central division of the

army, to place himself at the head of the Würtembergers and Bavarians. As soon as he arrived amongst them, he told them that he had come to fight in their midst, to prove to them how great was his confidence in the courage and loyalty of his allies, and to remind them of the many glorious actions in which their ancestors had won renown in times past.

The Prince Royal of Bavaria translated into German one sentence after another as the Emperor spoke, and officers repeated the translations throughout the ranks. A general cheer was then given for the Emperor, making him feel secure of victory.

The Bavarian General, Von Wrede, opened the attack on the enemy's lines at Siegenburg. At about two o'clock Marshal Davout on his side engaged the corps of the Archduke, which was advancing towards Abensberg, putting it to rout and compelling it to retreat towards Ratisbon. Marshal Lannes then charged the Austrians, vigorously driving them back as far as Rohr, and forcing them to retire upon Roffenberg. Thus pressed on every side they withdrew towards Landshut pursued by the Bavarian divisions under Lefebvre and by the Würtembergers under the French General Vandamme. The battle only lasted a few hours, and cost the Austrians eight flags, twelve pieces of cannon, and 18,000 men, who were taken prisoners some by the Bavarians and others by the Würtembergers, who all fought most valiantly. I never saw our French soldiers so covered with blood or so excited as these brave Germans were, but they had fewer opportunities of distinguishing themselves than we had, and eagerly availed themselves of this chance.

The result of the battle of Abensberg was to cut the forces of the enemy in two; one half under Prince Charles on our left withdrew towards Ratisbon, whilst the other on our right under General Hiller made for Landshut. This first success was of vital importance, for through it Prince Charles lost all the advantages he ought to have gained in taking the initiative, scattering his forces to points widely distant from each other, whilst at the same time it concentrated those of the Emperor on an area a few leagues in extent, and led up to the other victories which were to follow it in rapid succession.

On the 21st the Emperor slept at Rohr in the lodgings prepared for the Austrian Archdukes, and at seven o'clock on the morning of the 22nd he started for Landshut. Major-General Prince Berthier ordered me to go and urge on Marshal Davout's and Marshal Lannes' pursuit of the Archduke, who was on his way to Ratisbon, and to return quickly to tell the Emperor what amount of resistance the French were likely to meet with. I joined and marched with our advance guard, following the rear guard of the enemy as far as beyond Langwahl, where they made a fairly long stand, and I was leaving Marshal Lannes about two o'clock to go back to the Emperor, when I heard the noise of prolonged and continuous firing. Eager to get to the scene of action, I left the deep lanes, where I could not see more than a hundred yards on either side of me, cut across the fields, and making straight for the direction in which I heard the cannonade, I gained a height from which I could see in the distance below me the course of the Isar, the town of Landshut, with the French troops in pursuit of General Hiller's corps retiring on Landshut, where he defended the suburbs, attacked on the right bank by the French cavalry under Marshal Masséna, and on the left by the forces under the Emperor. The grand spectacle spread out beneath surprised and delighted me, and I felt like a second Moses looking down from Mount Sinai upon the Israelites in the plain. But the scene before me was far more imposing even than that which had met his eyes, for the infantry and cavalry were moving, and the clouds of smoke were rising up in one of the most beautiful and fertile valleys of Germany, the whole lit up by the bright spring sunshine. I tried to make out the exact position of the various corps which were manoeuvring over meadow land nearly surrounded like an arena by the hills, from the top of one of which I was looking down. I recognised the cavalry of the advance guard of Marshal Masséna engaged with General Hiller's corps defending the town of Landshut, where he was covering the retreat of the great convoys of artillery and baggage endeavouring to escape by way of the Vienna road. The ramparts bristled with the Austrian guns, the smoke from which prevented my seeing the heads of the columns of French troops with whom the enemy fought as they debouched along the right bank of the Isar.

From the side where I was, that is to say on the left bank, the suburb of Landshut was hemmed in by the Morand division, who were trying to get in before the enemy had burnt the two bridges across the river, here divided into two arms, flowing between the suburb and the town. Attack and defence were alike supplemented by a brisk cannonade.

Behind our infantry lines the cavalry, under Marshal Bessières, was grouped in divisions in two masses on the vast grassy plain, in the centre of which I recognised the group I sought, that surrounding the Emperor. Without losing any more time I set off again to join him, and as I cast the last look behind me I thought I could make out a considerable body of troops, in white uniforms, advancing along the Isar, and raising about them great clouds of dust. From the colour of their uniforms I gathered that they were enemies, and I guessed that they could not be seen from the valley, so I made all the greater haste to warn the Emperor, lest he should be taken by surprise. When I was halfway down the hill I completely lost sight of them myself, and I soon reached the Emperor quite out of breath and with my horse covered with foam. When I had given him an account of what I had seen, he asked me several times if I did not think it must be the corps under Prince Ferdinand, or that under the Archduke Maximilian, on their way to surprise him. I knew no more than he did, and dared not express an opinion one way or the other. I only insisted on the necessity of immediate precautions being taken. Without showing the slightest emotion, he sent several officers to reconnoitre the enemy's columns, and ordered his aide-de-camp, General Mouton, to go and press on the attack on the suburb and bridge of Landshut with several battalions, pointed out the positions to be taken up on the hills of the amphitheatre above us by the two divisions of infantry at hand, had batteries of artillery stationed halfway up, hid reserves behind inequalities of the ground, and, having turned every advantage to the account of those who were to receive battle, and arranged everything for the crushing of any enemy which should dare to enter the arena, he put himself at the head of General Dallemagne's cuirassiers, and started at a gallop to meet the enemy and draw them into the ambush just prepared for them.

In about a quarter of an hour the Emperor caught sight of the same clouds of dust and the same column as I had seen from the hill, and pausing to look at them through his field glass, he asked me the same questions as he had done before. We were soon able to make out the officers he had sent to reconnoitre galloping back, and they told us that the troops in white, whose rapid march was raising such volumes of dust, were several Bavarian and Würtemberg regiments which had surprised a great Austrian convoy of pontoons, ammunition, baggage, and provision wagons, which had been retreating towards one of the bridges on the Lower Isar, but whose drivers were now being made to go at their topmost speed with blows from the flat of their escorts' swords, for fear of their being retaken by the enemy. The wagons were covered with white canvas, which had led to my error when I saw them in the distance.

The Emperor was very much put out with me for misleading him as I had done, and said I might have led to the failure of the attack on Landshut; but we were all glad to have furnished him with an occasion for giving us such a masterly lesson in tactics.

We quickly returned to Landshut, where the enemy was desperately defending the bridges, firing from the windows of all the neighbouring houses, and I feared that I was about to witness a repetition of the bloody scenes of Saragossa. I turned to account the experience I had won in that terrible siege, and I was preparing to make our troops defile behind some walls, to protect them from the numerous projectiles, when General Mouton, impatient at the prolonged resistance, led the grenadiers of the 17th regiment through the flames consuming the first bridge, and established them in the houses of that very block. Our fusillade now became in its turn unbearable to the Austrians, and without losing a moment our pioneers pressed on with skill as great as their courage over the burning beams of the second and more important bridge, and reaching the entrance gate, broke it in with blows from their hatchets. Following close behind them, our engineers re-established the passage by extinguishing the flames and flinging on the smouldering beams the doors and planks torn from the houses of the village. The French carried Landshut at the bayonet's point. It would be difficult to describe the disorder into which we had thrown the Austrians, who, as they fled along the Vienna road, fell beneath our blows and the charges led by Marshal Masséna. The town was encumbered with carriages loaded with the sick and wounded, provisions and baggage; with ammunition wagons, and with several pontoon trains, of all of which we took possession, together with thirty pieces of cannon and 9,000 prisoners.

After this great day (April 22nd) the Emperor slept at Landshut, and during the night several of the Archduke Charles's friends and aides-de-camp, not knowing that the town was occupied by the French, entered it and fell into our hands.

On Sunday, April 23rd, the corps under Marshal Masséna passed through Landshut before daybreak, on its way to join that of Marshal Davout, which was advancing on our left in the direction of Eckmühl, keeping on its right the divisions under Marshal Lannes and General Oudinot, with the confederates led by Marshal Lefebvre. At ten o'clock in the morning the Emperor started for Eckmühl. He was as yet in ignorance of the fact that the enemy were masters of Ratisbon, and he meant to drive Prince Charles in that direction, thinking that he would find the town closed against him. The Archduke was already quite cut off from the corps of General Hiller, who, in consequence of the defeats related, was retreating by the Vienna road.

The army of Prince Charles was, however, still larger than ours, for it numbered more than 100,000 men. Moreover, he had at his command a few leagues beyond the Danube the still unbroken force of the Count of Bellegarde.

The enemy's troops, protected by the Danube, were extended along a line perpendicular with that river, and were stationed on heights approached by marshy slopes which made our advance extremely difficult, whilst clumps of woods dotted about on the hills prevented either side from judging of the numbers of the enemy. This last fact greatly influenced the events of the day. The enemy saw but a very small portion of our army, but they were greatly discouraged by our previous successes, and supposed that there were ten times as many of us as there really were behind the woods, so they never dared call out their reserves, but kept them back for a moment of yet more urgent need. We, on the contrary, though a little anxious about the attack we were threatened with on our left, which was anything but strong, were emboldened by three days of victory, and seeing but a small party of the enemy before us we threw prudence to the winds, and full of confidence in the skill of our great leader, we showed a bold front everywhere, and that carried us through.

The Emperor arrived at the head of the Lannes and Masséna corps, the Würtembergers, and two divisions of cuirassiers, and about two o'clock he was on the heights above Eckmühl. He had no sooner got there than he saw Marshal Davout's corps approaching, and learnt that when that general had reached the woods at eleven o'clock, he had met the enemy and at once opened fire; Davout had already gained some ground, and his cavalry, led by General Montbrun, had several times successfully charged that of the Austrians before Dunzling, when he made out the whole position of the enemy's army, their white lines stretching in zigzag fashion for a distance of two or three leagues between the numerous clumps of verdure crowning the heights. The formidable artillery with which the Austrians were provided replied to our cannonade, and raised long clouds of smoke above the marshes and meadows, which were ploughed up by the balls.

Thus far Marshals Davout and Lefebvre, fearing that they would not be supported in time, had hesitated to cross the streams and marshes still separating them from the principal line of the enemy, but when they saw in the distance the smoke of the cannonade from the Saint-Hilaire division rising from the heights of Lindach, which told them of the approach of the corps led by the Emperor, they urged their troops forward, and the struggle at once everywhere became very fierce.

Meanwhile Marshal Lannes' division on our right had crossed

the Laber stream, to take the village of Roking, which was hotly defended by the Rosemberg Corps, and climbed the heights, driving the enemy before them on to the Ratisbon road.

The Würtembergers, directed by the Emperor, tried to penetrate into Eckmühl, from which they were vigorously repulsed but without being discouraged; the French officers leading them three times resumed the offensive, and making fresh efforts they at last took the bridge, village, and castle of Eckmühl, the windows of which were crowded with troops.

The enemy, beaten in these two villages, now retired by way of the Leuchling heights on the two villages of Upper and Lower Leuchling. Then crossing the valley they debouched rapidly under the fire of Marshal Davout, and climbed towards him in close column, but the Marshal swept down from the wooded heights where he had taken up his position, joined hands with General Friant's division, himself led it to the charge, and drove the Austrians before him; after which the Marshal rallied his attacking columns, and climbed to the assault of the village of Upper Leuchling. There a fierce struggle took place. The Saint-Hilaire division attacked the wood covering the village, and met with a stubborn resistance.

On the right the Nansouty division of cuirassiers, with whom I was at the time, protected the Saint-Hilaire attack. This division crossed the meadow at a gallop, the horses often sinking in the mud up to the chest, and falling in the deep ruts which hundreds of balls were tearing out beneath our feet, covering us with splashes of black peat and mud; but though these impediments led to our arriving in great disorder on the firm ground occupied by the enemy, whose squadrons charged us fiercely to prevent our reforming, our action supported that of General Saint-Hilaire, whose division had great difficulty in taking the village. This charge of our 4,000 cuirassiers was so brilliant and successful that we heard the French infantry on our right shouting enthusiastically, "*Bravo, bravo! Vivent les cuirassiers!*"

At the same moment General Friant, on the left of General Saint-Hilaire, pressed on the attack on Upper Leuchling, the two generals succeeding in simultaneously entering the village, every street and garden of which was strewn with the dead.

The Austrians, driven from all the positions they had taken up, were now exposed to a cross fire from the corps under Marshals Lannes, Lefebvre, and Davout.

At about half-past four, Prince Rosemberg was almost surrounded in the two villages of Upper and Lower Leuchling, but he set his troops an example of extraordinary valour and devotion, defending his position for nearly an hour, and repulsing with the bayonet several charges and assaults. Nearly all his Hungarians fell in this action, and at last the position was given up to us, the enemy retiring in disorder. The taking of the villages of Eckmühl and Leuchling was the most glorious of the day's achievements by our brave regiments. The 10th, 19th, 59th, and 72nd Regiments held the most advanced positions throughout the day. These regiments seemed to be inspired with a bold spirit of emulation, vying with each other in their intrepidity; and in the despatches the praise they so well deserved was liberally accorded to them.

After the charge of the Nansouty cuirassiers, I was on my way back to the Emperor, who was directing the whole of the battle from a height above Eckmühl, when I met a gentleman on foot wearing a simple blue frock-coat and a military cap, with nothing about him to indicate his rank. He asked me if I could tell him where the Emperor was, and as I was pointing to the spot where I hoped to find him, one of the many bullets aimed in our direction pierced his breast. Indifferent to a fate which we each of us expected at any moment, I did not trouble to find out who he was, but went on to join the Emperor. When I reached him, he asked me if I had met General Cervoni. I replied, "I do not know him." The Emperor then added, "I have sent for him, and he left Marshal Lannes to join me. I can't think where he is." "Sire," I answered, "a gentleman asked me a minute or two ago where you were." "T that must be he," said the Emperor. "Go quickly and bring him here. I am anxious to speak to him." "But, sire, the gentleman was killed as he was speaking to me. That corpse stretched on the ground about a hundred paces off has a blue coat on." The Emperor sent at once to ascertain if it were indeed General Cervoni, and it turned out that it was that unfortunate officer. He had for two years commanded the Marseilles division, and had just arrived post haste to take up a command under Marshal Lannes, for which he had long been asking. The Emperor expressed the most lively regret at the loss of this meritorious gentleman, whom he pitied deeply for being killed just as he left his carriage, and without having had any share in the victory.

The army of the enemy retired in disorder on Ratisbon, availing themselves, however, of every clearing in the woods to reform their ranks and harass our march. At every step our light cavalry had to charge, whilst that of the Austrians also attacked us with considerable courage, though almost always without success. In one of the cavalry *mêlées* the Archduke Charles, who had placed himself at the head of the Austrians to encourage them, was surrounded and all but taken prisoner.

Our masses of cavalry, flanked on the right and left by the infantry marching through the thick woods, advanced by the main road, and it was nearly eight o'clock in the evening when they came upon a formidable body of cavalry and infantry drawn up in line before Egolfsheim to bar our passage. The only light was that of the moon, which was reflected from the sabres, helmets, and breastplates of the imposing arrays of the thousands of horsemen who were about to cross swords. The Austrian cuirassiers attacked our Nansouty and Saint-Sulpice Corps with the fury of despair, and a terrible *mêlée* ensued, in which the artillery did not dare to fire for fear of shooting down their own comrades. A few gunners cut down at their posts gave the alarm to the whole of the artillery of the enemy, who fled pell-mell with the routed Austrian cuirassiers, who, wearing no armour but their breastplates, lost many men, as soon as they turned their backs on us, our cuirassiers thrusting them through and through. The Austrian infantry, hoping to check the united torrent of fugitives and their pursuers, quickly formed in several squares, but were overturned without daring to use their weapons, as they could not distinguish in the gloom between friends and foes, so that thus defeated the squares were taken prisoners en masse. The rest of the Austrian army, with their corps broken up and hopelessly mixed together, passed the night in retreating in the greatest disorder towards Ratisbon. If Colonel Coutard, who had been left to defend that town, had had the sense to burn the bridges before capitulating, Prince Charles's army, deprived of those bridges and of an easy way of retreat to Bohemia, would have fallen entirely into our power, whereas as it was a large part of it managed to escape.

The Emperor ordered our cavalry to pursue the enemy at the sword's point, but the darkness increased and the march became more and more arduous. Presently, therefore, remembering moreover that his troops must be exhausted with fatigue, many divisions having marched twelve leagues that day before they began to fight, and being anxious to reserve their strength for the next day, he ordered the pursuit to cease and the army to bivouac beyond the village of Koffering, which had been taken and occupied at nine o'clock in the evening.

The Emperor took up his head quarters at Egolfsheim, where he hoped to get a little rest, but he had hardly had time to spread out his maps, and Major-General Prince Berthier had scarcely opened his portfolios to issue his orders for the next day, when the village was found to be on fire from some of the shells thrown into it in the evening, It would have been difficult to extinguish the flames, so it was left to burn, and the fire served to warm us. We passed the night in the gardens of the village beneath the stars; but our sleep, which we found all too short, was several times interrupted by our duties as aides-de-camp. When daylight returned we found we had about 20,000 prisoners, including the wounded who had been abandoned, and that we had taken fifteen flags, a good deal of artillery, and a great many first-rate horses. Our soldiers sold the best of these horses at four or five *Louis d'or* each. I bought three, but an hour afterwards some horse fanciers relieved me of my purchases without my knowledge, with the result that my part of the booty of the day of Eckmühl was the loss of fifteen *louis d'or* and the gain of many a pleasant memory.

At daybreak on the 24th, Marshal Masséna received orders from the Emperor to make for Straubing, and there cross the Danube so as to harass the retreat of the Austrians through Bohemia, whilst Napoleon himself, with his cavalry and the corps of Marshal Lannes and Davout, marched on Ratisbon.

It was nine o'clock when our advance guard met that of the Austrians in the plains about the town. The numerous cavalry of the enemy awaiting us in order of battle presented a most imposing appearance. Our regiments of carabineers (the elite of the French cavalry, not only on account of their height, but of their chivalrous bearing) had had no chance of crossing swords during the previous days, and their leaders, anxious to show off their skill, begged for them to have the honour of taking their share in the fighting. This request was granted, although they belonged to the reserve. The carabineers, wearing broad felt hats and uniforms turned back with red, were drawn up in columns of squadrons, and when the trumpets sounded the signal they dashed forward at a gallop; the earth shook beneath the onrush of 2,000 horses, and the gaze of all was riveted upon the intensely interesting evolution, whilst every heart beat high with expectation. The Austrians received the shock with great courage, but they could not stand against it; they were overturned, swept away as by a thunderstorm, and this charge of our carabineers outside Ratisbon will ever be engraved alike on our memories and in the annals of our wars as one of the most brilliant feats of arms of the age.

Two other charges from our cuirassiers completed the defeat of the Austrian cavalry, who fled pell-mell like a flock of sheep, not all of them succeeding in entering the town. If our infantry had only had time to follow these rapid movements, they would have got in with the enemy's cavalry, and as it was there was only just time for the Austrians to barricade the gates before our artillery came up and began bombarding them, whilst the enemy crowned the top of all the crenelated walls with infantry, and placed cannon in all the embrasures.

After all our efforts and our pursuit of the routed cavalry, we discovered that during the night the enemy had constructed a bridge of boats above the town. Marshal Lannes sent some infantry and artillery to attack this bridge, and the fugitives were thrown into great disorder. Our fire shattered and sank several boats, the bridge was broken, and retreat in that direction became impossible; all who were not able to get back into the town were taken, in spite of their being protected by a considerable number of guns, which fired on us from the heights of the left bank of the river.

Our efforts were now concentrated on the gates of the town, which we tried to enter. Our infantry, dotted about in the gardens at half range from the ramparts, riddled the artillerymen at their embrasures with bullets, and protected the troops who were bringing ladders from the neighbouring village, with which to climb to the assault as soon as a practicable breach had been made. Whilst this was going on the Emperor, who was on horseback near the town, was struck on the heel by a ball. Either the pain was not very great or he managed to hide it, for he merely sent for his surgeon Yvan, not even letting us take him out of range of the falling balls. He sat down on a drum, and Yvan dressed the wound, which was really a mere contusion. The Emperor then remounted his horse, and it was not until some hours afterwards that the army knew of the danger their chief had been in. When the troops did hear of it they hastened up from every direction and surrounded the Emperor, who to reassure them galloped through their ranks in the midst of enthusiastic cheering and touching expressions of devotion.

The day, a most laborious one, passed without our having succeeded in effecting a practicable breach, and we were beginning to be afraid we should have to go through a regular siege. During the confusion several quarters of the town had been set on fire, and many of the buildings of the luckless city were wrapped in dense clouds of smoke. As night approached these clouds became dashed with crimson, and the whole place was illuminated by the lurid glow of the flames. The atmosphere was perfectly calm, and there was no wind to disperse the smoke, which rose in majestic-looking columns to the sky.

I can still see in imagination the crests of the partly destroyed walls, dashed with a thousand varying tints, and crowned with eager, desperate defenders, standing out against the sombre glow of the conflagrations, whilst above the heads of the besieged rose masses of black smoke assuming many a different form, tongues of flame and columns of steam, as yellow as sulphur, shooting up here and there. At a considerable height above it all floated light vaporous, ever shifting clouds, lit up by the silvery beams of the moon.

The ancient walls of Ratisbon had not been built to resist artillery, and after our twelve-pounders had been firing on one spot for some few hours, we at last saw the fall of a house adjoining the enceinte, succeeded very soon by that of a large piece of the wall itself, making a wide opening. The chief difficulty now was to get to the base of the wall, for to do so we had to cross, without any cover, the wide promenades or boulevards surrounding the town. These boulevards were lit up as brightly as by day by the light of the moon and the conflagration, and moreover the enemy swept them with grape shot. Our infantry had been stationed under the shelter of a few houses, and when they had to cross the open to march to the assault the first ranks fell, and there was some little hesitation amongst the others. A second attempt was not more successful. Their chief, the impetuous Marshal Lannes, impatient at the delay, now exclaimed, "I am going to show you that I am still a grenadier!" and flinging himself to the head of the column he crossed the esplanade, followed by the assailants carrying ladders.

Captain Beaulieu, of the engineers, who had previously reconnoitred the way and the state of the breach, led the Marshal and his aides-de-camp to the right spot, and they were the first to arrive at the edge of the ditch, the counterscarp of which had fortunately not been put into a good state of defence. A few soldiers were able to climb the wall and jump into the fosse, others went down on ladders. Beaulieu and Labédoyère, leading the way, climbed up by the most practicable portions of the breach, repulsing a few Hungarian grenadiers who made an attempt to defend it. In a few seconds all the ladders were placed in position without disorder, the soldiers following their brave officers, and the column scaled the ramparts and got down into the town in the midst of a hot fusillade. As they advanced towards the Straubing gate our grenadiers came upon a body of terrified Austrians crouching against a wall, who laid down their arms. The Marshal's orders were to march direct upon the bridge, to cut off all possibility of retreat; but our men did not know the way, and had got wrong, when they met a French vivandière of the 65th Regiment, who had stopped in the town, and who, delighted to see her fellow-countrymen again, offered to lead them right, and took them towards the bridge through the thick of the firing. The streets and squares were encumbered with carriages and all manner of property which the inhabitants had been trying to save in the terrible conflagration. Our troops were, however, advancing rapidly through the burning streets, when they came to a dozen wagons and some carriages loaded with barrels. They were about to pass them, when an Austrian officer ran up to them and shouted in a distracted kind of way, "Don't go on! they are full of powder!" Every one shuddered, and, no longer thinking of fighting, our men joined the Austrians in a helter-skelter attempt to remove as far as they could the thousands of pounds of powder which were likely soon to blow the whole town to pieces. Our haste did indeed save us from that disaster, but when we at last got to the bridge the gates were already barricaded and defended by the whole Austrian artillery, massed upon the other bank and pouring a terrible fire upon the town.

Marshal Lannes, compelled to abandon the idea of taking the bridge, now contented himself with making the five or six thousand Austrians scattered about the town lay down their arms and ordering them to aid our troops in putting out the fire. A few minutes later a big suburb on the left bank of the river burst into flames. Very soon there remained not a single house, and it was by the melancholy light of the flames that we made our way to the Imperial head quarters in the Carthusian Abbey near the gates of Ratisbon, where we were able to take a little rest. Thus about midnight ended the fourth day of the new war, the sixth since the arrival of the Emperor. Even ancient history contains no record of so remarkable a series of events in so short a space of time. Four victories achieved in four days! A splendid opening of the campaign of 1809, the most brilliant of all the campaigns of the Empire!

On the morning of the next day—the 25th—we went over the unfortunate city, a great portion of which was still on fire. What had once been an extensive suburb on the left bank was now one huge furnace. The streets of the town were strewn with the Austrian dead and wounded, some of the bodies partly consumed by the flames. Our hearts were torn at the sight of the inhabitants wandering about amongst the smouldering ruins, and the Emperor was so much touched by all the terrible misery that he promised the poor creatures that he would have the homes they had lost rebuilt at his own cost.

The rest of the day was spent by Napoleon in having the wounded seen to and in reviewing his troops.

I was present at this review (at which I received a money grant—I had been made colonel of engineers two months before), and I was near the Emperor when he was nominating those who were to fill up the vacant sub-lieutenancies in the 52nd Regiment. He had asked the colonel to order out from the ranks the most deserving of the non-commissioned officers; and as the Emperor passed before them the brave fellows proudly presented arms, answering his questions and receiving with delight the Imperial baptism, "I make you an officer." When he had reached the seventh or eighth sergeant the Emperor noticed a handsome young fellow with fine but stern-looking eyes, and of resolute and martial bearing, who made his musket ring again as he presented arms. "How many wounds?" inquired the Emperor. "Thirty," replied the sergeant. "I am not asking you your age," said the Emperor graciously; "I am asking how many wounds you have received." Raising his voice, the sergeant again replied with the one word, "Thirty." Annoyed at this reply, the Emperor turned to the colonel and said, "The man does not understand; he thinks I am asking about his age." "He understands well enough, sire," was the reply; "he has been wounded thirty times." "What!" exclaimed the Emperor, "you have been wounded so often and have not got the cross!" The sergeant looked down at his chest, and, seeing that the strap of his cartridge pouch hid his decoration, he raised it so as to show his cross. He said to the Emperor, with great earnestness, "Yes, I've got one, but I've merited a dozen!" The Emperor, who was always pleased to meet spirited fellows such as this, pronounced the sacramental words, "I make you an officer!" "That's right, Emperor," said the new sub-lieutenant, as he proudly drew himself up; "You couldn't have done better!"

Meanwhile Archduke Charles had begun his retreat on Vienna by way of the wretched Bohemian roads, hastening his movements the more because he had heard of the forced marches of our troops on the same town, where we were likely to arrive before he could, as we were going thither by a more direct route and also by less steep and better roads.

The Masséna Corps was advancing between those under Lannes and Davout, so that it protected both. Masséna had had orders to march on Ebersberg, and the Imperial Staff followed that movement. Having been sent with an order, I was on my way back to head quarters, when I came upon Marshal Masséna just as he was leading the Claparède division against several battalions of the enemy's rear guard, posted in a hamlet on a branch road, and it was in the midst of a shower of bullets that I gave an account of my mission to the Prince, watching meanwhile the conflict I am about to describe.

The first brigade of the Claparède division was commanded by General Cohorn, who met the Austrians on the branch road mentioned above. A few battalions only had been stationed there to protect from a distance the approaches to the bridge of Ebersberg. They were easily repulsed and pursued as far as the narrow road which leads down to the bridge. This road, raised from about twelve to fifteen feet above the sandy meadows, often apparently flooded by the Traun, and with clumps of wood here and there, was rather more than half a mile long. The river, which was deep and rapid, here divided near the town into several arms, each spanned by a wooden bridge. The largest of the bridges, which was more than 1,200 feet long, abutted on to the gates of the town, and the Emperor had given orders that every effort should be made to prevent the enemy from destroying this bridge, which was so necessary to our advance. The Austrians had already piled up faggots and smeared the bridge with tar ready for setting it on fire, when Cohorn's troops dashed down the roadway pell-mell with the fugitives they were pursuing.

Hitherto our troops had been deploying in woods, where they could not see more than a hundred yards before them, but when they debouched from the forest the sight which met their eyes may well have surprised them. Beyond the long causeway on the other side of the bridge spanning the river and leading to the very walls of the town, the houses rose as in an amphitheatre, every window crowded with troops, whilst the terraces of the castle bristled with artillery, and every height overlooking Ebersberg was covered with batteries of artillery, and more than 30,000 men stood ready to fire down upon us if we got into the town. Under any other circumstances it would have been wise to pause and at least organise our attack on the formidable preparations for defence, but our troops were already launched against and mixed with the enemy. Their onslaught was tremendously vigorous; any manoeuvring to the right or to the left was impossible, retreat would have been even more perilous than advance, and Cohorn, recognising that his only chance of success was in audacity, urged his men on, encouraging them by himself marching at their head. As soon as the enemy's gunners caught sight of us they concentrated all the fire of the artillery upon the roadway and the bridge, the gates of which were immediately closed even against fugitive battalions, who, finding themselves exposed to the fire of their own comrades, flung themselves from the bridges and the roadway on to the islets in the river, where they were compelled to lay down their arms. All the killed or wounded on the bridge, whether French or Austrians, were pitilessly flung into the water, even carriages laden with the Austrian wounded encumbering the way were flung over, and a dash was made for the gates, which were barricaded from within the town. They, however, very soon gave way beneath the blows from the hatchets of our pioneers.

Cohorn's intrepidity had saved the bridge, and it helped us to secure the town also. After the terrible dangers they had escaped his troops debouched into a square full of infantry, and found themselves exposed to the fire from them as well as from the windows of the houses and castle above them. Cohorn's brigade suffered fearfully, and defended themselves with their bayonets only, but Claparède's second brigade came to their aid at double quick pace, crossing the bridge in a continued hail of grape shot. Many French generals were wounded, and had their horses killed under them.

Our artillery, which promptly arrived on the left bank, answered that of the Austrians, which was working such havoc amongst our men that they would really have had to give way and lose ground had not General Legrand's division come to the rescue. It was on this occasion that Legrand made his stern reply to General B. who came up to make a suggestion to him as to whither he should lead his column. "Eh!" he said, "get out of my way now; you can give me some advice later; we are not here to make phrases!"

When General Cohorn saw that he was supported, he led his men rapidly up towards the castle, whilst the battalions left behind drove in the doors of the houses and killed all those who had been firing at there from the windows. Claparède also pushed on for the castle, but he and General Cohorn were both repulsed and compelled in their turn to take refuge in the houses and fire at the Austrians from the windows. General Hiller meanwhile flung a number of shells into the town, and on every side fire broke out in the houses, the wounded Austrians, with which they were crowded, dragging themselves out into the streets to escape the flames.

General Legrand, eager to put an end to the struggle, in his turn led his men to the assault of the castle, whilst Claparède attacked it on the flank. Our pioneers drove in the gates, and opened a passage for us; the Austrians shut up in the castle tried to defend themselves, but ended by laying down their arms, whilst others got out through the gardens to the hill behind Ebersberg, where they were pursued, a bloody desperate conflict taking place, in which first one and then the other side was successful.

Whilst this was going on above the castle, shells were poured by the Austrians into the little town of Ebersberg, with a view to driving us out of it. On every side we were surrounded by flames; our position became no longer tenable, and we were compelled to withdraw from it. One regiment of cavalry which had got into the town, but could penetrate no farther, had already had to retrace its steps over the bridge to save the men and horses from annihilation. We wanted to avoid going up by the long arduous ascent to the castle, and the only other way out was by the gate opening on to the Vienna road. At this gate there were a number of vaulted arcades, beneath which the road, only wide enough for a single carriage, passed, debouching at the base of the steep heights covered with gardens enclosed within hedges, behind which the Austrians were in ambush, and thus protected were able to fire at almost close quarters upon the heads of the French columns as they issued at quick pace from the narrow defile. A scene as terrible was enacted here as that at the passage of the bridge. The street leading to the gateway was of a good width, but the houses were on fire, and burning brands fell upon the wounded Austrians, who were trying to save themselves. Cohorn, however, had no choice, and he ordered the head of his column to keep together, fix bayonets, and charge for the gardens, trampling down all the unfortunate wretches in the way. Our brave fellows, shouting "Forward! forward!" with one voice, flung themselves in good order and at quick pace beyond the arcades, the first rank to issue receiving such a volley of bullets that not a man remained standing. The second rank climbed over the bodies of their comrades, only to be in their turn thrown down. Imbued with the same zeal, the same cry of "Forward! forward!" continued to ring out, and twenty ranks went down in succession, without checking the advance of those pressing on behind, with burning brands upon their backs, which they were trying to shake off as they struggled over the masses of the dead and dying, forming such a terrible hindrance to their progress. Presently, however, the Austrians no longer had time to reload either muskets or cannon, the struggle was continued with the bayonet, and General Hiller's troops, no less courageous than their assailants, did not yield their position until they found themselves threatened in the rear by the cavalry of General Durosnel and Marshal Bessières, who had crossed the Traun at Lambach and at Wels when they decided to retreat.

The Claparède and Legrand divisions, with the whole of Marshal Masséna's corps, their artillery, ammunition wagons, and the cavalry of the advance guard, now made their way at a gallop through the same gate, crushing to pulp and powder beneath their wheels and the feet of their horses the bodies of from five to six hundred French and Austrians, piled up in a space but a few feet wide, as they pushed on to bivouac in the gardens on the hill of Ebersberg.

As we, with the Emperor, followed the advance guard, and our horses' feet sank in the mud made up of the still warm flesh and blood of the dead, a feeling of intense horror and disgust, of which I have never been able fully to shake off the memory, came over us. The street was strewn with terrible-looking corpses, half consumed by fire, and even our glory in victory could scarcely enable us to choke down our emotion at having bought that victory so dear. Bearing in mind the narrow space in which the struggle had taken place, it had been more bloody than any of our wars, though we had seen a good many more victims reduced to a similar condition in the bogs of Pultusk and Golymin.

In the order sent to Marshal Masséna on May 1st, the Emperor had foreseen the resistance we should meet with here, for he had said, "the enemy will take up an advantageous position at Ebersberg, but will be driven from it by the corps which will cross the Traun at Lamsbach." The advanced guard of this corps was confided to General Durosnel, whose march had been retarded by the many streams and ravines he had had to cross, for he had made his way straight across country in the direction from which he heard the firing, having failed to find the roads on the right bank of the Traun. If he could only have arrived two hours earlier, he would have saved the lives of many brave grenadiers.

The Emperor was much moved by all the suffering he had witnessed, and it was with a heavy heart that he passed the night in the gardens of Ebersberg surrounded by his soldiers, like some father who finds the best consolation for his sorrows in the bosom of his family; and our brave fellows were in their turn comforted for the loss of their comrades by the presence in their midst of their Emperor, sharing their couch of straw, their fatigues, and their privations.

The pretty little town of Ebersberg was still burning at the foot of the mountain, and the Austrian prisoners were employed to put out the flames. The night was calm and fine, the moon-lighting up the gardens. Our troops gathered in groups to chat together round some thousands of bivouac fires at very short distances from each other, the wood of the hedges and the trees, the bright-looking summer houses, arbours, and refreshment rooms—everything combustible, in fact—serving for fuel, and by their merry crackling making us forget, as we warmed ourselves at them, the absence of the supper which would soon have made us go to sleep if we had had it. I don't suppose any nocturnal fête was ever more brilliantly illuminated, or that there was ever more eager talking at any bivouac, for each one was congratulating himself on his escape in one or another episode of the awful struggle of the day. The names of Cohorn, Masséna, and Legrand were the most often quoted with admiration. Then each survivor spoke of the comrades killed here or there at his side; regretted the loss of a coat-sleeve or cloak which had been burnt, a shako which had been lost, or told of the explosion of his cartridge box as he made his way through the flames of Ebersberg, and the words, "Did you see this? Did you see that?" were passed from mouth to mouth, followed by an account of the episode referred to.

The Emperor, feeling the need of doing something to assuage his compunction at the thought of all the blood he had seen flowing in the horrible butchery, gave up several hours to the good work of consolation, and summoned to his aid the Comte Daru and M. Maret, Duke of Bassano, who had been with him as his secretaries since the commencement of

212

the campaign. Seated on piles of fagots brought for the fires, and by the light of candles set upon drums, the Emperor and these gentlemen worked for some hours in this rural council chamber, the secretaries holding their paper on their knees, preparing decree after decree for the Emperor's signature, ordering the construction of roads, the excavation of canals, the foundation of hospitals, &c., rewards to be given for great services, and so on. It was eleven o'clock when the Emperor, having given his instructions for the next day to Prince Berthier, ordered the Count and the Duke to open their portfolios, and at two o'clock they were still at work.

Owing to my absence at Salzburg, M. Maret had not seen me for some time, and when he was asked for a pension for the widow of Colonel Lejeune, who had been killed, it was said, a few days before, he thought I had fallen, and showed considerable interest in the matter when, at the bivouac I am describing, he presented the order for this pension to Napoleon for signature. The Emperor seemed surprised and grieved at the news, expressed a regret which did him honour, and added to his signature these generous words, "I double the pension." The double pension thus ordered was duly paid to Mme. Lejeune, and she enjoyed it from that time until two years ago! A few days after the incident just related occurred, the Emperor, having issued some orders which it would be difficult to execute, said to Prince Berthier, "Send a colonel of engineers;" and the Prince replied, "I will send Lejeune." "Oh, no, you won't," exclaimed the Emperor; "he is dead—so dead, in fact, that I ordered a double pension for his widow three days ago." "But, sire, I have just been speaking to him." "Well, I never! Send him to me." So they fetched me, and directly I appeared the Emperor began to laugh, and said, "Well, I see I was wrong; I thought it was he!" Then resuming his grave manner he gave me his orders without further explanation. A little later Prince Berthier and the Duke of Bassano told me all about this fortunate mistake, and I was able to thank the Emperor myself for his generosity.

CHAPTER 9

The Taking of Vienna—Essling

Those to whom was assigned the melancholy task of clearing Ebersberg of the human remains encumbering its streets, and opening a passage for the rest of the army, had not time to dig a grave anything like large enough to hold the many officers and men forming the elite of our troops who had fallen in the struggle. More than two-thirds of the bodies were therefore with infinite regret flung into the river and carried down by the rapid waters of the Traun to the Danube, where they were rolled over and over in the many windings of that great river till they found a final resting-place in the depths of the Black Sea. No prayers could be offered up for their repose at their sad funeral. History will—at least so I hope—preserve the memory of all that we owe to those who won the admiration of the whole army at a period rich in brilliant feats of arms, and point out as a useful lesson for the future the fact that all this blood would not have been shed if the division which the Emperor had ordered to advance by way of Steyr to attack General Hiller's forces in the rear, and compel him to retire from Ebersberg without fighting, had come in sight of his army in time to cause him uneasiness, or if the news of the powerful diversion about to be effected in his favour could have reached Masséna at the right moment.

The right wing of the invading army was covered by the Italian contingent under Prince Eugene, who had against him the Austrian forces commanded by the Archduke John, whom he had beaten at Piava and Saeile.

Our forces were divided from that army by the mountains of the Tyrol, into which the Austrian Marquis von Chatter and the

Count von Giulay had penetrated with their corps, each with a view to encouraging the revolt of the Tyrolese, and placing them once more under the domination of Austria.

Marshal Lefebvre with the French and two Bavarian divisions fortified Salzburg, and marched upon Innsbruck, the capital of the Tyrol. Our flanks on either side were therefore well covered. At Augsburg in our rear the Emperor had formed an army of all the troops which had not been able to arrive in Bohemia in time for the opening of the campaign. It was, therefore, with a sense of being secured on every side that we were about to begin our march on Vienna. We expected to give battle on a grand scale on the heights of Mölck or St. Pölten, where we supposed the enemy to be awaiting us in the best possible positions for the defence of Austria.

All the Emperor's dispositions were made with that expectation, which, however, was not realised. The Archduke Charles did not try to recross the Danube to take up a position behind the Enns by way of the bridge of Mautern, of which he was still master; and General Hiller, who with 40,000 men in the advantageous position of Ebersberg had failed to defeat us, dared not await us alone on level ground, on plains where he would need to deploy far larger forces than he now had. Our troops, irritated at all the losses they had sustained, set out on the pursuit of General Hiller with feelings of irritation and indignation, which made things very unpleasant for the inhabitants of the Austrian province we were entering. The good Germans, whom we all liked on account of their hospitable ways, had been kindly treated during our first invasion, but they were not so fortunate this time, so they all fled before us, and we often had a good deal of trouble to prevent our men from being too exacting and revenging themselves on those compelled to entertain us. When we entered Enns, I was wounded by some of our own people in one of the scuffles which so often occur in which an officer feels obliged to interfere to prevent wrong-doing. Only ten days before the people of Enns had been talking of soon devastating France! and today their protectors had fled, and they themselves were experiencing all the horrors of war. One of the sad vicissitudes of fate which overtake monarchs and victors in the midst of their most brilliant successes was recalled to our minds a few days later, when about thirty leagues from Enns we came in sight of the towers of the castle of Dirnstein, rising from the summit of a huge rock, as if to defy from afar any approaching assailants, however victorious hitherto. On the day when we drew near Dirnstein, the Emperor, noticing its towers rising up into the sky a few miles off on our left, pointed them out to Prince Berthier and Marshal Lannes, who were riding near him, with the words, "It was there that Richard of England was treacherously seized on his way home from Palestine, where he had vanquished the Saracens, and was shut up for a year by order of the Emperor of Austria, who demanded a great ransom. King Richard had been more fortunate than any of us three at Saint Jean d'Acre, but not more courageous, although he did receive the nickname of Coeur de Lion, which I think I might also well bestow on you two. With the confidence and loyalty of a noble nature he was marching through a country at peace with him when he was betrayed by an Austrian Archduke, and sold to the Emperor Henry VI., who kept him captive. How far removed are we now from those barbarous times! I have had princes, kings, and emperors who were my enemies in my power, and far from tampering with their liberty, I have not exacted from them a single sacrifice of their honour. Will they do as much for me?"

After these words the Emperor remained silent, and as he rode on, kept his eyes fixed on the ruins of the castle. Six years later he was himself to be held captive on an arid rock in mid ocean, far from France and from all who were dear to him.

General Hiller had burnt the bridge over the Enns when he retreated, and our troops were compelled to spend the whole of the 4th in preparing for the passage of the river. The artillery set to work to construct a bridge on piles, and the engineers having succeeded in seizing several boats on the Danube which had belonged to the enemy, had them brought up to the Enns and made a bridge of boats which was ready before that on piles. Our army then rejoined us at Enns, Marshal Lannes having reached that place by way of Steyr on the right bank of the river. The Emperor waited at Enns till the bridges were finished, and the next day, May 6, I followed him to Amstetten, and on the 7th to St. Pölten.

Our columns had already crossed a portion of the Danube, down which boats laden with provisions for us were making their way, but at Mautern, opposite Krems, the enemy still occupied both banks and a bridge across the river. Marshal Lannes now received orders to go and take that position and to seize the boats forming the bridge, or if he could do no more at least to burn them. I was at the same time sent off to expedite as much as possible the landing of our provisions lest they should fall into the hands of the enemy, and to get them conveyed to us by other routes. This task was promptly executed, and on the evening of the 8th I was able to enter Sigarskirchen with the Imperial staff, only some five leagues from Vienna.

As ordered by the Emperor, the position at Mautern was taken and the bridge burnt, but General Hiller had been able to use it the evening before to cross to the left bank. As the Archduke Charles would not now dream of attacking us on the right bank, and as there were no more obstacles for Marshal Lannes to overcome, he began his march that very night so as to arrive at Vienna at daybreak.

The suburbs of Vienna are completely enclosed within a huge entrenched camp, built in former days as a protection against the Turks and Hungarians. We expected to meet with a hot resistance, and I was told off to lead one of the assaults, but the fortifications were not defended at all, and a few discharges from our artillery were enough to win us possession of the whole of the suburbs, where part of the inhabitants quietly awaited our arrival in their homes. The Emperor took up his head quarters on the same evening (May 9th) at Schönbrunn, the Saint-Cloud of the Emperors of Austria.

The town of Vienna, protected on the northern side by one of the minor arms of the Danube, is surrounded by a strong *enceinte* of twelve curtains relieved by bastions at the angles of the polygon; where these terminate are as many grand *façades* with *demi-lunes*, dry ditches, alarm-posts, and covered ways, the glacis of which forms a beautiful esplanade enclosing the whole city. This esplanade between the town and the suburbs is used as a promenade by the inhabitants. When debouching by way of the streets of the suburb known as that of Maria Hilf on to this promenade, we attempted to march into the town, the garrison, the greater part of which was looking down on us from the ramparts, poured out such a hail of bullets and grape shot that we were compelled to be careful. This showed us that Vienna meant to close her gates upon us, and that we need not count upon the passive obedience she had shown us in our first invasion in 1805. The Archduke Maximilian found himself at the head of from fifteen to sixteen thousand men of proved valour, and in addition to that a numerous body of well-armed citizens, who gave proof of the greatest devotion to their princes. Public feeling, which was very bitter against us, urged the most stubborn resistance on the military chiefs, but most fortunately for us all this eager patriotism was entirely wanting in the skilful guidance necessary to turn it to really good account. During the fifteen days which had elapsed since the news must have reached him of the defeat of the Austrians at Landshut, Eckmühl, and Ratisbon, the Archduke Maximilian had failed to utilise either the inhabitants or the well-stocked arsenal for the organisation of a formidable defence. The approaches to the principal gates were not even palisaded. For all this, however, if the defence were only sustained for a few days it would give Prince Charles time to arrive at Vienna before we could take possession of it, so it behoved us to hasten its fall by every means in our power whilst his army was far enough off for our task, though still difficult, to be not altogether impossible. The Prince lost a good deal of time in Bohemia, whilst we wasted not a moment.

Marshal Lannes, no longer able to doubt that a stout resistance would be offered, now sent two officers with a flag of truce to ask that the gates of the town might be opened to us to avoid the horrors of an assault and a siege. No sooner had the envoys reached the promenade than they were assailed by the populace and charged by hussars with drawn swords, and M. de Saint-Mart, engaged though he was on a pacific mission, barely escaped with his life, and returned minus one cheek, which had been slashed off by a sword.

The Emperor, hearing of this treatment of a messenger bearing a flag of truce, ordered a regular attack to be made at once with a view to forcing the enemy to abandon the town, or at least to prevent the Austrians from shutting themselves up in it. Whilst our preparations were being made, a continuous fire was kept up from the ramparts on the suburbs with a view to dislodging us. The inhabitants of these suburbs, finding themselves deserted by their natural protectors, sent a deputation to the Emperor to beg him to intercede in their favour. The Emperor received the messengers graciously, and had a letter from Prince Berthier to the Archduke Maximilian given to them, charging them to deliver it themselves, as after the incident of the morning he could not send one of his own officers. Instead of receiving a favourable answer to this letter, the people of the suburbs only found the firing redoubled, absolutely no consideration being shown even for the numerous women and children.

We therefore set to work to place some twenty howitzers in the houses overlooking the esplanade, keeping them masked until nightfall, when we meant to sweep the ramparts and deal out death with the shells from them. Whilst we were preparing this attack, the troops under Marshal Masséna broke into the town on the north-east, took possession of the Prater, and held themselves ready to bar the passage of all who attempted to leave the town and escape by the way of the bridge over the Danube, or of any Austrians who should attempt to come to the aid of the town.

The day of the 10th passed in a cannonade from both sides, one to check our preparations, the other to protect them. Meanwhile, the Emperor having learnt that one of the young Archduchesses had been unable to leave on account of illness, issued orders that we were to avoid pointing our cannon in the direction of the Imperial palace.

At nine o'clock in the evening a hot fire was poured out from all our howitzers, to the great surprise of the inhabitants. The sky above the esplanade was immediately lit up by numerous far-reaching streaks of vivid light, resembling a brilliant display of fireworks, and ere long the flames of some eight or ten conflagrations, which continued to burn in different quarters of the town throughout the night, revealed many a terrible scene of desolation. The Archduke Maximilian, having learnt before daybreak that we were so placed as to cut off his retreat by way of the main bridge, sent some battalions to attack us, but they were beaten and pursued. The Prince then lost hope of being able to defend the burning town, and fearing to be made prisoner in it, he spent the whole morning in sending out all his troops, and every one who could escape, before the passage was completely closed to them. He resigned all his power to the Count von Urbria, Grand Chamberlain of the Emperor of Austria, and as soon as further retreat had become impossible without risking the great danger of running the gauntlet of Masséna's artillery, the few troops still remaining in the town hoisted a white flag. It was at noon on May 11th that this signal appeared, and messengers were sent to our outposts with proposals for capitulation.

Marshal Lannes at once ordered the firing to cease, and a parley was begun. A deputation of superior officers, clergy, nobles, and chief functionaries of the town waited on the Emperor at Schönbrunn, and demanded of him oblivion of the past, security of life and property, and the restoration of order in the town, where the populace had given themselves up to anarchy and pillage. The capitulation was accepted, the terms were drawn up in accordance with the wishes of the deputies, and our troops took possession of the town. At nine o'clock on the 12th, our battalions entered Vienna in good order, where they at once assumed the idle of protectors against the populace rather than that of conquerors of a taken city. The Emperor then issued an order of the day to the army, in which the following passages occur:

> Soldiers! the people of Vienna, widowed and forsaken, will be treated with respect by you; I take them under my special protection. Be good to the unfortunate peasants, and

to the good citizens who are so worthy of your esteem; do not be proud of your success, but see in it only the result of the Divine justice, which has made you the instruments for the punishment of the ungrateful and the perjured.

The Emperor had not forgotten that in the former invasion of 1805 the civic guard of Vienna had behaved with admirable loyalty and self-control, and he therefore now again allowed them to retain their arms, and aid us in protecting their fellow-citizens. General Andrassy, who a month before had still been ambassador at Vienna, was named governor of the town, where his generous and upright character had won him the esteem of all, and this choice was a proof to the Viennese of the Emperor's friendly sentiments towards them.

Thirty days only had elapsed since the Emperor was called from the peaceful festivities of Paris to place himself at the head of his army, and during this brief space of time he had conquered and dispersed 300,000 enemies and taken possession of their capital.

Chance and luck had really nothing whatever to do with all these miraculous successes, which were entirely the result of the genius of Napoleon, whose wisdom and foresight, with his patient unwearying activity, prepared everything and settled every combination beforehand, and who, though he was well able to insure prompt obedience, yet knew even better how to inspire all his subordinates with a confidence and devotion which made nothing appear impossible to them when they were working for him and carrying out his instructions. These feelings of confidence in their chief were so deeply engraved on the heart of all his soldiers that they laughed to scorn the word "impossible," which the Emperor had struck out of his vocabulary.

The taking of Vienna was, however, but the prelude of yet greater tasks awaiting us. In retreating the Archduke Maximilian had burnt the main bridge over the Danube, so that it was no longer possible for us to occupy both banks. The Emperor's next care was therefore to arrange some means of getting over the river, so as to go to meet Prince Charles, who was marching on Vienna with all his forces.

The great width and depth of the Danube, with the rapidity of the stream, made it seem as if any attempt to span it must fail, and this was very evidently the opinion of the enemy, but for all that everything was prepared for the bold undertaking, which was immediately put in hand.

Already on the 11th, even before the town was taken, Marshal Lannes had received orders to occupy the islands of the Danube a little above Vienna and opposite Nusdorff, so as to make a bridge there. Five or six hundred men did land on the islands, but were repulsed with great loss by the Austrians under General Nordman. This partial success restored the confidence of the enemy, making them more than ever sure that we should never succeed in taking a bridge; and this, perhaps, led to their placing fewer obstacles in our way than they might have done during the succeeding days.

Reconnaissances were made about three miles below Vienna, and the village of Ebersdorff, opposite Aspern and Essling, was pointed out to General Bertrand of the Engineers, and to General Pernetti of the Artillery, as the point at which the bridges were to be made. A narrow but deep creek served as a floating dock for our pontoons and boats, and we were able to launch them without being seen. The town was so near that we could easily obtain all it contained of any use to us, and of the many islands about us we chose the largest, called Lobau, which was more than five miles in circumference, as the best base for our operations, which were very soon begun.

During the few days when the Imperial Staff occupied the palace of Schönbrunn, I went several times to see the treasures of Vienna, such as the statues by Canova, and also to look up my old friends. Many of our officers were doing their best to console the young ladies who had been left behind in the precipitate flight of the princes and the notables of the Court and of the army, who had bequeathed to their conquerors the task of wiping the tears shed at the loss of husbands or lovers.

I also very often went to the much-vaunted promenade of the Prater, and was so delighted with the remarkable beauty of its trees that I made many sketches in the shady woods, getting as much pleasure out of doing so then as I do now in looking at them when I can get time to open my old portfolios. They call up again the charming impression made on me by those solitudes, where the only sound to break the stillness was the trickling of water or the chirping of the birds making love in this sweet month of May. The freshness and the quiet contrasted indeed with the noise and confusion of conflict, and with the terrible hurly-burly of that awful and still recent day at Ebersberg, and I counted myself lucky to be able to forget it all, if only for a moment, in the profound quiet which surrounded one here.

It was three days since I had had more than a few moments of rest, and my duties already called me to go and help in the construction of the bridges being thrown across the Danube at Ebersdorff.

In the first instance I was sent by Prince Berthier to press on the work, and to return and report to him what was going on in the docks. I passed the day there, and towards midnight, when the weary workers were resting for a few minutes, I started in pitchy darkness to return to Schönbrunn to give an account of my mission. I did not know the way, and wandered about for a long time in the swampy meadows, which had been flooded by the Danube six weeks before. I could no longer see where I was going, my horse began to tremble, and his nostrils were inflated with terror as he felt the ground giving way beneath his feet. In a fury of rage he resisted my efforts to spur him on, and whilst I was struggling with him the mud suddenly opened before us, the horse fell, and for a quarter of an hour I was in a most critical position. But apparently my time had not yet come, and I managed to scramble out unhurt. I remounted the noble animal, who had done his best to save me from the catastrophe, and I arrived at Schönbrunn at two o'clock in the morning. I woke up Prince Berthier, told him how far the work had advanced, and he went to the Emperor with the news of the progress of the bridge, taking leave of me with the words, "Well done! Go and change your clothes now; you are covered with mud."

On this same day, which had begun so badly, I experienced several other annoyances such as are all too numerous in war, and are more felt then than at any other time. When I left Strasburg, I had confided the three fine horses I bought from the Jew Levi for one thousand and several hundred francs to one of my servants, a man named Graf. He had been told to take special care of one of the horses, the most expensive of the three, which had been wounded in the foot; and proud of the confidence I had placed in him, the man had promised to prove himself worthy of it. The army had, however, advanced so rapidly, that he had so far not been able to join me. I was awaiting his arrival with impatience, and on this unlucky day, May 16th, when I was at dinner with my comrades, I saw Graf come in at the door with a face lit up with pleasure at seeing me again. His happy expression made me feel sure that he brought good news, and I asked him if he had had a pleasant journey. "First-rate, sir," was the reply. "And Zephir has quite recovered?" I said. "Ah, sir," he answered, his bright expression unchanged, "what a fine horse! Everyone stopped to admire him, and such a good-tempered beast too." "Well, then, my good fellow, he is quite cured?" And Graf, still with a smile on his face, replied, "Ah, sir, what a fine horse he was! But his leg got inflamed on the march—it was a pity and he died at Stuttgart; I have brought you the certificate of his death." Very much annoyed at the loss of such a valuable mount at this critical time, I hastened to inquire, "And what has become of Sultana?" "Sultana? Oh, yes, what a proud, strong creature she was! She gave me no end of trouble. She jumped and sprang about to such an extent that she broke her thigh, and the veterinary surgeon had her killed." "What!" I shouted, "What do you say, killed?" "Yes, sir, at Lintz, and here is the certificate." "And Alezan?" "Yes, yes, sir, Alezan is a famous fellow, so brave and as strong as an ox. I was able to make him do anything I liked. You may pride yourself on having made a very good bargain when you bought him. He ate for four, and he is fat and no mistake. You must come and look at him." I was beginning to smile and to feel a little cheered, when the wretched fellow, still laughing and looking perfectly contented, added,

"Look out of the window, sir, there he is on the road, only some forty paces off. It was so hot he fell down in an apoplectic fit. I was not able to bleed him, and he is dead." "What a fool you are with your praises of the dead!" cried my comrades with one voice; but I, used to this sort of contretemps, for I had very often had to send my carriages on in Italy, Spain, and Poland, did my best to put a good face on the matter, and took from my belt what little money I had left to buy horses to replace those I had lost. Since then, in my campaigns in Spain, Russia, Saxony, and on the Rhine, I have lost no less than thirty horses in one way or another, four of which were killed under me, several were eaten by our soldiers on the isle of Lobau, in Russia and at Torgau, whilst the rest were taken or killed in battle at Dennewitz, Leipzig, and Hanau.

Part of the army had already got near to Ebersdorff, and reconnaissances had been made as far as opposite Presburg, six leagues lower down. Generals Pernetti and Bertrand had had everything they could get in the town taken down to the place where the bridge was being made, including timber, planks, beams, posts, piles, rails, anchors, chains, ropes, small boats, wherries, pontoons, forges, engines, workmen's tools, &c. &,c. The dockyard, where the preliminary works were carried on, was behind a little copse, which screened our proceedings from the enemy, alongside of the creek already mentioned, in which the boats, also well out of sight, were floated as the work proceeded, Hundreds of officers and thousands of soldier artisans were busily engaged in cutting up and preparing the wood, most of which was very unsuitable and of a heterogeneous character. The pontoon detachment and marines of the guard crept along the river at night in little boats, testing the depth of the water and choosing the best spots for anchorage. We had not nearly anchors enough, and we supplemented them by filling open chests with cannon-balls. Extraordinary activity prevailed day and night in the dockyard, and on the morning of the 19th the trestles, the rafts, with some eighty or a hundred boats, the baulks, the abutments, everything in fact, was ready to be placed in position in a few hours. Barges were prepared to send the advanced guard over to the opposite bank, and several boats were tied together in pairs as flying bridges to take the workmen to and fro. The Emperor, seeing that the work had advanced as far as circumstances permitted, now gave the order for the bridges to be thrown across, and that operation was attempted at the beginning of the night. The waters of the Danube had already risen, putting us to some inconvenience and causing us great anxiety, but for all that the battalions of the Molitor division crossed in rowboats and took possession of the island of Lobau, exchanging a few shots with the Austrians.

On the morning of the 20th the bridges were fixed, and we could communicate fully with the island of Lobau. Marshal Masséna's corps was the first to cross, followed by that under Marshal Lannes, with wagons laden with the necessary pontoons and boats for spanning the remaining arm of the Danube separating the island of Lobau from the plain of Essling on the left bank. This small arm, from about 120 to 150 feet wide, was pretty deep, and the swollen state of the river was likely to make the work of bridging over the last bit difficult enough. The point chosen was where the plain jutted out considerably towards the island of Lobau. This position projecting from our bank allowed our artillery to sweep its surface in both directions, and thus protect the troops who were about to land on the opposite bank. The Austrian troops opposing us were not numerous, but they contested the passage hotly, though they were finally repulsed by the battalions flung across to the left bank by General Molitor and led by M. de Sainte-Croix, one of the aides de camp of Marshal Masséna, who was well worthy to second a general so able. The indomitable courage of this young officer, combined with his bright and cultivated intelligence, his charming face and taking manners, had greatly pleased the Emperor, who, with a view to his advancement, had confided to him the leadership of these battalions. Sainte-Croix, advancing in front of his men, left them no excuse for hesitation, and everything turned out in accordance with the wishes of the Marshal.

Whilst our advanced guard was drawing off the enemy, our engineers hastily raised behind the skirmishers at the apex of the angle occupied by us, a retrenchment or breastwork in the form of a crown-shaped bridge head, whilst behind them again we were working beneath the showers of balls which fell amongst us, and launched the boats which were to make the bridge. We had very little wood left for this purpose, and we had to cut some on the island. Whilst we were thus engaged, the water continued to rise, increasing the rapidity of the current, and adding to our difficulties; but in spite of everything the little ten-span bridge was finished on the evening of the 20th, and the troops who had reached the island of Lobau began to cross over to the left bank. The rest of the troops hastened their march; but it was only with difficulty and by dint of very great caution that they were able to cross the long defiles of narrow bridges, still anything but firmly fixed.

As soon as the Molitor division was ready to pass on to the plain of hassling, the advanced guard, led by Sainte-Croix, promptly debouched from the little wood which screened the point of passage; but the cavalry of the enemy soon drove them back, compelling them to return to shelter. Slowly, however, the numbers of the French troops increased along the front, and they in their turn now repulsed the enemy's cavalry, which drew back to some distance on the plain. This manoeuvre led us to suppose that the Austrian force was small, or that the enemy were trying to draw us into an ambuscade, so we did not pursue, our light cavalry alone advancing beyond the villages of Aspern and Essling, in which they took up their quarters without opposition during the night.

At midnight the Emperor was still in a state of great uncertainty, ignorant whether he had the enemy in front or not. About one o'clock, however, news was brought to him that a far-stretching line of fires had been noticed on the heights in the direction of Bohemia, at a considerable distance from our left wing. There could be little doubt that they were the camp fires of a considerable force, and Marshal Masséna, who had climbed up into the belfry at Aspern to get a better view, was also of that opinion.

The whole of the night of the 20th I remained at the bridge, hard at work trying to strengthen it and aid the crossing of the troops who were about to take up their position on the plain in the following order of battle: Masséna's corps on the left in the direction of Aspern; that of Marshal Lannes on the right towards Essling; whilst the cavalry under Marshal Bessières was to take its stand between the two villages. The Emperor and his Guard also arrived before daybreak.

The darkness had not yet dispersed on May 21st, when our cavalry vedettes were compelled to retreat before a large body of the enemy's sharpshooters, heralding the approach of the Austrian army, some 170,000 strong, which had advanced upon us during the night without our having been able to perceive it. Of this force a body of 60,000 cavalry with 300 pieces of cannon were already deploying in a semicircle with a view to surrounding us.

At daybreak only 25,000 of our men had crossed the river, and the skirmishers were already engaged all along our line, which occupied about two miles and a half between Aspern, Essling, and Ebersdorff. The Danube had now risen more than three feet, and made our bridges very insecure. The soldiers would never have had the heart to venture on these rickety planks, washed and shaken by the rushing waters, but that they were inpatient to get to the plain to join the comrades who were already attacked, and whose danger they recognised. A body of Austrian cavalry, supported by a good many guns, advanced to retake the three villages we occupied to begin with. Ebersdorff being too farms off from our right wing, the Emperor ordered it to be abandoned before it was attacked, and the troops from it came up to aid in the defence of Essling, whilst the artillery of the enemy, eager to dislodge us from that position, showered shells and balls upon our cavalry drawn up in front of it. All these projectiles fell into the luckless village, which was soon on fire. On our left the village of Aspern was occupied by several battalions of the Molitor division, and moreover covered by our cavalry. A yet more formidable attack was directed by the Austrians upon this point; thousands of shells soon set fire to the village. Marshal Masséna perceived from the fierceness of the onslaught what the Archduke Charles was aiming at, and all the importance the enemy would attach to the possession of Aspern, from which they hoped to debouch upon our bridge, destroy it, and take us all prisoners in the plain by cutting off our retreat. On the discovery of this scheme the genius of Masséna rose to meet the emergency, and of the two terrible days which I am about to describe he was the chief hero. His example redoubled the courage of the 10,000 troops under him, and enabled them to withstand the obstinate efforts of the three Austrian corps which dashed themselves against us a hundred times at least in the forty-eight hours of the struggle.

Our one aim in this two days' battle was to end the war and obtain peace. We were not successful, but no victory could have been more glorious to our arms than the long-sustained, unflinching resistance which intimidated a force four times larger than our own, with every means at its disposal for completely crushing us, and prevented it from daring to interfere with our retreat.

We were soon wrapped in thick clouds of black smoke rising from the burning village of Aspern, through which the sun, as yet but little above the horizon, shone like a blood-red globe of fire, giving a crimson hue to the whole landscape. This phenomenon, which would have aroused the superstitious fears of the heathen, made us all say with a smile, "We are going to have hot work," and it turned out that we were right.

Whilst the Emperor was advancing slowly across the plain of Essling, so as to give the rest of his forces time to come up, General Hiller's corps was trying to pass between the river bank and Aspern, so as to make straight for our bridge; but the Molitor division barred his passage, and prevented him from reaching the Danube. Meanwhile, at about ten o'clock in the morning, an enormous boat which had got loose from its moorings was carried down by the current, and broke one of our larger bridges by falling on it, so that our communication with the plain was interrupted for several hours. The news of this serious accident was brought to the Emperor just as the aim of the Austrian movement upon Aspern had fully declared itself. Behind the enemy's cavalry we could now see a considerable column of infantry converging on the same point, the village was soon surrounded by a swarm of skirmishers on foot, and the attack became so vigorous that General Molitor was driven out of Aspern. These two untoward incidents occurring simultaneously, the Emperor thought it prudent to advance no farther on the plains; and though his troops had gained a good deal of ground in the centre, he ordered the movement to be suspended, and the troops to remain on the defensive only until the arrival of reinforcements. The enemy noticed this halt, and seemed also to have been aware of the breaking of our bridge. They at once became far more daring, and for several hours we were overwhelmed by a terrible cannonade from a battery of some sixty pieces, whilst the Rosemberg division, protected by the artillery, advanced fearlessly upon us. Marshal Lannes, however, repulsed every attack with the Boudet division only. The enemy's cavalry then charged several times with such tremendous force that we were in danger of being broken up; but the valiant General Lassalle, at the head of our light cavalry, fell upon the Austrians, putting them to rout and compelling the terrible battery of artillery to retreat for a moment at a gallop. This respite was, however, of but very short duration for the French centre.

On the left the Austrians had entered Aspern, and it was absolutely necessary to dislodge them. Masséna, therefore, who had had all his horses killed, marched on foot with drawn sword at the head of the grenadiers of the Molitor division, forced his way into the village, crowded as it was with Austrians, drove them out, and pursued them for some twelve or fourteen yards beyond the houses. But here the French troops found themselves face to face with the strong force under Hiller, Bellegarde, and Hohenzollern, advancing rapidly in their direction. It was hopeless for the division to attempt to engage such superior numbers in the open plain, so Masséna recalled the pursuers and ordered them to hold Aspern.

The enemy, ashamed apparently of this first defeat, returned to the charge with 80,000 men and more than a hundred pieces of cannon, which were soon pointed on the village. To make the more sure of victory, the Austrian troops, who were expected to carry all before them, were in ranks far too closely serried; and Masséna, noticing this error, opened fire with his few remaining pieces upon the densely packed masses of men, every shot working terrible havoc amongst them, though their onrush was not checked for a moment. In a very few minutes the village was completely surrounded by troops; and hidden from view in the dense clouds of smoke from the cannon, the musketry, and the fires which at once broke out, the combatants, almost suffocated by the stroke, crossed bayonets without being able to see each other; but neither side gave way a step, and for more than an hour the terrible attack and desperate defence went on amongst the ruins of the burning houses.

Whilst this horrible scene was going on on our left—where the French had also to drive back General Hiller, who was struggling to reach our smaller bridge news was brought to the Emperor that our men had managed to repair the large bridge and that reinforcements were beginning to arrive. These tidings were promptly made known to all who were interested, and greatly revived our hopes.

It was now a little after four o'clock, and the united corps of Hiller, Bellegarde, and Hohenzollern had succeeded in taking half the village of Aspern. Masséna still held the church and cemetery, and was struggling to regain what he had lost. Five times in less than three hours he took and retook the cemetery, the church, and the village, without being able to call to his aid the Legrand division, which he was obliged to hold in reserve to cover Aspern on the right and keep the enemy from getting in on that side. Throughout this awful struggle Masséna stood beneath the great elms on the green opposite the church, calmly indifferent to the fall of the branches brought down upon his head by the showers of grape shot and bullets, keenly alive to all that was going on, his look and voice, stern as the *quos ego* of Virgil's angry Neptune, inspiring all who surrounded him with irresistible strength.

No less fierce was the struggle in the centre. Marshal Lannes, with the Boudet division, protected by the village of Essling, formed the front line of our army between Essling and Aspern; whilst Marshal Bessières covered this line with the cavalry, the Emperor with his Guard forming the reserve.

When the news reached us that our bridge was broken, the wind was blowing the masses of smoke rising up from Aspern towards us, wrapping us in a black cloud, whilst the blood-red sun shed its lurid light upon the scene. Hitherto, as I have already said, we had been able to repulse the charges of the enemy's cavalry, and had even driven off the sixty pieces of cannon which had been pouring such a murderous fire upon us, but now we were forced to wait till our communications were reopened before we could continue to act on tine defensive. This enabled the enemy to rally. The Archduke again attacked the village of Essling, defended by Marshal Lannes, but he failed to enter it, and the Hungarian cavalry under him again charged that commanded by Marshal Bessières, but each time they were thrown into disorder and compelled to draw back for a considerable distance by the cavalry divisions under Generals Lassalle and Espagne. In the course of a few hours the last-named troops flung themselves at a gallop upon the enemy's squares, broke them up, and dashed several times right through their ranks, carrying off fourteen guns. It was in this capture of artillery that General Fouler was killed at the head of his men, and it was whilst carrying off the same guns that General Espagne fell mortally wounded by a cannon-ball. The Archduke, being unable to get the better of Marshal Lannes and General Boudet at Essling, Masséna now ordered some 90,000 men with 200 pieces of cannon to deploy to our front. We owe many thanks to the Austrian gunners, for, whether from nervousness or awkwardness or in haste, they certainly aimed very badly. I was very often close to the Emperor on the left of Essling whilst all these terrible projectiles were raining upon the centre of his army, and though his features expressed absolute indifference to his own danger, I could not help seeing that he was keenly anxious about his men, compelled to remain inactive under such a hail of missiles. The sound of the bullets crashing, not a hundred yards behind him, on the high felt caps, the bayonets, and the very breasts of his

Guards, seemed to tear his heart, and he evidently longed to be able to put a stop to the storm. But at last the repairing of the bridges was achieved, and part of General Nansouty's large body of cavalry came up to our support.

As the regiments of cuirassiers formed in order of battle to the sound of the cannon-balls falling on and penetrating helmet and breastplate, we could see the brave fellows under fire calmly closing up their ranks and awaiting without a sign of fear the signal to charge.

It was seven o'clock, the sun was just setting, and the enemy seemed to be about to outflank us on the right, when Marshal Bessières, still full of the zeal he had shown in the many extraordinary charges he had already led, received orders from the Emperor to advance at the head of the cuirassiers just arrived, and drive the enemy off before night.

The emperor would have preferred waiting to strike a decisive blow until more fresh troops, eager for the fray, had arrived; but it was so painful to him to see so many of his men struck down as they passively waited, that he decided to order three regiments of cuirassiers to be formed into three columns and led at a trot in the direction of the hottest fire from the enemy's artillery.

Marshal Bessières, General Saint-Germain, and Colonel Margaron, therefore, advanced with their cuirassiers, and after several gallant charges routed the artillery of the enemy, and put to flight the corps of infantry and cavalry which came up to support them. We thus remained masters of the ground, and having got rid of the enemy on one side we had the satisfaction of finding hostilities cease in that direction about eight o'clock, just as the night was beginning.

On the left, however, the struggle was far from being over, and an awful battle was still raging in the streets and behind the walls of the village of Aspern. The enemy, irritated at the stubborn resistance of so small a body of troops, redoubled their efforts to dislodge them before nightfall, and went on fighting by the light of the conflagrations alone. The history of our wars relates no more thrilling incident than this long and obstinate struggle, in which our troops, disheartened by the ever fresh difficulties with which they had to contend, worn out by fatigue, and horrified at the carnage around them, were kept at their posts by the example and exhortations of Masséna and his officers alone. General Molitor had lost some half of his men, and the enemy were hurrying up from every side. The struggle was maintained under these terrible conditions until eleven o'clock, when we remained masters of Aspern and of the whole line between it and Essling. At that late hour of the night the Carra-Saint-Cyr division succeeded in coming up to the support of Masséna's left, and in relieving that General of his anxiety as to the movements of General Hiller. The enemy withdrew to bivouac at a distance of about four cannon shots in our rear. Quiet was at last restored, and the silence was only broken by a few shots fired now and then in the distance to keep the sentinels on the alert. In the calm of the ensuing night columns of flame from the conflagrations in Aspern and Essling rose majestically on the right and left of our camp, as if to light up the scene of the struggle of the morrow, for which we must very soon prepare. Our pontoon detachment meanwhile was busy repairing the damage caused by the rising of the river, and by the various floating objects brought down by the flood, which had become entangled amongst our ropes. Our sappers were hard at work strengthening the reliefs of the bridge head, and the Emperor and his staff stretched themselves out upon the grass near by to snatch a few moments of repose, often interrupted to press on the passage of the troops.

During the night of May 21st and 22nd, the grenadier corps under General Oudinot, the Saint-Hilaire division, part of the Guard, several regiments of light cavalry, with quantities of artillery, ammunition, and provision wagons, crossed the bridge in one continuous stream, surmounting the greatest difficulties, whilst we were occupied in placing the small bodies of troops, as they arrived, according to the directions of the Emperor on ground which we had now been able to reconnoitre. We were filled with admiration for the eagerness with which the men pressed on to the aid of their comrades.

At three o'clock on the morning of the 22nd we suddenly heard the cannonade of the enemy all along our line, and we were afoot again long before daybreak. At four o'clock the Austrian columns took up their positions from one end to the other of our front, extending indeed beyond it on either side, and the battle began again. Audacity and skill alone could bring us through against such superior forces, and neither was wanting to the Emperor or to those under him. He very soon determined to concentrate his attack on the enemy's centre, so as first to divide the Austrian forces and then to crush the wing on our right, which would assure us the victory over the second wing on our left. We started to convey the orders to this effect.

I had to go backwards and forwards from the field of battle to the bridges, and from the bridges to the outposts, to keep the Emperor informed of all that was going on, so that I was able to get a very general notion of what occurred on this awful day.

The shape of the field of battle might be compared to that of a huge outspread fan, with the Danube forming the sides, and the bridge the radiating point. The French army occupied the small inner rays or ribs of the fan between the wider outer rays and the handle, whilst the Austrian army was advancing upon us from every point of the wide outspread semicircle, extending on the right to Essling and on the left to Aspern.

Marshal Lannes, retaining his position of the evening before, defended Essling with the Boudet division, having on his left the Saint-Hilaire division and General Oudinot with the corps of grenadiers, whilst the cavalry under Marshal Bessières, the Nansouty cuirassiers, and part of the Guard, were between Saint-Hilaire and Masséna, who still occupied Aspern with the Legrand and Carra-Saint-Cyr divisions supporting his left. General Molitor, who had suffered so much on the 21st, was placed in reserve behind Aspern with the few men left to him, and small parties of troops, arriving one after the other from the bridge, took up their stand as reserves at its head. On the right bank of the Danube, meanwhile, Marshal Davout with the great park of artillery, the ammunition, and all the remaining corps of the army, were waiting their turn at the entrance to the bridge, eager to cross it.

The enemy's troops manoeuvred as on the day before, advancing in a hesitating manner; the infantry and artillery firing continuously, the general impression conveyed to us being that they were intimidated by the extraordinary resistance they had met with.

When the Emperor perceived how far beyond our lines those of the enemy stretched on either side, he felt sure that he would find any individual point he might elect to attack weak, and harassed as we were by the terrible cannonade, which became more and more murderous as the artillery drew nearer to us, he ordered the whole line to advance, and told Marshal Lannes to attack with the utmost possible vigour the Austrian centre, part of which had already taken possession of a few houses on the right of Essling, whilst the other wing was making a furious assault on Aspern.

It was hardly light when Marshal Lannes commenced his movement, leaving General Boudet on his right to defend Essling; and forming his remaining divisions in columns according to regiments with the cavalry in the second line, he marched proudly forward in that order, and very soon came up with and attacked the enemy. General Saint-Hilaire and the 52nd Regiment led the way, the Oudinot corps and the columns moving up to his support, the enemy everywhere wavering and drawing back before our troops. We eagerly pressed on our advantage, and the Austrians were thrown into a disorder which insensibly spread all along their line. In a very few minutes we had broken the enemy's ranks, and their troops drew back in several divergent directions. The Archduke Charles thought from this that the whole of the French army had succeeded in crossing the bridges during the night and was advancing upon him, and for a moment he seems to have despaired of rallying his forces. However, by the most courageous efforts, in which he exposed his own person with a reckless contempt of death, he succeeded in leading back to the charge several corps which had withdrawn, himself retaking the flag of one of his regiments, that under Colonel Zack, and planting it almost in our ranks. Vain efforts only; for all who returned to the charge were overthrown or taken prisoners. Flags, guns, and some 500 men were in one moment taken possession of by the French, and all the Archduke's aides-de-camp were killed or wounded as they stood around him. He succeeded, however, in reforming several ranks, but they were soon broken up and driven back by General Oudinot, who continued to advance.

Marshal Bessières, at the head of several columns of cuirassiers, then made his way through our division, and several times charged the Austrian infantry and cavalry. Our cavalry threw the enemy's ranks into disorder, and drove them back upon their rear guard as far as the village of Breiteulée, which had been but an hour before the head quarters of Prince Charles. It was when he was leading one of these cavalry charges that the French army lost General Durosnel, one of the Emperor's aides-de-camp. His horse was killed under him, and he was taken prisoner. We had long thought him dead, when the signing of peace restored him to us. It was from him that we learnt into what disorder the Austrian army had been thrown, and with what devoted courage the Archduke had behaved at this critical moment, when our troops had cut the enemy's forces in two, and were advancing rapidly across the plain with enthusiastic cries of "*Vive l'Empereur!*"

This joyful signal of victory resounded all along our first line, rousing the jealousy of the second corps, which had not been able to take part in the charge. Essling had a momentary respite from the attacks of Rosemberg, Masséna had succeeded in repulsing Bellegarde, and the Guard, still small in numbers and held in reserve, had advanced on the plain to the support of the divisions engaged with the enemy. The Emperor now checked the zeal of Marshal Lannes, who was pressing on in advance of his men, and told General Oudinot to moderate his attacks so as to give time for the main body of the cavalry to come up with Marshal Davout's 40,000 men, some of whom were beginning to arrive. The Emperor had already issued orders for Davout's corps to take up their position in the centre of the battle, so as to crush first one and then the other of the enemy's remaining wings, the centre and the right wing being already routed. It was not yet seven o'clock, and everything promised the most glorious issue of the day for the French arms. The very heavens, which were still calm, seemed propitious to us; but Providence was about to put our courage to the most terrible proof.

The fine warm weather in which we had been rejoicing for a whole month had caused the premature melting of the snow, resulting in the periodical rising of the Danube taking place now instead of as usual in the middle of June. So far we had thought the increase of the volume of water to have been merely one of the effects of a passing storm, which would not interfere long with our plan. But instead of subsiding the inundation spread all along the river, and the wind, which blew strongly in the direction of the current, added to the force of the flood, which swept down with it all manner of objects torn front the banks, such as trees, stacks of fodder, rafts, boats, &c., which were flung violently amongst the slackened ropes of our larger bridges, breaking them and dragging away the anchors, which were not strong enough to resist such pressure. The force of the current became terrible, and at seven o'clock our brave pontonniers and marines, having done everything humanly possible to prevent the catastrophe, were driven to despair of being able to keep open communication, for it was cut off by the breaking of one of the bays of the large bridge. An aide-de-camp of General Bertrand brought this fatal news to the Emperor in the midst of our success, telling him that the state of the river and of our boats was such that he must not count upon the arrival of the 70,000 men waiting on the right bank.

This terrible contretemps came upon us like a thunderclap, but the Emperor received the tidings with resignation. Prince Berthier and Marshal Lannes also accepted it without uttering one word of discouragement, disguising the painful impression they could not fail to feel. We spoke in whispers of the catastrophe, taking care not to let the news be noised abroad, but we could not help being greatly dejected at the knowledge that our only hope of securing the victory was gone. The Emperor sent me at once to the bridges to find out whether it were not possible by means of row-boats or flying bridges to bring over at least some men and ammunition.

Napoleon, though the enemy were in retreat before him, now felt himself compelled to order Marshal Lannes to halt and take up a position supported on the right by Essling, and on the left by a stretch of undulating ground running in the direction of Aspern, and connecting him with Masséna.

In the thirty hours' struggle sustained by our infantry and artillery, our ammunition had been nearly all consumed, and the stores which our park of reserve artillery was to have brought to us could not now arrive. We were therefore obliged to slacken fire, so as to make the powder and shot still left to us last longer. The Austrians may have noticed this, but what probably opened their eyes to our critical position, leaving them in no doubt as to the untoward incident which had occurred, was the movement of concentration which now took place, our army, instead of further pursuing the enemy, though they offered no resistance, prudently assuming the defensive. Moreover, the Austrian spies stationed on the heights of Bisamberg saw all that went on at our bridges, and sent frequent messages to the Archduke, who thus learnt that our communications were cut off.

The Archduke, therefore, who had been much surprised at our halt, was reassured at the very moment when he thought all was lost, and set to work to stop the retreat, reform his lines, and lead his troops once more to the charge. His strong body of artillery, which had drawn back to avoid the capture of the guns, returned to the battle field, and the cavalry, refreshed by the rest they had had, reappeared at the front and made several charges, which were, however, without effect.

The Emperor had ordered Marshal Lannes gradually to resume his former position, whilst General Saint-Hilaire, who had been in the front, reformed his columns with a view to withdrawing them, and during that manoeuvre he was attacked, and for some time exposed to the fire of the whole of the Austrian artillery, numbering more than 200 pieces of cannon.

Under this terrible hail of balls and grape shot Marshal Lannes' corps slowly fell back, and their resolute attitude seems to have intimidated the enemy, for they did not dare come to close quarters, but endeavoured to crush our troops from a distance. The brave General Saint-Hilaire, the pride of the army, as remarkable for his wit as for his military talents, was so devoted to the Emperor, who returned his affection, that he had been fighting on for a long time in spite of a serious open wound, and he was now one of those who fell beneath the grape shot of the enemy. He was carried back to us in a dying state.

With the calm presence of mind which always distinguished him in danger, Marshal Lannes placed himself at the head of his troops in lieu of the friend who had just fallen, and imbuing the men with his own *sang-froid*, he reminded them with a laugh of the fact that he led their retreat at Marengo under just such a fire from the Austrians as this, but that for all that the day had ended in a brilliant victory for the French. "Come, come, my friends," he cried, 'the Austrians are worth no more, and we are worth no less, than at Marengo!" Marching quietly on foot amongst his men, who shared his confidence, the Marshal repulsed several charges of cavalry, and finally took up his position on the undulating ground already referred to, extending from Essling to Aspern. These two villages were still occupied by the French, but both were being vigorously attacked, for the Archduke, finding his centre so fiercely assailed, had ordered the wings of his army to redouble their efforts against Essling and Aspern in the hope of checking the impetuous charge of Marshal Lannes.

My duties having now called me to the bridges, I was unable to follow the further course of events on the battle field. The scene at the bridges was, however, not less intensely interesting than it had been on the plain of Essling, for the swollen waters were destroying everything, men and their work alike falling victims to its ravages. To reach the bridges I had to cross the island of Lobau, where our wounded were lying about amidst the brushwood, having dragged themselves thither in the hope of getting help. And they did get it; but, O my God! of what a terrible nature that help was! Everywhere limbs were being cut or sawn off to save the lives of their owners. The Larreys and the Percys, in spite of, or rather because of, their compassionate hearts, were hard at work in their blood-stained amphitheatre, their very mercy making them apparently recklessly cruel. How we should all shrink from the very idea of glory, if in seeking it we always had to cross such meadows as these, strewn with limbs cut off from the bodies they had belonged to, and to look on at the work of mutilation and dissection characteristic of what is called the ambulance department of an army! Fortunately, however, the brilliant results of the victory we always feel sure of gaining, generally make us quickly forget the horrors we have gone through in achieving it.

The bridges I had helped to construct and thought so firm, having crossed them already some twenty times, were all but completely destroyed, all that remained being a few portions which had been with difficulty made fast in the hope of saving them from being swept away by the current. Here and there five or six boats still held together, and in one place there were as many as twelve, but there were wide gaps between with absolutely nothing to bridge them over. The river, which had risen some eight feet, and was at least a third wider than when I had last come down to the bridges, was rolling along at a tremendous pace, carrying with it all manner of floating objects. Where the chains of the anchors had held they had been too short to save the boats, for they had been swamped and sunk. Our brave marines and pontonniers did their very utmost to arrest the worst mischief, but their little boats got entangled in the ropes, and many went down with those in them unable to rally from the collisions they were powerless to avoid. Big boats and rafts coming down stream at the speed of a galloping horse fell across the few portions of the bridges still intact, and the stream, impeded for a moment in its course, dashed over them with renewed force, great waves flinging themselves against every obstacle with a hissing thunderous roar. To complete our misfortunes, a big watermill built on two boats was first set fire to, and then purposelessly cut adrift and launched on the current by the Austrians. The huge burning mass, vomiting forth clouds of black smoke from the tar with which it lead been smeared, bore down upon us and added to our anxiety for what little was left to us of our bridge of boats. With admirable intrepidity a good many of our marines now flung themselves into small boats and hastened off to fling anchors, chains, and ropes on to the floating firebrand in the hope of bringing it to a standstill, though they knew it was probably filled with explosives, and would presently blow up and destroy everything near it. At whatever cost, its progress must be stopped before it fell upon our boats and set them all on fire. Our marines and engineers did not succeed in entirely averting the catastrophe, as several pontoons were set alight, but neither were their brave efforts quite thrown away, for they managed to turn aside the fiery furnace into an open space where a span of our bridge was broken away. When the burning mill passed me I was near enough to touch it, and the heat was so intense that I and the men with me could not help recoiling and feeling a momentary horror at finding ourselves at the mercy of fire and water at once.

The Danube had now risen so high as to inundate some of the woods of the Prater, and the deer from them were trying to escape by swimming, some of them passing under our bridges. Whilst we were all doing our best to extinguish the flares of the burning boats, a herd of deer was just passing, and our soldiers, who were always ready for a bit of fun whatever the danger they were in, flung a number of ropes over the fugitives, of which there were about twenty. A stag and two hinds, numbed with cold and terror, were caught and hoisted on board alive. The antlered stag, generally so proud and vigorous, so ready to defend itself, now remained motionless but for its trembling, whilst its great eyes, from which the big tears were rolling down, expressed its presentiment of the fate awaiting it, for of course a capture of game was looked upon as most lucky at this juncture.

I soon recognised the impossibility of organising a service of row-boats for taking troops and ammunition over, as they would inevitably have drifted into the hands of the enemy. The difficulty of getting skiffs over was not so invincible as for the big boats, which were carried quickly over such great distances that, in spite of every effort on the part of the rowers, they would shoot past the island of Lobau and run ashore far below it on the left bank, the ground occupied by the enemy. There was not the same risk in going from the island of Lobau to the right bank, because our troops were stationed all along it as far as beyond Presburg, and there was no danger of drifting boats falling into the hands of the enemy. The employment of flying bridges was still less possible, the current being far too strong for them. In spite of everything, however, we did all we could to remove the wounded at least by degrees. General Bertrand and the engineer officers and men did all in their power to mitigate the disasters overwhelming us, turning aside the fresh firebrands that were launched on us and saving the stores on the banks.

It was with the very deepest regret that I went back to tell the Emperor he must not hope for the arrival of the rest of the army. During my absence the struggle, which was still hotly maintained, had approached a good deal nearer to the villages of Essling and Aspern. The attack was still sustained much as before on Aspern, but it had been doubled and tripled on Essling. Many of our guns were already dismounted, whilst others, which had become useless from the exhaustion of our ammunition or the loss of our teams, which could no longer be replaced, had been carried off. The Emperor, having no more troops of the line to meet the masses of Austrians who had rallied to crush Marshal Lannes and General Oudinot, at last had recourse to his own Guard. Stationed as they were behind him, they had been suffering terribly from the long-sustained fire of the enemy, which had become so hot during the last few hours as to be all but insupportable, and they were all eager to take part in the fray.

A fresh and most heroic struggle now began. The Emperor ordered Marshal Bessières to lead the cuirassiers and cavalry of the Guard against the masses of advancing troops, and to charge them with a bold front, not so much in the hope of securing victory as of breaking their ranks and saving our own army. Whilst Marshal Bessières, at the head of the cavalry, was over-throwing several of the enemy's columns, the Archduke bravely led his own picked corps of Hungarian grenadiers, hitherto held in reserve, up to our guns, which they approached without drawing trigger, but a terrible hail of grape shot arrested their progress. The Archduke, however, did all he could to encourage them and urge them on; but the raw young grenadiers under Oudinot, many of them almost beardless, charged and actually drove back once more these seasoned Hungarian troops, whose waxed moustaches with ends twisted into the shape of horns gave them a most formidable appearance. The Archduke then called up his cavalry, which suddenly fell upon us and drove us back. Our retreating horse made their way between the lines of our infantry, so that their pursuers received our fire almost at close quarters. Our vigorous onslaught, which overthrew a large number of the enemy, at last checked the Archduke's attack upon our centre, and led to his leaving Marshal Lannes unmolested for a moment.

The course of events was, however, far more rapid at Essling. General Boudet's troops, worn out with fatigue, had been compelled to evacuate the village between three and four o'clock, and the Emperor, recognising what misfortunes would result from the loss of the position for the rest of the day, ordered his aide-de-camp, General Mouton, to go and retake it with four battalions of fusiliers of the Young Guard, whilst General Rapp, another of his aides-de-camp, was sent to the support of Marshal Masséna at Aspern, with some battalions of light infantry of the Guard. Just as these two generals were starting, one for the right, the other for the left, as ordered by the Emperor, M. Alexandre de Laville, an aide-de-camp of Marshal Bessières, returning from the cavalry scuffle in which he had been engaged, met General Rapp, and pointing out to him the masses of enemy advancing upon Essling, he said, "General Mouton will certainly be crushed if you do not go to his support." Rapp hesitated for a moment between obedience and his desire to save his fellow officer, and then, urged on by De Laville, he marched upon Essling. The Emperor was at first annoyed at this breach of discipline duly reported to him by De Laville, but later, when success had been secured by the disobedience, he rewarded those who had thus taken the initiative with promotion.

The village of Essling was already completely occupied by the enemy, but General Mouton's troops charged into it with fixed bayonets in spite of all opposition, and succeeded in entering the large farm, already on fire, which had been defended for a long time by General Boudet, and was now held by an Hungarian battalion. A second Hungarian corps was entrenched in the cemetery, which was taken by assault by the Imperial Guard under General Gros. As that general had not men enough to retain possession of prisoners, it would have been dangerous to take them, so no quarter was given, and 700 Hungarians were put to the sword amongst the tombs, after which two corps of the Guard took up their stand in the village, presenting an appearance as forbidding as their assault had been terrible, so that the enemy, discouraged by the loss of so many men, did not venture on any further attack of our position, though they still riddled us with bullets. This murderous fire also reached the two corps of the Guard held in reserve, and they actually lost more men than if they had been in action. The Emperor, full of admiration of their courageous calm beneath this terrible fire, to which he had himself also been exposed for two days, and anxious to do them justice, spoke of there in the gazette of the battle in the following terms:

> The skirmishers under General Curial burnt powder for the first time on this day, and proved their strength. General Dorsenne, commanding the Old Guard, placed them in the third line, forming a wall of brass which alone was enough to check every charge of the Austrian troops."

This General Dorsenne was, without exception, the handsomest man of the army. He was very particular about his *toilette*, and gave a great deal of time to the care of his beautiful long black curls. But this devotion to his appearance did not prevent him from being, as was Murat, who resembled him in this respect, one of the bravest soldiers of France. The seasoned troops under him followed his example in the carefulness of their get-up, and this gave to the Old Guard an appearance so brilliant that it set a mark upon the epoch to which they belonged.

Just when the pursuit on either side had everywhere ceased,

and it appeared as if the Archduke, fearing, perhaps, to be too venturesome, was beginning to be disposed, as the saying goes, to provide us with a golden bridge for the retreat he desired us to make, the fatal news was brought to Prince Berthier of the breaking of our smaller bridge. He at once sent me to try and remedy the mischief, which was a difficult task enough. However, by means of ropes, trestles, beams, chesses, and planks laid crosswise, I did manage to connect the pontoons and make our only means of communication with the island of Lobau bear for a short time longer. I then hastened back with this news to the Emperor, who ordered me to go to Marshal Lannes and ascertain how much longer he thought he could maintain his position. When I reached that officer his horses had been killed, and I found him crouching with a few officers behind a bit of rising ground which protected them up to the waist only. Between this group and the enemy were some 300 grenadiers, the little remnant of the gallant army with which Marshal Lannes had been defending the position since the morning. The scattered bodies of infantry were protected from the charges of the enemy's cavalry by a few hurdles only, which had served to mark the limits of different properties. The Marshal's reply to my inquiry was, "I have but the few men you see, and we will hold out to the end; but I have no more cartridges, and do not know where to get any." Then, vexed at seeing me exposed to the grape shot ploughing up the crest of the breastwork behind which he was to some extent sheltered, he made me dismount and tell him what was going on elsewhere, reminding me how, three months before, at Saragossa, we had been crouching together in a trench in an equally critical position, and that the town had yielded on just such a day as this. I left with him a handsome young fellow officer, since disfigured by wounds, De Septeuil by name, and went to give the Emperor his reply in the words, "I will hold out to the last." As I rode off, I was covered with the dust raised by the grape shot from the enemy, and I doubted very much if I should get back alive; but I was even more anxious about the fate of the Marshal.

I had scarcely reached the Emperor when Prince Berthier

said to me, "the small bridge is broken again. Go quickly and see what can be done." I hastened off, and we succeeded in mending it yet again, but the river was still rising, and we had little hope of maintaining it intact for any time. All our wounded were now dragging themselves to this small bridge, crowding the approach to it, each eager to be the first to cross. Driven back by the carpenters, whose work they impeded, their position was one to draw tears from the spectator. The less mutilated amongst them endeavoured to clamber up the ropes into the boats, but climbing one over the other they got in each other's way, and not a single one succeeded in getting over the bridge. Many wounded horses, abandoned by their owners but accustomed to follow them, added to the confusion by pushing in amongst the unfortunate fugitives. All huddled together on the banks and approaches to the bridge, they were soon overwhelmed by the water, which continued to rise. The crowd became so great that the wounded were unable to move back, and we had to look on whilst men and horses were drowned without being able to do anything to help them, for a way of retreat for the army must be secured before anything else. "Let us save the Emperor!" were the words which passed from mouth to mouth. In this terrible disorder that was our one hope; it behoved us all to do our utmost to save him from being either taken prisoner or killed, and I now hurried back to Prince Berthier to beg him to do all in his power to induce the Emperor to retreat to the island of Lobau whilst it was still possible. Napoleon was most unwilling to desert his army, and would not consent to leave until I had described to him the distressing state of things at the bridge. At last, slowly traversing on foot the little wood, which had also been turned to account as an ambulance, I had the satisfaction of leading the Emperor to the group of wounded accumulated near the bridge. All, when they saw us approach, roused themselves to cry, "*Vive l'Empereur!*" and tried to draw yet more closely together so as to leave room for him to pass. Hitherto the Emperor's features had maintained their absolute calmness of expression, but now they suddenly relaxed, and his cold bright eyes were dimmed as he fixed then on the ground before him. He only recovered his composure when the removal of the wounded began; and he was watching the long file moving away, when Marshal Lannes was carried up mortally wounded. Directly he caught sight of him Napoleon hurried to his side with an expression of indescribable grief.

As soon as I had left the Marshal, the remnant of his men had been put quite hors de combat by the grape shot of the enemy, and he had been the very last to retire, almost alone and on foot. One of the many balls still ploughing up the plain had carried off both his legs. Two or three officers accompanying him, wounded though they were themselves, with a few grenadiers and dismounted cuirassiers, had carried him to the little wood, where first aid was rendered. There he was joined by others of his troops less seriously wounded, and they made a litter for him with their muskets, a few branches of oak, and two or three cloaks. Bathed with sweat, their brows contracted with suffering, their complexions blackened with exposure to the sun and the fumes of the powder they had been burning for two whole days, and many of them bleeding from their wounds, everything about the brave fellows bore witness to their valour and devotion. Most of them had one arm at least in a sling, and used the other to help carry the litter. The head of the Marshal, who was all but insensible, had sunk upon the hands of one of the officers who with anxious care were carrying the precious burden. The melancholy procession halted on the little bridge when it came in sight of the weeping Emperor, hastening, all overcome with grief, to meet his dying friend. Every heart was torn at the sight of sorrow so sincere, and tears poured down the cheeks of veterans whom no personal danger could have moved to emotion. The Emperor flung himself upon the litter, threw his arms round his friend, and holding him in a close embrace as the tears rained upon his face, he inquired anxiously, "Do you know me, dear friend? It is Bonaparte, it is your friend." The Marshal, who had recovered consciousness, responded with a few affectionate words, and the doctor, seeing that this painful scene was likely to hasten the all too rapidly approaching end, expressed his fears to the Emperor, who retired after once more pressing in both his own the hand of the brave friend whose skill had increased with his experience, and who Napoleon had hoped would yet aid him in some hundred future victories. The Marshal was too exhausted to be taken farther then, and he remained for the night on the island of Lobau, which the Emperor did not leave without going to see him once more.

The enemy, worn out by the unexpected resistance they had met with at every point, kept at a distance from us now, harassing us only with the fire from their artillery, which in the course of a single day had poured out on us no less than from 3,000 to 4,000 pounds of iron in the form of balls and grape shot. No further incidents occurred before the night set in. The Austrian army, three times more numerous than our own, had from 8,000 to 10,000 men killed and 16,000 wounded, including amongst the former twelve generals, and amongst the latter 700 non-commissioned and 87 superior officers, whilst 1,500 prisoners, including one lieutenant-general, were taken, with fourteen pieces of cannon and four flags, trophies very dearly bought and forming but a poor compensation for the loss of the illustrious Marshal Lannes, such a general as Saint-Hilaire, and so many brave and valued officers and amen.

I was charged to devote my whole attention to the preservation of the little bridge, which was so much menaced by the rising floods that I really feared the island of Lobau itself would be presently submerged. The rise of the water not another two feet would bring about this result, and we could see from the marks on the trees that it had already once reached that height. Fortunately, however, our fears were not this time realised.

At ten o'clock in the evening, Major-General Prince Berthier told me to go to the main branch of the Danube and prepare a boat to secure the passage of the Emperor to the right bank.

It was the time of the new moon and it was pitch dark, black clouds so completely covering the sky that I had not even the light of the stars to guide me, and as I splashed through the puddles caused by the rising of the river, I began to be afraid I should lose my way. The wind too was beginning to rise, and the moaning of the trees stifled that of the many wounded lying near. I often stumbled over their feet as I made for the bank of the river at the point where there remained but a few relics of what had been our bridges.

The best of the boats was quickly manned with fifteen rowers, a couple of pilots, and a few good swimmers in case of accidents; and I started to go back to tell the Prince that all was ready. When I had got about halfway, and as I was groping along in this, one of the darkest nights I had ever known, with my hands outstretched to guard myself from running up against a tree, I came in contact with some one else advancing from the opposite direction, and using exactly the same precautions. Then a husky and weary voice inquired brusquely, "Who are you?" "It is I, sire," I replied, for I recognised the Emperor; and Prince Berthier, who was close behind the Emperor, whispered to me, "Is the boat ready?," "Yes," I answered; "I will take you to it."

When we got to the bank the Emperor sounded his watch, which struck eleven, and turning to Prince Berthier he said, "the time has come; give the order for retreat." My young fellow officer, Edmond de Périgord, now a lieutenant-general, then lit a torch, and with difficulty preventing it from being blown out by the wind, he held it whilst by its vacillating light and using my sabretache as a desk, I wrote the two lines which ordered Marshals Masséna and Bessières to withdraw to the island of Lobau at midnight and there take up their position. Prince Berthier signed the message, and the Emperor said to me, "Go and take that order." The next moment, showing no anxiety in spite of the pitchy darkness and of the rising storm, which was adding to the force of the wind and the waves, he stepped into the boat with the three officers attending him, the moorings were cast loose, the bark shot forward like an arrow from a bow, and in an instant it had disappeared. The torch was extinguished by the fury of the wind; some four paces from the bank there was nothing to indicate the direction taken by the fugitives, the new Caesar and his fortunes were swallowed up in the gulf of darkness, and night perhaps be sucked down into the abyss never to reappear, whilst I remained the sole witness to the catastrophe. I could not get over the terrible anxiety which seized me when the torch went out, and it troubled me greatly until quite late the next day, when I learnt that the Emperor, though the force of the current had carried his boat a long way down, had succeeded in reaching the opposite bank without accident, and was now engaged in arranging for the sending of provisions over to the island of Lobau.

After the departure of the Emperor, the terrible drama which had been going on for two days seemed drawing to its close, but it was by no means over for me.

I had not seen a sign of my men or my horses since sunset, and had no idea where to look for them. It would have taken too long to seek them, and besides I could not cross the battle field on foot and at night without losing a great deal of precious time. I was feeling very much put out at the contretemps of the absence of my people when I got to the bridge, but amongst the crowd hastening to cross it I recognised one of the sappers of our engineer corps, leading the saddled and bridled horse of an Hungarian hussar. "Who gave you that horse to hold?" I inquired. "Captain Français, of the mining corps," was the reply. "Do you know me?" "Oh, yes, Colonel." "Well, tell the Captain that I take this horse for the service of the Emperor. I will return him tomorrow, or if he is killed pay twenty-five *louis d'or* for him;" and seizing the bridle I sprang into the saddle and dashed off at a gallop, my only fear now being that I might be shot by our own men, who would, perhaps, take me for a *Uhlan* or Hungarian hussar.

A few scattered bivouac fires dimly lit up the paths of the little wood and those across the plains, and making my way along the wide spaces between the fires, I soon arrived at Aspern. The glow from the red ashes of the houses which had been burnt was not bright enough for me to ascertain to whom to apply for information as to the Marshal's whereabouts. I had already had to turn back from one street, too much encumbered by debris for me to get through it on horseback, and was trying another, when a sentinel challenged me with "*Wer da?*" the "Who goes there?" of the Austrians, to which I answered without hesitation, "*stabsofficier*" (Staff officer). A young officer, deceived, no doubt, by the trappings of my horse, then came forward and said politely, "*Darf ich fragen wie viel Uhr es sei?*" (May I ask what time it is?) "*Mitternacht*" (midnight), and without further explanation I put spurs to my horse and galloped off as I had come. Some twenty Austrian bullets immediately whistled about my ears. I dashed back into the little wood, lying flat on my horse, and there I was received with more bullets, for I was supposed to be part of a cavalry charge. The darkness and Providence preserved me, however, and I shouted as I drew rein, "Don't fire; I am French!" A terrible voice then suddenly shouted angrily, "Who is the d——d fool who ventures to pass my outposts?" "Oh, it is you, General Legrand!" I exclaimed, recognising the voice. "I am looking for Marshal Masséna; I did not know you had left Aspern, and I have just come from there!" "My dear fellow, what imprudence!" was the reply. "I don't know exactly where the Marshal is, but he ought to be quite close to us in the little wood near one of those fires." I asked several other people, but the answer was always the same, "I don't know." I was still wandering about in the wood, my horse treading often on cinders still simmering, little dreaming that the heat from them was all the warmth the hero of these two terrible days could find, when I came upon some one lying alone on the ground wrapped in his cloak, without so much as a bit of straw to serve as a couch. A brusque voice cried, "Don't ride over my legs." "Why, it is the Marshal himself!" I exclaimed. "What a hunt I have had for you!" Then dismounting I said to him in a low voice, "I bring you the order for retreat." "I expected it, and I am ready," was the reply. "Does Bessières know?" "No, Marshal," I answered, "but I am going to tell him." "Very well, be off, and mind the bridge is ready; it is midnight, and I shall cross at once." I easily found Marshal Bessières, surrounded by his cavalry, and before daybreak all had silently retreated to the island of Lobau, except a few companies left to defend the entrance to the bridge, which, however, the enemy made no attempt to attack.

Back again on the island, Marshal Masséna took command of the army, remaining there for three whole days, during which it was impossible to obtain anything like provisions enough from the right bank of the river, so that we were obliged to kill and eat our horses. All our efforts were concentrated on finding some means to remove the wounded and to obtain provisions. Marshal Lannes was one of the first to be taken to the other side, and for two days we hoped his life might be saved, but he died at Vienna on May 31st. On the evening of the 23rd the Danube began to go down, and I went all over the island to the different spots where our troops were encamped beneath the grand old trees, and our brave fellows, after going through such terrible experiences, were at last able to indulge in a little repose, and to stretch themselves to sleep beneath the far-spreading branches, secure in the knowledge that the Emperor was doing everything in his power liberally to supply all their needs.

Meanwhile the Italian contingent had arrived, the Viceroy in command met and embraced the Emperor at Ebersdorff on the 25th, and the union of all the forces of the Grande Armée cheered us all with the hope of being able soon to achieve a brilliant revenge. Thus ended the great battle of Essling, which reflected so much glory on the French arms, inasmuch as by dint of marvellous courage and perseverance 50,000 men, cut off from all hope of succour, and short of ammunition though they were, yet kept back for three days an army 160,000 strong backed by a river in flood, and with all the resources of a patriotic country at their command.

CHAPTER 10

Wagram—Znaim—Klagenfurth

I was not able to cross the Danube and return to Ebersdorff until the 25th. After having shared the fatigues and privations of the army during the preceding days, I was glad enough to get back to plenty and to be able to have a little repose, but the last was of very short duration. The Emperor was not a man to lose any time. He always aimed at rapidly concluding a glorious peace, and all his energies were directed to winning that peace by some decisive victory. The first thing done was to restore the bridges and withdraw the wounded and artillery still remaining on the island of Lobau. The Guard and those corps which had suffered most passed over to the right bank, where they were quickly reorganised, the gaps being filled up by the fresh troops which had arrived from France, so that in a short time the Emperor was at the head of a larger army than he had had before the battle of Essling.

The Archduke Charles had also received reinforcements, and was encamped with his increased forces a little distance from the banks of the Danube. He seemed anxious to alarm us by threatening to cross the river to Neuburg above Vienna, and to Presburg below that town, where he had had a very strong bridge head constructed.

General Pajol, commanding our light cavalry, being thus threatened by this feigned passage of the river at Neuburg, I was sent to him on May 27th with orders to reconnoitre the state of the enemy's works and advise our General on the best measures of defence to adopt. The Austrians, I found, had made very extensive entrenchments on the left bank, but they were all of a purely defensive character. I climbed on to the Leopoldsberg, from which I got a good view of the works, of which I made a plan. I was in full sight of the enemy, who poured a regular volley of shot upon me; but I relied on the clumsiness of the marksmen, and was able to complete my sketch. I had also to pass in review and report on the state of the newly arrived troops in the same district, and the enemy cannonaded us for ever so long without hitting a single man. On the evening of that very day the monks of the Closterneuburg Abbey entertained me at a banquet as sumptuous as any that could have been given in a big city in time of peace. The orchestra of the convent, accompanied by the music of a fine organ, was supplemented by the band of our Regiment, and it seemed to me a truly wonderful experience to pass in a few minutes from the tumult of war to the pleasures of the table and the enjoyment of the finest music.

Our time was now chiefly occupied in military works outside the gates of Vienna, such as the reconstruction of the bridges and the reorganisation of the army. Being so near the town, where many of the richest families still remained, we were able to avail ourselves of the generous hospitality of the inhabitants, and the arduous toil imposed upon us by the war was relieved by many a pleasant recreation. I was able, for instance, to indulge in doing a little painting at the house of the venerable Casanova, the painter of battle scenes, who had long been well known in Paris, and had now retired to Vienna, where he was engaged in painting incidents of the wars of the Austrians with the Turks. I went, too, sometimes to the clever engraver, Mansfeld, who lent me his burins; and to the residences of the Princesses of Staremberg, Czartoriska, Trautmansdorf, Bathiany, &c., who got all the members of the staff who were able to draw or to write poetry to contribute something to their albums.

The construction of the bridges was confided to General Bertrand, General Rogniat, of the engineers, General Lariboisière, of the artillery, and the pontonniers and marines of the Guard. The same site was chosen as before, but the bridges were wider and constructed in a much more scientific manner. For the passage of the infantry strong pile bridges were constructed, capable of withstanding the force of the river freshets; stockades were firmly planted at distances of about 300 feet in the bed of the stream, so as to protect the bridges from the shock of floating bodies, whilst bridges of larger boats provided crossings, well protected from every kind of accident, for the use of the cavalry and the passage of all the material of war. These parallel bridges thus rendered traffic to and fro between the banks as easy as in the streets of a town. Fortifications were erected on the islands of the Danube, the most zealous activity reigned in every department of the various works, and it was easy to see that it would not be long before the Emperor was ready to advance upon the army of the Archduke, and attack the enemy on the very same battle field as before.

Meanwhile the Austrians seemed to be still uncertain what to do next, and had evidently arrived at no plan for a grand attack. They appeared to have some idea of threatening our rear in the direction of Hungary, and made great preparations for crossing the Danube opposite Presburg. Marshal Davout was ordered to oppose their passage, and I was sent to him to urge him to compel any Austrians who crossed to return to the left bank.

Nothing could be more picturesque or quaint than the appearance of the fine town of Presburg perched on the hills, looking down on the river and the islands with which its course is dotted. These islands had been clothed with thick forests of lofty trees, but the last floods had torn up thousands of venerable giants, many of which lay prone or were being carried along by the current. Only the saplings, too weak to resist, which had bent to the storm, remained growing; but though they had risen again now the tempest was past, they had as yet but little foliage. The trunks lying about, stripped of their foliage and their bark by the water or by the floating objects which had been dashed against them, made the islands look like great timber yards, full of wood waiting to be sawn. The Austrians had made use of the trunks thus encumbering the ground, as if they had been an abattis of impenetrable wood, to fortify the approaches to the entrenchments of the bridge head they had constructed on the largest of the islands opposite the big bridge. At first sight it seemed as if it would be very difficult to dislodge them from this position. I wanted to give the Emperor an idea of the state of things, so I climbed to a lofty spot, and I was making a plan of the fortifications, which I meant to let the Marshal have also, to help him to decide on the order of his attack, when, defying every obstacle in the way, he ordered the charge to be made (June 7). Springing from tree to tree, our grenadiers succeeded in less than half an hour in climbing up to the entrenchments, which they assaulted simultaneously at five or six different points, killing all who attempted to defend them. The entrenchments were then occupied by our men, the Austrians' bridge was burnt, and one colonel with thirty men were taken prisoners. The plan I had hastily made merely served to illustrate my account to the Emperor of the boldness of the successful enterprise. I did not leave till I had also made a sketch of the works the Marshal had had constructed opposite the bridge head, so as to blockade it. My notes on this occasion contain also a memorandum of the terrible fusillade and cannonade to which we were exposed not only when this coup de main took place, but throughout the whole of the day.

It was but sixteen days since our retreat from Essling, and the bad news had already spread all over Germany, completely changing the attitude towards us of those interested in the overthrow of Napoleon. The political horizon became everywhere overclouded, and distressing tidings reached us at Ebersdorff. Prussia hastened to renew the preparations for war which had been suspended when at the news of our victories at Eckmühl the Tyrol again revolted, and the Bavarians had been compelled to abandon Innsbruck. Austria endeavoured to spread the insurrection, whilst England pressed on her own armaments, aided Austria with subsidies, and landed troops in Italy opposite Naples, threatening Rome. King Murat was even obliged to carry off the Pope on July 6th, and in France fresh revolutionary plots were formed against Napoleon.

Without quitting Vienna, however, the Emperor was clever enough to frustrate all the efforts made against him at a distance, and the skill and energy with which he pushed on the preparations for his next attack confirmed the confidence of his troops in him, a confidence which even all that had occurred at Essling had failed to shake.

Marshal Davout's corps, opposite Presburg, protected us from any attempts the Archduke John might make to pass from the left to the right bank of the Danube, whilst the army of Italy covered us at a distance from any attack which might threaten us from the direction of Hungary.

The work on our bridges was pushed on with extraordinary rapidity. The huge chain which had been forged by the Turks for barring the passage of the Danube, and had for two centuries hung as a trophy of victory over the Ottoman power from the roof of the arsenal of Vienna, was taken to Ebersdorff and fastened across the river to strengthen the stockades raised in advance of the bridges to protect them from being set on fire or injured by floating objects.

Lobau, with the islands near it, full as they were of troops and encampments, forges, rope factories, repairing sheds for mending the boats &c., resembled the big arsenals of the chief French ports just before the starting of some maritime expedition. The month of June was spent in completing these extensive works, and during it I was able to snatch a few hours for my favourite pursuit of painting. In one of my recent excursions in the service of the army I had witnessed one of the too frequent acts of pillage which it had been my business to endeavour to repress, but it had struck me as tragi-comic rather than horrible, for at thirty one laughs at everything, and with no idea of doing anything more than enabling my fellow officers to share my amusement I had made a sketch of the scene. I only relate the insignificant little episode of this drawing of mine to illustrate how much at heart the Emperor had the honour of France on every occasion, however trivial.

To maintain discipline and repress pillage had always been one of the duties of the leaders of the army, but during a war so many fortuitous circumstances make it necessary for soldiers to forage for their provisions that a general is often obliged to be blind to their excesses. Often enough indeed such generals as Mansfeld and De Broglie, with others as severe as they, who had mercilessly hanged men for stealing a cabbage or a chicken from the peasants in an enemy's country, have soon afterwards lost battles through the disaffection of their troops. When by the Concordat concluded by the First Consul in 1801 he re-established the Church in France, Napoleon had taken a great step towards the restitution of public morality, and he was very severe on any tampering with it. During the disorders of the Revolution he had been very indignant at seeing the mob decked out in priestly vestments, and at the desecration of the sacred ornaments of the Church in profane orgies. Young soldiers like myself had been accustomed to seeing misguided men behave in this manner, and were in the habit of laughing at them. I was no wiser than my comrades; I did not realise that to deserve respect one must honour that which others revere, and I thoughtlessly made a water-colour sketch of the scene I am about to describe.

On the day when our army was approaching Ebersdorff, our soldiers with the excellent appetites travelling gives had gone some distance from the camp to get provisions. In the midst of the confusion into which the unexpected visit of our troops threw the village, a cottage took fire and the flames spread to the neighbouring houses. The first thought of our young soldiers was to rescue the villagers, but in throwing out the objects they were anxious to save they came upon the provisions &c. which had been hidden from us by their owners, and which had attracted so many unwelcome visitors. Loaves of bread, lumps of lard and vegetables, were now piled up out of the reach of the fire, mixed helter-skelter with the clothes, household linen, furniture, kitchen utensils, jars of wine, and casks of beer of the luckless peasants. The fire was scarcely extinguished before our thirsty soldiers fell upon the liquor and drank more than was good for them. Then, having quickly taken their fill, and seeing that nothing but trouble would come of further delay, they started to go back to the camp laden with provisions, which in their very unstable condition they found much too heavy to carry.

The road to the camp was soon strewn with the debris of the booty, each man throwing away what he could not take with him, till the track was marked with a long uneven line of scattered fruits, ducks, saucepans, hams, linen, fat geese, clothes, and even books, for some of our soldiers were educated men, who cultivated literature when their brains were not muddled with wine. In their reckless gaiety, many of the high-spirited young fellows had decked themselves out in women's clothes, putting the petticoats on over their uniforms, and the blackened faces of the grenadiers, with their huge moustaches, presented a most comic appearance beneath the caps and above the bodices and short skirts of the peasants as they capered, shouted, and roared with laughter, whilst near them stood the owners of the stolen property, weeping in angry bitterness. One soldier, mounted on a donkey which had belonged to some peasant, and wearing a saucepan as a helmet, was dragging back to camp a lamb, a sack of vegetables, the curé's spit with his joint of meat on it, and a doll; another, his clothes all in disorder, had made a luckless villager don his helmet and breastplate, and drive in front of him the pig fattened for the use of the family, whilst he himself, with the peasant's cap on his head and so tipsy he could hardly keep himself steady, was trying to console the weeping daughter of his victim, who would not leave her old father in the hands of the intoxicated troopers. What shocked the Emperor most, when, thinking to please him, some one showed him this sketch of mine, was the fact that in the midst of the scene of fire and pillage with the grotesque medley of dancing and weeping figures such as is only seen in times of war, some of the soldiers were amusing themselves with sacred objects taken from the burning sacristy. One was wildly brandishing in the air a barber's wooden block with the curé's tonsured and powdered wig upon it; another, reeling with intoxication, had put on a stole embroidered with silver, with other sacerdotal ornaments, in which he was preaching wisdom and sobriety to his comrades. The Emperor was annoyed at this profanation of religion, and, angry with the author of the sketch for seeing anything comic in such a scene, he sent a message to me to the effect that I had better employ my brushes in the perpetuation of beauty and of noble actions. "Lejeune," he said, "has distinguished himself by many deeds of brilliant courage; it would be more worthy of his talent if he were to represent them."

On June 14th the army of Italy had gained a great victory over the Austrians near Raab, and, in ordering his aide-de-camp General Lauriston to go and besiege that town, the Emperor also gave instructions that I was to be sent first to reconnoitre the position, to press on the siege, and then to push a reconnaissance as far as possible in the direction of Comorn and Pesth, the latter being the chief town of Hungary. Raab capitulated on the evening of the 22nd, and at daybreak on the 23rd I was already ten miles away from it on the heights opposite Comorn.

I had taken from our outposts of the army of Italy General Montbrun's light cavalry division, which the Viceroy had placed at my disposition to echelon along the road I had to take, so as to insure me everywhere a point of support to meet every contingency which might arise. I came in sight of the town on a beautiful morning; the bayonets of the defenders and the new brass cannon mounted on the ramparts of the suburb on the right bank of the Danube gleaming in the sunshine.

Having placed my troops in a position from which they could observe my movements and come to my aid if necessary, I started to reconnoitre the place in broad daylight, an operation always difficult and requiring great audacity. The venture was of the most absorbing interest to me, and all the young officers who were to be left behind out of danger were eager to accompany me. The discussion with them was really touching, but it behoved me to go alone, so as to attract less attention, and I was obliged to be content with choosing the fleetest of their horses, on which I could skim along like a swallow and brave the firing on the glacis of the town as I examined its enceinte and fortifications. By a lucky chance the sentinels and the troops in the town, still absorbed in thinking of their last defeat, and never dreaming that the French could be so near, mistook my party for a corps of Austrians who had escaped after the battle of Raab, and at first paid little attention to the officer scudding along the crests of the covered ways as he examined the shape and condition of the walls and ditches.

Profiting by this lull in the enemy's vigilance and the extraordinary swiftness of my steed, I pushed on for several leagues along the road to Pesth, from which I was not more than some ten miles distant. I saw no troops whatever, so riding back I halted on a plateau commanding a view of the greater part of Comorn, of which I made a plan. I had to hurry over the last lines, however, for some horsemen had meanwhile been sent out from the town to reconnoitre my party, and the news they took back led to my work as an engineer being cut short by a sharp cannonade, draughtsman and plan being covered with dust as the balls ploughed up the ground. I thanked General Montbrun's division and the officers who had accompanied me for their help, and remounting my post-horse I set out for Raab, arriving there on the 24th. I was present at the parade which took place in that town when the Viceroy allowed the imprisoned garrison to march past him with their arms, their flags, and all the honours of war. I also accompanied Prince Eugène on a reconnaissance of the interior of the town and of its fortifications. The next day, the 25th, I went to Schönbrunn, fifty leagues from Comorn, where I gave an account to the Emperor of the happy way in which I had turned to account the few days of my absence, during which I had not had one night's rest. Apparently insignificant as this trip was, I treasure up the memory of it more than of any other because it enabled me to boast that I was the only Frenchman who had the honour of penetrating, arms in hand, to the very heart of Hungary. Thousands of Frenchmen, it is true, reached Pesth, but it was as prisoners. It was this feat which in 1810 won for me the distinction of the Order of St. Leopold of Hungary, of which the Emperor of Austria made me a knight.

I was scarcely back at Vienna before I had to help at the works for the passage of the Danube. Everything was progressing rapidly; the various corps of the army were approaching ebersdorff, and the Emperor was concentrating all his great resources. The Archduke Charles, still unable to make up his mind what it would be best to do, seems to have hoped that some such occurrence as that of Essling would draw us again into this net, and with his army considerably increased he awaited us in the same positions as those he had occupied a month before, which he had now covered with redoubts and entrenchments.

The news received by the Emperor from his armies at a distance was most satisfactory, and calculated to encourage him in his ulterior schemes. In Spain and Portugal, Marshals Soult and Ney with General Suchet had beaten our enemies a few days before at Lugo, Oviedo, Gallegos, and Belchite. In Dalmatia, Marshal Macdonald had entered Layback, General Marmont had won a victory at Gospich on the 21st, and taken possession of Fiume on May 28th; the victory of Raab had followed on June 14; that town had been taken on the 22nd; on the 26th General Broussier had entered Grätz, and on June 30th Marshal Davout defeated the troops of the Archduke Ferdinand outside Presburg.

Amongst all these battles and victories there was one action so remarkable and so brilliant that I feel impelled to describe it here from the accounts of eyewitnesses. During the taking of Grätz by General Broussier, and when the struggle was at it fiercest, Colonel Gambin, of the 84th Regiment, was ordered with two of his battalions to attack the suburb of Saint-Leopold, where he made from four to five hundred prisoners. This vigorous assault led General Giulay on the enemy's side to imagine that he had to deal with a whole army, and he hurried to the aid of the suburb with considerable forces. Gambin did not hesitate to attack them, and he took from them the cemetery of the Graben suburb, but was in his turn invested by the Austrian battalions, and found it impossible to rejoin the main body of the French. He accepted the situation, spent the whole night in fortifying the cemetery and the adjoining houses, and, his ammunition being exhausted, he actually kept at bay some 10,000 assailants with the bayonet alone, even making several sorties to carry off the cartouches on the dead bodies with which his attacks had strewn the ground near the cemetery. General Giulay now directed the fire of all his guns and of five fresh battalions on this handful of brave men, who had already for nearly nine-teen hours withstood a whole army. General Broussier was at last able to send Colonel Nagle, of the 92nd, with two battalions to the aid of the 84th. The enemy vainly endeavoured to prevent the two regiments from meeting. Colonel Nagle overthrew every obstacle, got into the cemetery, and after embracing each other the two officers with their united forces flung themselves upon the Austrians, took 500 of them prisoners, with two flags, and carried the suburb to Graben by assault, finding no less than 1,200 Austrian corpses in the streets. When the Emperor heard of this feat of arms he was anxious to confer the greatest distinction he could on the 84th Regiment, and ordered that its banner should henceforth bear in letters of gold the proud inscription, "One against ten." It was with men such as these we were now to march on Wagram.

Every day, except when Napoleon himself visited the island of Lobau, a young officer named De Sainte-Croix came from Marshal Masséna to give the Emperor an account of all that was going on there. The brilliant and intelligent young fellow often climbed the loftiest trees to watch from a distance the preparations going on on the plain for rendering impregnable the approaches by which the Archduke expected the French army to attempt to advance. The Emperor took great delight in hearing about all these details, and ordered the erection of entrenchments and batteries in the same direction, so as to confirm the Austrians in their error. He even made us take from the enemy an island occupied by them, the possession of which really would have been necessary to us if we had meditated an attack on the old battle field of Essling. It was on July 2nd that Major Pelet, aide-de-camp to Marshal Masséna, was ordered to take this position. At the head of 600 skirmishers he went to the island in boats in broad daylight, killed or took prisoners all its defenders, and then raised an entrenchment to protect his own men from the artillery fire at once directed on them by the Archduke. A number of Croats were sent to dislodge our troops, but they were driven back, and whilst the fire from some twenty pieces of cannon was concentrated upon the newly taken island our pontonniers succeeded, beneath a hail of shot, in establishing a bridge in the rear of our skirmishers, so as to insure to them the arrival of succours, or, if need were, a way of retreat.

Our preparations were now complete. The island of Lobau was well fortified; the double stockades and the pile bridges were well consolidated; all the boats destined for the rapid construction on emergency of seven or eight bridges over the narrow arm of the Danube separating the island of Lobau from the left bank were hidden upstream, where they could easily be put together in a moment and flung across the narrow space. In a word, everything was just as the Emperor wished it to be. Most of those wounded at Essling had resumed their places in the ranks, and were amongst the most eager to secure a victory after their previous defeat. The Emperor then ordered the combined forces waiting some twenty leagues off, to join him, and in thirty hours his whole grand army of 200,000 men had assembled with admirable precision within sight of the ramparts of Vienna. Nothing could be more solemn or more deeply interesting than this gathering of forces before a great battle; and in the case of that of Wagram, the hour, the scene, the circumstances of the time, all combined to make it one of the most remarkable, whether of ancient or modern tunes. Many and most striking were the vicissitudes to be witnessed in its course by the numerous spectators, for during two long days victory vacillated between the two armies before it was finally assured to the French flag.

In the afternoon of July 3rd, the Emperor, having issued his orders with the greatest foresight, took up his head quarters beneath the tents on the island of Lobau, so as to be within sight of the final preparations, the aim of which was to put the enemy on the wrong scent, and to draw their attention with their chief forces upon the old point of passage opposite Essling, where the Emperor meant to make a false attack only. This would lead the Archduke really to expose his left wing, whilst protecting it in the direction of our right on the side of the castle of Enzersdorff, which the Austrians had fortified like a citadel. Everything succeeded according to the Emperor's wishes, and a circumstance which at first sight appeared disastrous for us, in the end seconded our enterprise at the point above indicated. The elements, so cruel to us six weeks before, now came to our aid and fought on our side.

It had been intensely hot all day on July 4th, and never, perhaps, was the air more fully charged with electricity. On either side the troops waited in vigilant suspense, resting under arms, and oppressed with the weight of the stagnant atmosphere. The sun set behind heavy masses of cloud torn by occasional flashes of lightning, followed by the distant rumbling of thunder, prophetic of that of the battle to come. So far the storm only threatened our adversaries, but it slowly gathered about us, wrapping us in an obscurity so dense that it seemed to us better suited to slumber than to war. Each one was doing his best to protect himself from the rain, which was beginning to fall, when at about ten o'clock in the evening the Emperor had the order to attack silently communicated to us. Our pontonniers and the marines of the Guard immediately loosened the boats and put them together across the little arm of the Danube, without being either seen or heard by the enemy's sentinels.

Captain Baste, of the navy, commanding the marines of the Guard, with five gunboats, threw 1,500 skirmishers on to the left bank, who had orders to advance with the bayonet without firing a shot, so as to escape notice in the darkness. The wind drove our boats in the right direction, and the noise it made in the branches of the trees prevented the enemy from hearing us. Flashes of lightning and claps of thunder rapidly succeeded each other, the clouds were rent asunder, and a downpour of rain of extraordinary violence baffled the vigilance of the sentinels, and when they at last gave the alarm we had gained a footing on their ground, and 3,000 men led by Sainte-Croix were arriving in columns behind our advanced guard. The bridges had been so well prepared beforehand that one of them, consisting of twenty-five boats tied together, was by means of a very simple evolution flung in less than five minutes across the water, in the form of a quarter of a circle, the two end boats being fastened one to either bank. The sullen roar of the enemy's cannon and the flashes of fire from their guns now began to mingle with the thunder and lightning from the sky. A flash suddenly revealed to me when I least suspected it that I was standing side by side with the Emperor, whose profile with the little cap and the grey cloak stood out distinctly for a moment. It was really like a scene of apotheosis, for thousands of balls of the largest calibre were raining upon us. It is thirty-seven years now since that awful day, and yet the grand scene still rises vividly before me.

Our batteries replied to those of the Austrians, and it was under a terrible fire of bombs, shells, round shot, and grape, which crossed each other above our heads, that we made our way over the bridges below Enzersdorff, which we left behind us on our left. Neither the darkness nor the storm, which continued to rage with fury, nor the deluge of rain, which drenched us to the skin, checked the advance of our columns for a moment, and long before daybreak the whole army had arrived on the plain, Marshal Masséna being on the left, General Oudinot in the centre, and Marshal Davout on the right, whilst the corps of Marshal Bernadotte, the Viceroy, General Marmont, and the Guard formed the second line and the reserve.

A bright and glorious summer's day succeeded the awful night of storm, and when the sun rose on July 5 the enemy had the painful surprise of finding that instead of arriving opposite to the batteries which were to work their destruction, the French forces were drawn up in battle order on the extreme left.

The Emperor had thus turned and avoided all the entrenched corps, and rendered the elaborate and costly works of defence absolutely useless. This compelled the Archduke to alter all his plans, to leave his fortified positions, and, losing all his advantages, to come out to fight half a league from his redoubts. The French, on the other hand, joyfully recognising the skill with which the Emperor had managed to evade the terrible obstacles prepared to check their advance, augured the very best results, and marched on with renewed confidence to the victory of which they now felt assured. The stronghold of Enzersdorff was bombarded so vigorously that it was soon unable further to defend itself, and was completely destroyed, being literally reduced to ashes. Colonel Sainte-Croix had orders to take possession of it, and he took prisoners the battalions defending the crenelated walls. General Oudinot, leading the French centre, came upon the well-fortified castle of Saxengang, defended by 900 Austrians, whom he forced to capitulate, taking from them twelve pieces of cannon. These two feats of arms were achieved before nine o'clock in the morning, on the right of the ground where the fighting was to go on for the rest of the day.

Whilst the advanced corps of the Austrians were drawing back to change front and prepare to receive battle, the Emperor was advancing across the plain, protected on the left by the Danube, his line of battle being perpendicular with that river. The two armies thus soon faced each other, and the battle began immediately after the troops had deployed. On our left, Marshal Masséna marched along the Danube upon Essling, leaving Oudinot on his right; Bernadotte made for Rasdorff, and Marshal Davout on our extreme right for Neusiedel, the light cavalry covering the whole of the right of our army, and the other corps marching in serried ranks behind that first line. The artillery parks and reserves had completed the transit of the bridges, and towards noon the Emperor had all he needed at hand concentrated in a small space.

About two o'clock we saw the Austrian army taking up a position on the heights beyond the Russbach stream, and preparing to contest its passage. Thus far the resistance on the Austrian side had been feeble, and it was only with the Bernadotte corps that the struggle had been at all severe, the enemy having for a moment hoped to beat the Saxons, whose cavalry had received several vigorous charges, each time, however, repulsed with great courage.

Marshal Davout had orders to outflank the enemy on our right in the direction of Neusiedel. General Oudinot took possession of Groshoffen. The fire of both armies now came into brisk play all along the line, and between five and six o'clock the battle became general. The struggle lasted for several hours, and after terrible carnage Wagram and Baumersdorff were taken by the French. The Archduke Charles then carne up with fresh troops, and, rallying the fugitives, he assumed the offensive. At the same moment the Saxons under Marshal Bernadotte penetrated into Wagram on the opposite side to that by which General Oudinot had entered it, and in the darkness, intensified by the smoke from the firing, these two parties of Frenchmen mistook each other for enemies, and inflicted great losses on their own comrades. Thanks to this cruel mistake, the Austrians were able to retake Wagram and Baumersdorff, where they passed the night.

The battle raged till ten o'clock in the evening, and never was I in a more terrible fusillade. It seemed simply impossible for any one to escape; but Major-General Prince Berthier and his officers remained in the thick of the fight for two whole hours. Prince Berthier and two of my fellow staff officers had their horses killed under them.

The Emperor and his staff spent the night at Rasdorff, and our outposts occupied a curve of more than three leagues in extent between our extreme right and left. Nothing decisive had as yet occurred, and we expected that the next day the Emperor would strike a great blow at whatever point of the enemy's line he thought best.

At two o'clock in the morning of the 6th, Prince Berthier ordered me to go all along the line of our vedettes, beyond Aderklaa to our extreme right, and to penetrate as far as possible into the Austrian lines to ascertain whether preparations were being made for attacking us or for retreat. I obeyed these instructions, and having passed Aderklaa, occupied by our troops, I managed, screened by the tall wheat with which the plain was covered, to reach the enemy's lines without being seen. Complete repose reigned everywhere, and I had reached the heights of Neusiedel, almost in the centre of the Austrian encampments, when I saw their troops noiselessly resuming their arms, and advancing slowly in battle order towards the French army. Day would soon break, and I must avail myself of the twilight to escape the vedettes and take the news to the Emperor of the approaching attack. The danger of my position was extreme, and in order to cross the stream of Russbach I had to make a wide detour, so that it was nearly five o'clock before I got back to head quarters. A hot fusillade was already being exchanged with our centre, and our troops were so vigorously attacked that they abandoned Aderklaa, and drew back on Rasdorff. The Austrian corps under General Bellegarde dashed upon us with an audacity which nothing could withstand, and our ranks suffered greatly under the terrible cannonade. It is really no exaggeration to say that I saw balls rush through the air and ricochet from the ground much as hail rebounds in violent storms. In this part of the battle field we lost a good deal of ground with many men, and I felt very anxious as to the result of the day.

On our right the Prince von Rosemberg endeavoured to drive back the French under Marshal Davout occupying Groshoffen and Glinzendorf. This attack, at first extremely vigorous, gradually slackened, for the Prince had relied on the support of the Archduke John, who was to have joined him from Presburg, but he never came up at all that day. Marshal Davout, noting the irresolution of the enemy, redoubled his resistance, overthrew the Austrians and drove them back to the heights of Neusiedel.

It will thus be seen that a fierce cannonade was going on all along the semicircle formed by our line. Though on our right Marshal Davout was gaining a dearly bought success, the enemy was continuing to advance on our centre, riddling us with projectiles, whilst on our left the Austrians were rapidly gaining ground, and approaching our bridges, of which they were endeavouring to get possession. It was in this direction that the struggle, which lasted to the very end of the battle, was fiercest, and the idea appears to have occurred to the Emperor that he might reap an advantage from this very circumstance by in his turn wheeling Marshal Davout's corps upon the extreme left of the Austrians so as to turn them, and, cutting them off from the reinforcements they expected from Hungary, drive them back upon Bohemia.

The Italian, Bavarian, and Saxon contingents were engaged between our centre and our left in endeavouring to repulse the vigorous assaults of the Kollovrath corps, which had joined forces with those under Bellegarde and Klenau. The Carra-

Saint-Cyr division, which had tried to retake Aderklaa, had been beaten and driven back. The Saxons had endeavoured to support the French, but they had been compelled to retreat in the greatest disorder, and had only been able to reform their ranks behind the Legrand and Molitor divisions, which checked the enemy's pursuit.

The Emperor's head quarters were at Rasdorff, which occupied about the centre of our operations, and it seemed to us there as if Klenau had already reached our rear, and was threatening our bridges, which he seemed likely to take, as he had driven General Boudet back upon them. The Emperor, however, showed no uneasiness about Klenau's movements, but allowed him to lose time and ground by thus withdrawing from the principal point of the battle field, he himself meanwhile giving his whole attention to what was going on at the centre, where the corps under Kollovrath and Bellegarde seemed ready to surround us.

The Emperor had kept in reserve close at hand the Macdonald corps, the heavy cavalry, his Guard, and nearly 300 pieces of cannon, but the balls of the enemy were already beginning to fall amongst these troops. Marshal Bessières, one of the group immediately surrounding the Emperor, was wounded by a ball, which killed his horse; several distinguished officers were carried off by a fire which we were eager to silence, and the enemy's cavalry, gallantly led by the Prince von Lichtenstein, charged us furiously. We were all anxious and intensely annoyed at being compelled to remain inactive.

The very moment when the Archduke seemed confident of success, and those under him, in the intoxication of victory, neglected the necessary precautions in case of defeat, when we were beginning to lose heart, whilst our pressing danger made us wild to take part in the struggle, was also the moment for which the Emperor had waited to surprise the enemy by an unexpected attack. He seized the opportunity by ordering General Lauriston to advance at a trot with sixty pieces of artillery, the Guard commanded by General Davout, and forty guns of position led by Aboville to within pistol-shot range of the centre of the Austrian line, and there to pour upon the enemy such a terrible fire of grape shot as should make a great gap in their ranks. The corps under Macdonald and Oudinot, the cavalry of the Guard, and the heavy cavalry were sent to cover this movement, to dash into the gap and mow down all the troops which might otherwise rally and return to the attack on us. This bold manoeuvre was executed with extraordinary promptitude and precision. The huge column of 200 teams, dragging the cannon and ammunition wagons, deployed in less than five minutes over a space of some 2,200 yards. At the same moment the showers of balls which had been raining upon us ceased to worry us, we resumed the offensive, put the enemy's artillery to flight, cut down their cavalry, and pushed on without opposition over ground strewn with the dead. The terrible fire from 100 cannon in a restricted space set light to the standing corn, and the conflagration spread all over the plain. The village of Aderklaa, which the Austrians to hold, became a prey to the flames, which rose to an immense height, and our cavalry, deploying in the midst of the enemy's squadrons, spread the ravages of the fire and carried off many prisoners.

At the same time General Macdonald and General Reille, with the infantry of the Guard, advanced in columns at the double, overthrowing all before them and retaking Wagram at the same time as Marshal Davout outflanked the enemy's left, threatening to turn them and cut off their retreat.

At this critical moment of the battle I received orders to go to the road to Hungary and reconnoitre what was going on beyond the Archduke John's position; and it was still broad daylight when I got back at eight o'clock in the evening, having seen nothing of any kind to cause anxiety. Suddenly, however, I saw some of our foragers returning to the camp stripped almost naked, and all but out of breath with running, shouting as they came, "*sauve qui peut!*"

I at once tried to ascertain what had terrified them, but I could see nothing, and those I questioned were as much in the dark as I was. Braving the cavalry of the enemy, which could rapidly scour across the vast plain, I made all possible haste back to camp, where I found every place in a state of confusion. The terrified men were upsetting the saucepans on the fires; mules and horses were being hastily laden anyhow; tents were being overturned, drums and trumpets were sounding on every side. The cavalry mounted, the infantry formed in squares, and everybody eagerly inquired of every one else, "What is it? What is it?" I galloped at full speed to the Emperor's tent, found him as much taken by surprise as any one, and as I drew up he was just flinging himself on to his horse, half dressed, without his cap, and with slippers instead of boots on his feet; for when he was told of the alarm he was being rubbed with a rheumatic brush by his Mameluke servant Roustan. I approached him and. told him that though it was still quite light and I could see a long distance off, I had noticed absolutely nothing alarming. Charles de Périgord, one of the Staff officers, now came running up, exclaiming, "sire, it is really nothing, only a few cowards who——" "What do you call nothing?" answered the Emperor. "I tell you there is no such thing as a small matter in time of war; nothing compromises an army so much as a careless security. Go and find out what it really is, and come back and give me a more sensible report." Then, having sent some other officers to reconnoitre, the Emperor completed his toilette and awaited their return.

Meanwhile the greatest confusion prevailed in the rear of our army, for those waiting with the carriages, provisions, and all the paraphernalia of war, hearing the noise, began to run away in disorder. For a moment there seemed to be a regular rout, and if it had continued we might well have been anxious. It was just at the entrance to the bridges that the panic was greatest amongst the non-combatants. Many even of those who had the Danube between them and the enemy fled, abandoning their carriages and baggage, which had been overturned in the strange scuffle, and did not consider themselves safe till they were behind the ramparts of Vienna.

Our messengers returned at last to assure us that the enemy were nowhere to be seen, and order was restored before the cause of the alarm was discovered. Later however, it was ascertained that some fifty Austrian horsemen, whose retreat to the main body of their army had been intercepted in trying to join that at Presburg, had cut their way through a little village where our unarmed foragers had been collecting straw. The blows they received when they were least expecting them inspired them with such terror that they communicated it to every one else, and as they ran away shouting at the top of their voices the alarm spread with incredible rapidity.

An army less lucky than ours generally was marches with far less confidence than we did, and I cannot help thinking that we should have been wiser to take precautions to guard against these blind panics, which a skilful enemy could turn to such great advantage.

The panic led to several very comic scenes, the one I am about to relate amongst others. Meal time being near, a superior officer of the Guard had climbed into the baggage wagon of his battalion to get out some delicacies of diet for distribution to his fellow officers, but the cry of *"sauve qui peut!"* which the officer himself was too busy to notice, made the driver run to his horses, which had not been unharnessed, spring into the saddle and start off at a gallop. The shock threw the officer down, the cover of the wagon shut upon him, stifling his shouts, and there he had to remain, half-suffocated amongst the bottles and provisions, till a league further on the vehicle was brought to a standstill in the block at the entrance to the bridge, and the driver opened his prison and set him free. Absent when his corps resumed their arms, he was supposed to be dead; and his account of his mis adventure, when he had been engaged in fetching something to add to the cheer of his battalion, was greeted with shouts of laughter from his comrades.

All the corps under the Archduke continued to retreat, and the next day the Emperor took up his quarters at Volkersdorff, a few leagues beyond Wagram. Here he created princes, counts, barons, and knights, and gave increases of pay. I shared in the rewards, for it was then that I received my title of Baron.

Before resuming his pursuit of the enemy, the Emperor gave orders that all the wounded should be seen to. The Austrians were as well cared for as our own men, and the inhabitants of

Vienna turned out in crowds to seek the sufferers and carry them off the field of battle. Count Daru, chief commissary of the army, and Baron Larrey, chief surgeon, superintended with generous zeal the attendance on the wounded, but their numbers were so great that in spite of every effort many who were hidden amongst the corn were not found until after five days of terrible sufferings beneath the burning sun of July.

Some were dreadfully burnt by the fire which had consumed much of the crops during the battle; others, too weak to drag themselves away from the decomposing bodies of the men killed beside them, were consumed by a wasting fever and had had nothing to assuage their thirst but their own tears of despair, which fell upon their dry parched lips, and the sweat which poured from their brows. Others, I shudder to relate, drank the water they passed themselves to relieve their horrible thirst. They cried aloud for help, and those who sought them also shouted, but the closely growing crops covering the wide-stretching plain, trampled down and broken though they were, stifled the sound of their feeble voices, and the charitable persons anxious to bring help to the dying had in many cases the greatest difficulty in finding them. It was heartrending work for us who had to go the day after the battle to the aid of the unfortunate creatures.

As at Marengo, I came upon several Austrian officers lying on the plain who had had parts of their bodies carried away by balls, and who, though they still retained all their mental faculties, could not hope to survive. They entreated me to cut short their suffering by a pistol shot, and I, who would have killed them if I had met them sword in hand the day before, had not the courage to render them this cruel service. I would have begged Larrey to give them a draught which should lull them into the painless sleep of eternity, had I not known that it is wrong to doubt the power of God, who is able to restore even those whose lives seem hopelessly doomed. It never does to despair, as is proved by a thousand happy examples, for Larrey, who was often accused of cruelty, and who would not have used the knife so often if there had been time to await the result of milder but less certainly efficacious measures, did indeed save some whose cases seemed most hopeless.

The victory of Wagram, which once more plunged Austria into mourning and consolidated the power of the Emperor, did not secure peace, and we had to make yet further efforts to win it. The Austrian forces, though in retreat, were still very numerous, and the insurrection in the Tyrol was assuming a serious character, which might be turned to account by our enemies.

The Emperor having heard that the principal forces of the Archduke were returning by way of Znaim on Moravia, determined to follow them.

The French daily gained marked advantages over the Austrians, who, hotly pressed by the corps under Marmont, Oudinot, and Marshal Masséna, tried to make a stand at Znaim, which the Archduke was strongly fortifying and had covered by his artillery, and which was originally so strongly situated at the junction of the rivers Taya and Lischen as to be considered impregnable.

Marshal Masséna was the first to be engaged at Znaim, and his position was critical enough during the whole of the 10th whilst the other French corps were still a long way off.

The fighting was resumed on the 11th. At first a storm accompanied by heavy rain damped the ardour of the combatants, and restored to the Austrians certain advantages of the ground by inundating the field of battle. Our cavalry, however, at last succeeded in crossing the Taya at several different points in spite of the rain of the day before, and the Legrand division followed it. The Masséna and Marmont corps in their turn crossed the river under the eye of the Emperor, who had just come up with his Guard, his cavalry, and the infantry under Davout and Oudinot. The Archduke Charles, finding himself attacked on every side, now recognised that, in spite of the success he had just achieved at several points, it would be impossible for him to maintain the fine position he had taken up at Znaim, and without further hesitation he ordered the retreat.

His army retired in good order, whilst the fusillade was kept up as hotly as ever.

In the midst of the scattered firing all along the line—some hundred different little combats were going on—the cry was heard, "Cease firing! Cease firing! Here comes the bearer of a flag of truce to sue for peace."

It was very difficult to transmit this order to cease firing, for both sides were eager to continue the struggle and many of the French and Austrian officers who were sent with the news of the demand for peace were themselves wounded.

The Emperor's tents were quickly pitched on the plateau opposite to and overlooking Znaim, the camp was established around then, and the last rays of the setting sun lit up a scene of unrivalled beauty. At the base of the wooded hills flowed the pretty river, and beyond stretched a smiling landscape dotted with gardens, just now rendered animated by the numerous soldiers, some of whom were eagerly climbing the cherry trees and devouring the fruit, which I believe they would have been just as ready to pick if the firing had still been going on, though this pause in hostilities in such a delightful neighbourhood was a regular fête for them.

The Archduke Charles, seeing that nothing but a treaty of peace could now save the Austrian monarchy, had decided to demand an armistice for negotiations. The Emperor, no less desirous to conclude peace, received the Prince von Lichtenstein, who had been chosen as envoy, with every possible distinction.

July 12th was spent in the going to and fro of couriers between the two camps, to arrange the conditions of the armistice which was to precede the treaty of peace, and as soon as the preliminaries were signed, the Emperor entered Znaim. He admired its site and its surroundings so much that he asked me to make a sketch of the whole scene, with a view to the exhibition later of a panorama of the grand battle field, such as that of the interview between the Emperors at Tilsit with the crowds who witnessed it, to which every one was then flocking in Paris.

On June 12th the Emperor ordered his troops to occupy the cantonments abandoned by the Austrians, in accordance with the articles of the armistice.

Before starting for Vienna on June 13th, the Emperor, unwilling to leave the army without some public expression of his gratitude to God for all the brilliant successes his arms had achieved, addressed a circular to the bishops from his camp at Znaim, telling them to have a public thanksgiving in all the churches.

"Jesus Christ," said the Emperor, "although He was of the seed of David, tells us that His kingdom is not of this world, and He ordered Christians to render unto Caesar the things that are Caesar's. I," he added, "am the inheritor of the power of Caesar. I shall persevere in the grand work I have undertaken, and of which I have now all but achieved the completion, that of restoring religion and public worship; I shall maintain the independence of thrones and nations, I shall wean the church from things temporal and perishable, whilst leaving to her the care of our eternal interests, of the affairs of the soul with the direction of consciences, and her ministers, thus set apart to her service shall be compassed about with the reverence which we alone are able to secure to them. Such is our will."

One must know what war means to be able to appreciate the joy of returning to a peaceful roof, beneath which one can give oneself up to repose without dreading the sound of the trumpet calling one to horse. It was with this sense of relief that we all returned to Schönbrunn, and were able for a whole day to wander about its fine conservatories and gardens, and to visit our friends in Vienna. The next day we made a pilgrimage to Ebersdorff, recalling many a touching memory of the bridges, islands, and battle fields of Essling and Wagram. It is impossible to describe the immense interest, fraught alike with pain and pride, with which I gazed once more on the ashes of the twenty villages burnt down in the plains during those terrible days, and the still recent traces of the grand evolutions which had ploughed up the ground in every direction, death claiming the while so many victims. The freshly disturbed soil everywhere marked the sites of the graves of our brothers, our friends, and our enemies. The whole landscape was wrapped in a melancholy silence, the ground was strewn with rags which had once been uniforms, and with broken armour, whilst the only moving figures were those of a few soldiers here and there engaged in picking up muskets, swords, breastplates and balls, with a view to earning the reward promised by the Emperor for every weapon brought into camp. There were no other crops to be gathered in, and the cultivators of the fields only visited them now to mourn over their losses. There was but one consolation for us—the princes of the land had themselves brought this desolation upon their people, which they might easily have spared them. Not a curse was muttered against us by the good-natured Germans, and we on our side respected their natural grief.

I was often sent by the Emperor to the hospitals to give comforting messages from him to the wounded, to ask if he could do anything for their families, and to see that nothing was lacking which could hasten their recovery. Of course I appreciated the confidence shown in me by choosing me for these visits of inspection, but I should have greatly preferred the perilous honour of going to take a redoubt by assault in the open air to having to make the round of the wards in the magnificent hospitals of Vienna, crowded with the wounded, hundreds of whom were daily carried off by typhus fever. The effects of this fever on its victims were like those of the cholera, for they quickly became delirious, and so disfigured as to be unrecognisable. I saw several in the convulsions of tetanus fall out of bed and roll about naked on the floor, suffering the most horrible tortures. It is appalling to think how many perished in this way.

Percy and Larrey set an example of great courage to their young fellow surgeons compelled to spend whole days in the polluted atmosphere, and the survivors were not at all intimidated by the death of those of their comrades who succumbed. I never left the hospitals without admiring their steadfastness and thanking God for guiding me to choosing a profession less sad than theirs, and above all for saving me from having to invoke their aid on my own behalf.

I was now commissioned to go to the Tyrol to insist on its evacuation by any Austrian troops which might still remain there, and to take over the fort of Saxemburg, which was to be given up to us. Nothing could have been more delightful to an artist than to be ordered to cross the beautiful mountains and valleys of the Tyrol in the most beautiful season of the year. I very soon secured an equipage to my mind, and I had reached Mürrschlag, situated on the lofty pass separating Austria from Styria, when I noticed that a great stone was gathering. It was but noon, yet it soon became as dark as at midnight, and the rumbling of the tempest echoed through the mountains, whilst in the obscurity the forests assumed a hue of the deepest gloom as the wind bent their branches to the earth and stripped them of their foliage. A heavy downpour of rain deluged me in my open carriage; but drenched to the skin as I was, I enjoyed watching the magic effects of nature in this angry mood, though I must confess that I felt a little nervous amongst these wild districts when the fury of the blast drove my horses and carriage in the direction of the precipices with which they are intersected. This brilliant display of superhuman grandeur was, however, perhaps specially got up for my benefit with a view to impressing me with the beauty of nature, even when wrapped for a moment in the sombre colours of a tempest.

The storm did not last long, and the sun came out again. The rain drops reflected its beams like diamonds. The valley was bathed in light, and, warmed by the flood of rays, was converted for the nonce into a celestial land, from which ethereal vapours rose on every side. The scene filled me with a kind of ecstasy, and my soul seemed to take to itself wings and float away into space with the clouds of mist. I wondered how any one, free to do as he likes and with plenty of money, could help loving to travel, for it is only those who do who can see Nature under her best aspects, and enjoy the vivid impressions they produce. When I think of the lovely valleys of the Tyrol, and recall the effect they had upon me, I felt sure that the gate of heaven is at the brink of the waterfalls of the Mürr at Klagenfurth, at Villach or at Spital on the Drave, and I have not the slightest doubt that Homer, Virgil, and Dante, when they described the entrance to hell or to the Elysian fields, were thinking of the spots on earth which had seemed to them most luxuriantly beautiful or most savagely forbidding.

The sturdy inhabitants of the Tyrol, whose passionate indignation at their separation from Austria and incorporation with Würtemberg and Bavaria in 1805 was ever on the increase, waged war upon us from their mountain fastnesses with indomitable courage and skill, harassing us the more as they attacked us in the rear, and the insurrection even seemed likely to spread to the route by which our reinforcements were expected from France. The Kings of Würtemberg and Bavaria, the greater portion of whose troops were with us in Austria, were for a time very uneasy about the revolt in the Tyrol, where the news of our luckless defeat at Essling had been greeted with the greatest enthusiasm, no one supposing that we should be able to recover from it. The people indeed were so much emboldened by it, that a general rising took place throughout the whole of the Tyrolean Alps, the Austrian General Buol and the Marquis de Chateler doing all in their power in the name of the Emperor of Austria to foment discontent and spread the insurrection. Many able men, such as Andreas Hofer, Hartel, Arco, Speckbacher, Schmidt, Adel, and others, with the Capuchin monk Haspinger, placed themselves at the head of the insurgent peasants, giving their orders in the name of God and the Holy Virgin, and fighting with extraordinary courage. Several French detachments were taken prisoners on their way across the Tyrol. Innsbruck was retaken, the Bavarians were repulsed, and the enthusiasm of the Tyroleans over these few isolated successes, achieved during the months of June and July, rose to its highest pitch.

The Emperor, who was always generous to the French *émigrés*, had had the Marquis de Chateler's sequestrated estates in France restored to him but two years before, and he was very indignant to find that this man, forgetting all the claims of gratitude, was one of the most eager in stirring up enemies against him. He therefore now sent to De Chateler a message to the effect that the decree of the Republic condemning to death any émigré who should bear arms against his country would be put in force in his case. The Marquis was at first greatly dismayed, but he soon recovered courage, and redoubled his efforts, showing the most bitter *animus* against us. It was in the midst of the success his efforts had won for the Austrians and the insurgents, that the news reached them of the armistice of Znaim, and they received orders to conform to its conditions. But the Tyrolese had already begun to look upon themselves as the saviours of the Austrian monarchy, and they could not bring themselves to relax their efforts. The Austrians alone, and that most reluctantly, agreed to retire and relinquish the country to us. Such was the state of things in the districts for which I was bound, where a contingent made up of French and Russians was under the command of General Rusca.

On July 30th I left Klagenfurth, the picturesque situation of which I greatly admired, and I found General Rusca at Villach. We went together as far as Spital, and there he gave me several of his officers with the men under them to go and take over the fortress of Saxemburg, where I arrived at daybreak on August 1st. The Austrians were fully prepared for our reception, and the meeting was far more friendly than I had expected it to be. I passed the day in examining the state of the ramparts, magazines, &c. I did not notice anything very remarkable about this fort, and though it is situated at the top of a mountain I think I could have taken it quite easily if it had not been given up to me, for it is closely overlooked by several quite accessible heights from which it could be at once disabled by our modern projectiles. I drew a plan and made several sketches of the position, which I sent the next day to Prince Berthier with an account of my mission, not forgetting to acquaint him with the bad disposition towards us of the people of the country, who might have incited the Austrian soldiery to maltreat us. The latter, however, though they greatly outnumbered us, behaved with far greater loyalty than was agreeable to the Tyrolese. With but a few hundred Italian soldiers, I was in the midst of eight or ten thousand Austrians, who, under the leadership of General Schmidt, now evacuated the Tyrol and withdrew to Hungary. The grave courtesy of generals, officers, and men was really remarkable under the melancholy circumstances in which they found themselves. The gallant fellows wanted peace as badly as we did, and if their columns had been made up of Frenchmen I could not have been better or more fraternally treated.

In the rear of the troops, however, the attitude of the people was very menacing, and the heights were covered with peasants, who watched with regret the departure of their protectors. I thought it prudent therefore to hasten to rejoin General Rusca, who was now advancing upon Lientz. the chief place in the Pusterthal.

We passed the 4th and 5th of August with General Rusca and the Italian Generals Souqui and Arrezi, and during these two days a terrible storm raged around us, completely covering our camp and the neighbouring districts with snow. We wanted to push on towards Brixen, but we heard that the Austrian General Buol was escorting several hundred French prisoners to us, and that the Tyrolese threatened to kill them all if we advanced further into the valley. To avoid rendering it impossible for the Austrian General to protect them by approaching nearer, we awaited them at Lientz, enduring agonies of suspense as to their fate till they were safely amongst us, expecting every moment to have the pain of hearing that some of them had been murdered. During the 6th some of the inhabitants of Lientz and the neighbouring villages went to their houses and brought out their arms, which they gave up to us. This apparent submission was, however, as we shall see, only intended to lull our jealous vigilance.

On the same day—Sunday, August 6th—General Rusca placed his division, all in full dress, in order of battle, on the heights to receive the troops under General Buol, who had just passed our outposts and were to halt for the evening on the plain below our position, where we had already marked out their encampment. General Buol handed over to us the two hundred prisoners he had brought with him, and as soon as his eight or ten thousand men had taken their places in the meadow below, General Rusca sent me to invite their leader and sixty of his officers to come and share the dinner we were having prepared. He also sent wine and bread to the Austrian soldiers, which were accepted; but the more important affair still to be settled was not arranged quite so easily. One of the conditions of the armistice was that no artillery should be taken out of the Tyrol by the Austrians, and when I asked General Buol to have the twelve pieces of cannon he had brought with him taken to our camp, he found it very difficult to obey the orders he had received on the subject, and his staff did all they could to induce him to refuse. I insisted, however, and the irritation against me became intense when I ordered four pretty little pieces of cannon of small calibre, ornamented with very fine sculptured designs, to be placed with the regular war artillery. A colonel with a very ugly face and absolutely no nose at all advanced upon me with flashing eyes and said to me in French, in a very gruff and arrogant tone, 'those cannon belong to me, and they won't be taken away whilst I draw breath!" Then, placing his hand on his sword with a threatening gesture, "If you want them, come and take them."

Without moving, I answered with a smile: "the treaty in question says cannon, without specifying their calibre. Later, if you like, I will give these gentlemen the entertainment of watching a single combat between you and me, if they think that will amuse them; but before I do anything else I have got to fulfil my mission. When I have the honour of knowing your name, I can ask the Emperor to give you back your cannon." "I am the Prince of Linange," was the reply, "and I shall take away my cannon." The dispute became hotter and hotter; the group closed in round me and my comrades, whilst other officers joined it, and presently one of them, who spoke French very well, and to whom all the others gave place, although he wore nothing to indicate his rank, came up and began doing all he could to increase the irritation against me. In spite of the uproar I managed to preserve my presence of mind, turning a deaf ear to all offensive epithets which I could not otherwise have passed over, but my position was momentarily becoming more critical.

General Rusca, who from his position on the heights saw with anxiety the excitement in the camp below, where the soldiers were arming and preparing to attack us, now sent an Italian officer to me to find out what it was all about. That gentleman, being on horseback, was able to see me as I looked down from my steed on to the angry group of officers surrounding me, and recognising the danger I was in he waited but to meet my eyes and thus telegraph encouragement to me before he galloped off again. The authority of General Buol was already being set at defiance, and the new-comer, who was evidently a Frenchman, kept urging the Prince of Linange to insult me further. I realised that if I lost my temper my life would be the forfeit, and I was still calm when I caught the name of the man who had made my position so dangerous. It was General the Marquis de Chateler, and directly it fell upon my ears, I of course remembered what the Emperor had told me about him. Rallying the courage which was perhaps beginning to fail me, I looked fixedly at the Prince and the Marquis, and said, 'the taking away of your cannon is not the most painful part of my mission, but to deliver over to a court-martial any émigrés I may happen to meet with, especially the Marquis de Chateler, whom I will feign not to know, that his life may be saved." These words produced far more effect than I expected, for both officers remained mute and apparently confounded. At their sudden change of expression, the rest, who did not understand French well, waited to have my words translated to them, and there was a moment of hesitation, but what really brought me safely out of the affair was that the Italian officer, Seroni by name, had lost no time, and we now saw a cloud of dust approaching, raised by eight pieces of cannon being driven up at a gallop, the gunners with matches lighted. In some four seconds they were drawn up, pointed and ready to pour forth grape shot, protected by our division, which was also on the alert to attack at a signal from me. This prompt arrival of artillery, with our energetic action generally, did more than all my arguments; the crowd dispersed, the pretty little cannon were given up with the rest of the artillery, and when they were amongst our ranks, I repeated to the officers my invitation to dinner. They made no reply; the Marquis de Chateler was the first to withdraw, and the Prince remained to the last, watching me with his repulsive eyes. I thanked him, however, for the honour he had been willing to do me in measuring swords with me in the presence of the two armies, and placed myself at his disposal if he still cared for a meeting with me. He took no notice of what I said, and I retired. I heard the same evening that the Prince of Linange was an émigré from Alsace, and was surnamed the Monster because of his ugliness, perhaps also on account of his character, for he was alike the cleverest and most troublesome bully in the Austrian army. Order was completely restored, but when the dinner hour arrived not one of our invited guests appeared, so sixty French officers took their places, and we merrily drank the health of the sulky fellows.

We spent the 7th at Lientz in gleaning information as to what was going on in the villages near, and learnt that the insurgents were gathering in large numbers it certain points preparatory to attacking us in the town and in our camp. I at once took all possible measures for the defence, had barricades erected at the weakest points, and on the side of the camp caused ladders to be fixed on either side of the walls, so as to facilitate our communication with the outlying troops, and ordered the removal of various blocks of rock encumbering the ford of the Drave between the camp and the gate of the town. General Busca also took necessary precautions, and we awaited the enemy.

A little before daybreak on August 8 the peasants swept down from the mountains and attacked us on every side at once. They thought to surprise us, and were, in their turn, greatly disconcerted at meeting with such unexpected resistance. The hordes flung themselves upon us with the greatest fury, but in such disorder that their losses were very pinch greater than ours. One of the attacking columns penetrated into the quarter of the town where I happened to be, and for a moment I was in a very awkward position, but I soon saw half a battalion of our men climbing down the ladders referred to above, and, falling on the rear of my assailants, the French troops had soon destroyed them all, not one being left alive. I shall never forget the horror with which I saw so many white or fair-haired heads fall beneath our blows in the mêlée, for it was patriotism alone which had inspired their owners to attack us, and I hated to be compelled to order no quarter to be given to those who would have assassinated us. "Kill the devil lest he should kill you," says the proverb;

and the enraged peasants, as they dashed upon us, rolled over, and fell at our feet, continued to strike at us even when mortally wounded. I lost ten of my Italians, and had a good many more wounded at this one point.

The next day I climbed up to the ruins of a strong old castle on the heights above the town, and remained sitting amongst them for some time. Just at the entrance to these ruins rose a gigantic lime tree, some thirty feet in circumference, its huge roots deeply embedded in the crevices of the rock; sole survivor, it seemed to me, of its contemporaries of two hundred years ago. Seated beneath the shade of this veteran of the valley, I had a splendid view of the surrounding country. On my way back to the town, I heard that the insurgents, relying on their thorough knowledge of the country, were preparing to surprise and murder us all in the night. We therefore kept watch till the morning, but nobody came.

General Rusca, anxious to show his gratitude for my co-operation, made me a present of a very fine horse and overwhelmed me with attentions. The General, noted for his combined culture and courage, was an Italian by birth, having been born at Nice, where he began life as a doctor. When the Revolution broke out in France in 1791-92, he hurried to take part in it with extraordinary enthusiasm, and his audacity soon led to his rising to the rank of general in the French army. He prided himself on being able to keep a more vigilant watch than any other man of his time, and as a matter of fact he did not go to bed once during the fortnight I was with him. Still I must admit that when he did not keep himself awake by repeating the passages he knew by heart in Homer, Horace, Virgil, and other authors, he would often fall asleep at table or even when engaged in conversation. He told me that one day when he was in the department of Var, the Austrian General Scharf sent an envoy to him to summon him to evacuate the district which the Austrians, invited by the inhabitants, had just occupied. "We were in my garden," said the General, "near a flower bed full of tulips, many of which were in seed". This made me think I would imitate the conduct of a certain King of Rome, and with my riding-whip I cut off the heads of the flowers, saying to the officer, "If what you tell me is true, that is how I should treat the inhabitants, and that," I added, as I trod down the stalks which had remained standing, "is what I should do to the enemy!" This pantomime quite dumbfounded the Austrian, and put an end to the interview. I already knew what a terrorist General Rusca was, and I quite believed his story; but I contented myself with silently thinking, "*se non è vero, è ben trovato.*"

LEONAUR

ALSO FROM LEONAUR

AVAILABLE IN SOFTCOVER OR HARDCOVER WITH DUST JACKET

SEPOYS, SIEGE & STORM *by Charles John Griffiths*—The Experiences of a young officer of H.M.'s 61st Regiment at Ferozepore, Delhi ridge and at the fall of Delhi during the Indian mutiny 1857.

CAMPAIGNING IN ZULULAND *by W. E. Montague*—Experiences on campaign during the Zulu war of 1879 with the 94th Regiment.

THE STORY OF THE GUIDES *by G. J. Younghusband*—The Exploits of the Soldiers of the famous Indian Army Regiment from the northwest frontier 1847 - 1900..

ZULU: 1879 *by D.C.F. Moodie & the Leonaur Editors*—The Anglo-Zulu War of 1879 from contemporary sources: First Hand Accounts, Interviews, Dispatches, Official Documents & Newspaper Reports.

THE RECOLLECTIONS OF SKINNER OF SKINNER'S HORSE *by James Skinner*—James Skinner and his 'Yellow Boys' Irregular cavalry in the wars of India between the British, Mahratta, Rajput, Mogul, Sikh & Pindarree Forces.

TOMMY ATKINS' WAR STORIES 14 FIRST HAND ACCOUNTS—Fourteen first hand accounts from the ranks of the British Army during Queen Victoria's Empire Original & True Battle Stories Recollections of the Indian Mutiny With the 49th in the Crimea With the Guards in Egypt The Charge of the Six Hundred With Wolseley in Ashanti Alma, Inkermann and Magdala With the Gunners at Tel-el-Kebir Russian Guns and Indian Rebels Rough Work in the Crimea In the Maori Rising Facing the Zulus From Sebastopol to Lucknow Sent to Save Gordon On the March to Chitral Tommy by Rudyard Kipling

CHASSEUR OF 1914 *by Marcel Dupont*—Experiences of the twilight of the French Light Cavalry by a young officer during the early battles of the great war in Europe.

TROOP HORSE & TRENCH *by R. A. Lloyd*—The experiences of a British Life-guardsman of the household cavalry fighting on the western front during the First World War 1914-18.

THE EAST AFRICAN MOUNTED RIFLES *by C. J. Wilson*—Experiences of the campaign in the East African bush during the First World War.

THE FIGHTING CAMELIERS *by Frank Reid*—The exploits of the Imperial Camel Corps in the desert and Palestine campaigns of the First World War.

Lightning Source UK Ltd.
Milton Keynes UK
14 November 2009

146236UK00001B/93/A